Ballots and Trade Union Democracy

Ballots
and Trade Union
Democracy

Roger Undy and Roderick Martin

With the assistance of R. Blackwell and J. Hutton

Basil Blackwell

First published 1984
Basil Blackwell Publisher Limited
108 Cowley Road, Oxford OX4 1JF, England

British Library Cataloguing in Publication Data

Undy, R.
  Ballots and trade union democracy.
  1. Trade-unions – Law and legislation – Great Britain
  I. Title   II. Martin, Roderick
  344.104'188   KD3050
  ISBN 0–631–13539–1

Typeset by Katerprint Co. Ltd, Oxford
Printed in Great Britain by T J Press Ltd, Padstow

Contents

Tables

Preface

The research upon which this book is based would have been impossible without the full cooperation of trade unionists, politicians and representatives of employers' organizations. We are extremely grateful for the time and courtesy extended to us. Since many interviews were off the record and on politically contentious matters, we are unable to acknowledge our debt to all individually; we hope that the accurate presentation of different points of view will be regarded as a substitute.

We also wish to acknowledge the special contribution of Richard Blackwell, research officer on the project 1980–82 who, with the authors, was responsible for writing chapters 2 and 3. Our second major academic debt is to John Hutton, who was research officer on the project between April 1980 and August 1981, before leaving to take up a tenured teaching post at Newcastle Polytechnic. His role in the early stages of the project was indispensable. We are also grateful for the secretarial help given by Trinity College, Oxford (especially Mrs Pat Rogers) and the assistance of the secretarial and library staff of the Oxford Centre for Management Studies who helped at all stages of the research and writing.

Finally, we would like to thank the Social Science Research Council, and especially the Monitoring of Labour Legislation Panel, for their financial and other support during the project. However, responsibility for the contents, opinions and conclusions expressed here rests with the authors and not with the SSRC or its Panel.

The order of authors appearing on the title page was decided by lot.

Roderick Martin
Roger Undy
Oxford, November 1983

Introduction

This study owes its existence to an initiative by the SSRC Monitoring of Labour Legislation Panel, which invited the authors in 1979 to submit proposals for a research project on the legislation on ballots proposed in the 1979 Working Paper *Support from Public Funds for Union Ballots*. The study was thus conceived as an attempt to monitor the effects of legislative changes on union behaviour. However, we believed – like many others – that the effects on trade union behaviour of the proposed legislation on ballots would be slight, since unions would be unlikely to be attracted to a scheme launched by a government which regarded trade unions as, at best, a major hindrance to economic growth and, at worst, a major constitutional threat: there would, therefore, be little impact to monitor.

In view of this, we proposed to focus on the use trade unions made of ballots in elections to union office and in collective bargaining and the consequences of their use, both because of the intrinsic interest of the role of different decision-making methods and because existing practices would give an indication of likely future trends if balloting were to become more widely used. This was especially desirable since there was no systematic evidence on the role of ballots in unions when Parliament was discussing the balloting provisions of the 1980 Employment Act.

The origins of the project explain its focus. The starting point was the 1979 Working Paper. Since 1979, there have been significant shifts in the Conservative governments' policy, some of which were anticipated and taken account of, others which were anticipated but could not be taken account of for practical reasons, and others which were not anticipated. Hence, we anticipated the extension of financial assistance to balloting on collective agreements, and indeed had argued from the beginning that discussing strike ballots without discussing ballots on collective agreements was nonsense. We also anticipated the concern with workplace ballots, but were unable, with the means available, to investigate systematically the role of workplace ballots, especially in collective bargaining: the survey of plant-level union activities required was beyond our resources. Workplace ballots may be used more extensively as a method of consulting union members than we have suggested, although we think it unlikely. For the same reason we have not investigated the use of workplace ballots by employers, with or without union cooperation. Finally, we did not anticipate the role of ballots on the closed shop, as provided for in the 1982 Employment Act, or on the political levy, as proposed in the 1983 Trade Union Bill. However, although the mechanism is the same, the issues involved in ballots on the closed shop and on the political levy are different from those involved in ballots on elections to union office or in collective bargaining.

Research into policy issues on the current political agenda presents major difficulties, intellectual as well as practical. There are differences in perspective between researchers, approaching issues from within an academic tradition of research and reflection, politicians, anxious to correct what they see as remediable abuses, and practitioners, anxious to get on with resolving day-to-day problems without too much interference from outsiders who are unlikely to do good, certainly not in the short run, and might do harm, intentionally or otherwise. There is the problem of maintaining rapport with respondents in widely differing circumstances, and with widely differing values. There are also major practical difficulties. Organizations do not always regard the collecting (or retaining) of information as a major priority, especially when administrative resources are limited. Where the information does exist, it may be difficult and time-consuming to unearth and collate; where it is accessible, it may be confidential and not disclosed or disclosed in such a way as to be incapable of being used in a public document; where the information is able to be reported publicly, it may be presented in a partial manner, designed to influence discussion in a particular direction.

Notwithstanding these difficulties, we have attempted to outline in a coherent form the development of Conservative policy on union ballots, and to present evidence on the use trade unions make of ballots. We do so believing that legislation ought to be formulated in the light of its impact on the issues to which it ostensibly relates, and not solely in terms of its effects in Westminster, in the media or on the electorate. That obligation upon policy makers is more difficult to carry out if researchers are not in a position to provide the information required, if only in an inadequate and not always appropriately structured form. Practitioners in industrial relations would, we are sure, wish to be less politically salient than they are, perhaps hoping for a period of benign neglect. Since they are unlikely to achieve that political obscurity, we hope we have done something to inform the political debate which is inevitable in such a contentious area.

The term 'ballot' is a generic term, covering all circumstances in which the individual union member records his or her vote on paper on a specific policy issue or in an election. The ballot may be more or less secret; the votes may be counted at the workplace, branch, union office or outside premises; the ballot paper may be returned via the steward, branch officer or through the postal services. The 'ideal– typical' ballot is conventionally regarded as one in which the administration of the process is carried out by a neutral outside body, with papers despatched and returned through the post, and the member voting as an individual in secret. However, few union ballots fall into such a category. More characteristically, the ballot is administered by the union itself, the voting is carried out at the workplace or branch and the papers forwarded either by the steward or branch official or returned through the post. The unqualified term 'ballot' is used to cover all circumstances; 'secret ballot' where the ballot is obviously in secret; 'postal ballot' to refer to arrangements involving the despatch and return of ballots through the post; and 'half postal ballot' to refer to arrangements involving only the return of ballot papers through the post.

The union rule books examined relate to the 1970s. Since the survey was carried out, some unions have merged and others will have changed their rules. In general, however, the situation as presently outlined, holds true.

In this discussion of trade union ballots, we begin by examining the origins and purposes of Conservative proposals to encourage secret postal ballots, continue by assessing the actual and potential effects of such ballots on union behaviour and conclude by discussing the overall importance of ballots for union democracy. The Conservatives had both political and industrial objectives in encouraging the use of ballots in unions. In the short term the policy produced substantial political benefits; however, the long-term effects on union behaviour and hence on industrial relations are less certain, and may run counter to Conservative objectives. Postal ballots do not inevitably increase union democracy, nor do they guarantee the election of moderate union leaders. The influence of different union structures and procedures and of bargaining contexts makes the impact of postal or workplace ballots on union decision making problematic. Because of the uncertain effects of ballots on union behaviour, and the threat to pluralist democracy posed by government intervention in union affairs, the overall long-term consequences may not be justified by short-term gains.

1 Conservative Industrial Relations Policy and Trade Union Ballots

Both Labour and Conservative governments of the 1960s and 1970s saw industrial relations problems as a major obstacle to increasing Britain's rate of economic growth. Industrial relations issues were therefore at the centre of political concern. One strand of government policy concerned macro level economic management, with measures taken to control the rate of increase in earnings, whether by incomes policies or by control of the money supply. A second strand, with which this study is directly concerned, involved structural reform of the industrial relations system. Both Labour and Conservative governments believed that this was required: Labour governments, especially in the 1970s, believing that the role of the trade union movement should be enhanced as a means of securing positive union involvement, Conservative governments that the trade union movement's actions should be more legally regulated. This study is concerned with the development of one aspect of Conservative policy, the use of ballots; this chapter places the development of that issue in the context of overall Conservative industrial relations policy.

Conservative industrial relations policy was moulded by five major considerations, the importance of each varying with changes in political and industrial circumstances. It was not simply a single-minded effort to undermine the trade union movement. The most important consideration was the Conservative belief that the unions were major obstacles to economic expansion; trade unions were seen as restricting economic growth by pressing for 'excessive' wage settlements and opposing technological innovation, especially at shop-floor level. Linked to this, secondly, was a desire to restore the 'balance' between management and unions which the party saw as being disrupted at national level through the Social Contract (or similar corporatist policies) and at plant level through the growth of shop-floor power. Thirdly, the Conservatives were concerned at the close financial links between the trade unions and the Labour party, believing that many Conservative supporters were – often unwittingly – financing the Labour party through their payment of the political levy. Fourthly, Conservatives believed that the growth of union influence on the Labour party and the Labour government, through the Social Contract and related policies, undermined the constitutional supremacy of Parliament. Finally, Conservatives also believed that trade unions, through the operation of the closed shop, were a major restraint on individual freedom. The Conservative party therefore believed that trade union influence needed limiting on economic, political and libertarian grounds. These general concerns moulded Conservative policy throughout the period, underpinning the Industrial Relations Act 1971, as well as the Employment Act 1980, the Employment Act 1982, and the 1983 Trade Union Bill.

This chapter outlines the basic principles of Conservative industrial relations policy and their significance for legislation on trade union ballots. This necessarily involves a limited perspective: industrial relations policy is only one aspect of a comprehensive political–economic strategy, and ballot proposals are only one element in industrial relations policy – less immediately contentious than legislation on strike picketing, the closed shop and the political levy. Nevertheless, increased use of ballots was envisaged as leading to the long-term transformation of trade unions, increasing union democracy and thereby making union leaderships more responsive to membership opinion, a membership thought to be less militant industrially and more conservative politically than union leaders.

This chapter is divided into four sections. In the first section we discuss Conservative industrial relations strategy, and the role of union ballots in that strategy. In the second section we discuss the legislative process involved in the passage of the Employment Act 1980, concentrating upon the (largely unexpected) political importance of the balloting proposals for divisions within the Conservative party. Thirdly, we discuss changes in policy on union ballots after the Employment Act 1980, ending with the Trade Union Bill 1983: the detailed discussion of the scheme established under the 1980 Act by the Certification Officer is contained in chapter 4 below. Finally, we present brief conclusions on the significance of Conservative policy on ballots.

The discussion of policy developments is inevitably incomplete: it is not proposed to examine the changes in Conservative policy in fine detail; the precise contribution of different groups and individuals, especially within the civil service, to policy formulation remains confidential, and the policy itself is continuously developing.

CONSERVATIVE INDUSTRIAL RELATIONS STRATEGY

In their discussion of the 1980 Employment Act, *Striking a Balance?: Employment Law after the 1980 Act,* Lewis and Simpson outline what they describe as 'the dominant climate of opinion on industrial relations among Conservative politicians, boards of directors, financiers, top civil servants, judges, some leading academics, newspaper proprietors and, on the evidence of public opinion polls, a segment of the electorate including many trade unionists'. Trade unions have too much power, causing employers either to concede inflationary wage increases, which they cannot afford, or suffer industrial action, with resulting losses to the workers concerned, their companies, and the national economy. 'If trade unions attempt to maintain internal solidarity and discipline through the closed shop, they are charged with the imposition of unreasonable restrictions on the liberty of the individual. And if the trade union movement engages in political activity . . . the constitution and the sovereignty of Parliament are threatened.'[1] For Lewis and Simpson the Employment Act 1980 was a way of curbing the unions, and redressing the balance of power between management and labour. 'The Employment Act is in essence based on the single strategy of the restriction or coercion of trade unions. This strategy accords with the same individualist ethic which underpinned the Industrial Relations Act.'[2] Although the major elements in this strategy involved legislation restricting the closed shop and picketing, especially 'secondary' picketing, legislation on balloting played its part by encouraging internal political procedures likely to favour 'moderate' union policies. Moreover, the provision of public funds for ballots is seen as providing an entree for external oversight – and eventually even regulation – of internal procedures.[3]

Lewis and Simpson thus see Conservative industrial relations strategy as single-mindedly designed to weaken the power of trade unions as a means of strengthening the position of British capital. Conservative politicians are hardly likely to wish to *weaken* the position of British capital, but it is too limited to see Conservative policy as concerned solely with one issue. Such a view underestimates the importance of three additional Conservative concerns, which had importance in their own right: the need for economic growth, moral liberalism and the supremacy of Parliament. It also neglects the difference in attitude towards industrial relations between different groups within the 'dominant' consensus.

Conservative politicians were concerned to weaken trade unions as a means of restoring 'balance' between management and labour. Chapter 2 of the Conservative manifesto in the 1979 General Election was headed 'Restoring the Balance'. They saw this change as important for economic revival. Moreover, they were concerned to do so within the basic assumptions of a Conservative tradition: the tradition as well as the achievement of balance was important. Furthermore, not all Conservative politicians shared the same view of industrial relations: some politicians were more sympathetic to corporatist policies, with their encouragement of trade union involvement in national policy formulation, than others. Contrast, for example, the views of Robert Carr or Peter Walker with those of Sir Keith Joseph, Sir Geoffrey Howe or Mrs Thatcher.[4]

Conservative industrial relations policy was conditioned by long-term values and preoccupations, whose importance and prominence varied with changes in short-term political considerations. The first value was that of the freedom of the individual, interpreted in common law terms: what might be termed 'moral liberalism'. The common law conception of individual freedom was a major concern of the Inns of Court Conservative Lawyers Association, whose pamphlet *A Giant's Strength*, published in 1958, provided the basis for subsequent Conservative legislation. The party's concern with the closed shop, shown in the 1971 Industrial Relations Act, the 1980 Employment Act and the 1982 Employment Act, was greater than justified by the contribution of the closed shop to industrial relations problems or to trade union bargaining power: if Conservative politicians had been solely concerned with reducing union power they would have paid far less attention to the closed shop. The concern was justified by the importance the party attached to individual freedom, and the perceived threat to that freedom posed by the closed shop.

The second value was that of the sovereignty of Parliament. This sovereignty was seen as being undermined by the growth of 'tripartism' and, more especially, by the Social Contract, with its explicit allocation of a policy-making role to the trade union movement. In the words of *The Right Approach: a Statement of Conservative Aims*, published by the Conservative Central Office in October 1976:

> People . . . question whether the trade union movement is subject to the will of the democratic majority at Westminster. We believe that a strong and responsible trade union movement has an important role in a free society; it should be widely consulted and its interests acknowledged and understood. But the trade unions are *not* [italic in original] the Government of the country. We are not asking the electorate to return us to office so that we can hand over government to any group, however important, which has not been elected to govern. It is Parliament, and no other body, which is elected to run the affairs of this country in the best interests of all the people.[5]

In *The Conservative Manifesto 1979* the party stressed: 'We will see that Parliament and no other body stands at the centre of the nation's life and decisions.'[6]

Reflecting these concerns, Conservative thinking on industrial relations in the 1970s was summarized in *The Right Approach,* published in October 1976. Conservative thinking was still heavily influenced by memories of the February 1974 election campaign: 'Two and a half years ago we fought a General Election in which the central question was the relationship between parliamentary authority and industrial power. Much of what we said then has been borne out by events.'[7] The major source of concern was the Social Contract. For Conservatives, Labour's programme in the February 1974 general election had been 'dominated' by the need to satisfy the demands of a handful of union leaders and the party's left wing.[8] Unions had successfully demanded policies 'in exchange for restraint which either damaged the national interest as a whole or which they hope will further their own interests at the expense of the rest of the community'. The Social Contract had major economic disadvantages, but, more fundamentally, it undermined and supplanted the role of Parliament. Bargaining on policy matters had become a matter between trade unions and the Labour party, Parliament being bypassed, and wider community interests ignored, in the process. Conservatives aimed to restore Parliament's authority, for 'it is Parliament, and no other body, which is elected to run the affairs of this country in the best interests of all the people'.[9]

Individual freedom and the supremacy of Parliament were long-standing Conservative concerns, but they were not sufficiently urgent – or electorally popular – in themselves to cause industrial relations policy to play a central role in Conservative strategy. Urgency was provided by the contribution the trade unions were seen as making to Britain's relative economic decline. In February 1974 the Conservative party described industrial relations as 'the "Achilles heel" of the British economy', and as such responsible for 'our economic progress lagging behind that of most other industrial nations'.[10] The first of the five tasks the Conservative party set itself in the 1979 manifesto was: 'to restore the health of our economic and social life, by controlling inflation and striking a fair balance between the rights and duties of the trade union movement'. 'Sound money and a fair balance between the rights and obligations of unions, management and the community in which they work are essential to economic recovery. They should provide the stable conditions in which pay bargaining can take place as responsibly in Britain as it does in other countries.'[11] Sound money was to be achieved by reducing the rate of growth of the money supply and gradually reducing the Government's borrowing requirement. Industrial relations were to be improved by three immediate changes: restrictions on picketing; provision of the right of appeal to the courts for members expelled from their unions, with compensation for loss of jobs if dismissed; and provision of public funds for secret ballots to encourage wider participation.[12] For major Conservative politicians, 'Solving the union problem is the key to Britain's economic recovery', to quote the title of an address by Sir Keith Joseph to the Bow Group in February 1979.

These three concerns moulded Conservative thinking on industrial relations in the 1970s. All three concerns led the party to wish to restrict the power of trade unions, and in doing so to restore a 'balance' between the power of trade unions and of other social actors – the individual, Parliament and management. Conservative policy was not simply 'union-bashing': it was more complex and more cautious. On the other hand, the Conservative view of trade unions was based upon different assumptions from those common amongst many trade union members, and probably most union officials. The basic Conservative assumption is that trade unions are instrumental organizations, with no particular symbolic – much less constitutional – importance, and should not be regarded as any different from other private voluntary organizations: any differential treatment is grounded in political necessity, not principle. It is thus hardly surprising that Conservative policy should be seen as anti-trade union, since even amongst the Conservatives most sympathetic to trade unionism the implicit conception of trade unions differed substantially from that of trade union leaders; many less sympathetic Conservatives, who became more influential with Cabinet changes in 1981, regarded unions as dangerous organizations whose power ought to be curtailed, if possible permanently.

Although such values and preoccupations moulded Conservative policy, they did not determine the timing of legislation, nor its specific content: timing and detail were determined by short-term considerations, including political opportunism and the role of particular individuals. Hence the importance attached to trade union legislation itself was greater in February 1974 and May 1979 than in October 1974, reflecting perceptions of the contribution union unpopularity could make to electoral success. Similarly, and more specifically, the concern with picketing in the 1980 Employment Act was influenced by experience during the 'winter of discontent' in 1978–9 and the steel strike (1980). There was no mention of picketing in *The Right Approach,* published in October 1976, although other legislative proposals on industrial relations were discussed, and legislation on picketing was the first item mentioned in the 1979 manifesto. The timing and extent of legislation were also influenced by the political views of specific individuals: the 1980 Employment Act reflected primarily the views of James Prior, then Secretary of State for Employment, whilst the 1982 Employment Act, and even more clearly the 1983 Green Paper *Democracy in Trade Unions,* reflected those of his successor, Norman Tebbit.

The 1980 Employment Act, with which this study is primarily concerned, was influenced more by the views of James Prior than by any other Conservative politician. Unlike some other Conservative politicians, including Sir Keith Joseph, he believed that legislation could exert only a minor influence on industrial relations, and that governments should act cautiously. Mr Prior outlined his views on trade unions in a Guildhall lecture in 1980:

> There is . . . a limited amount that Governments can do to produce good industrial relations . . . On industrial relations matters I believe that Governments have two prime responsibilities. First, Governments must endeavour to establish the appropriate ground rules, so that those who work in industry can work with one another and negotiate freely with a sense of certainty and fairness . . . The second prime responsibility of Governments is to seek to create the right conditions which help people working in productive industry.[13]

The ability of the parties to work effectively depended upon 'responsible leadership' in both management and trade unions. More specifically, trade unions should move away from the 'Action Day' mentality, through reducing the use of strike action, 'reappraising' their political role and improving their organization.[14]

Conservative policy on union ballots developed within the context of a concern to limit the ability of trade unions to restrict economic growth and to discipline the individual without appeal, and to re-assert the supremacy of Parliament. At the same time, the party recognized that trade unions had an important role to play, if one more limited than that played in the 1970s. 'We see the trade unions as a very important economic interest group whose cooperation and understanding we must work constantly to win and to keep as we have done in the past.'[15] But the unions were not to be centrally involved in formulating economic policy, any more than any other interest group: 'Union leaders may well find it convenient (and refreshing) to deal at arm's length with a government which knows both its place and theirs.'[16] 'A strong and responsible trade union movement could play a big part in our economic recovery.'[17] The key element in Conservative conceptions of the role of unions was 'responsibility'. This involved union leaders acting in the national rather than sectional interests: responsibility involved moderation, both in the formulation of wage claims and in the use of industrial action to achieve them. A major task of industrial relations reform was thus to ensure 'responsible' leadership of the trade union movement: the problems involved in defining responsibility – to whom and for what – were not examined seriously.

Although there was agreement on the desirable qualities of union leaders, there was uncertainty about the best way of ensuring the emergence of responsible leadership. The prevailing view was that moderate union leaders would be obtained by increasing membership participation in union elections, since the majority of union members were moderates – many even voted Conservative. Ballots were therefore desirable as a way of increasing participation in union elections. An alternative view was that union members were themselves militant where their own interests were concerned, and that the role of union leaders was to hold militancy in check: ballots would not help, and might hinder, this process. The Secretary of State himself was ambivalent on the issue:

> Too many union officials, particularly at local level, have been reluctant to accept involvement in hard decisions. And this is part of the whole problem of union leadership and discipline. It is not leadership to be a shuttlecock bouncing backwards and forwards between employers and union members. Wider membership participation in the operation of trade unions is one thing – and a desirable one: abdication to anarchic minorities with whom the majority of the moderate union membership become fed up is quite another. I believe that it is quite wrong to adopt secret ballots as the means of relieving senior officials of the obligation to take responsibility. But secret ballots can and ought to be developed by union leaderships as a strong support and protection for the majority of members.[18]

Despite this ambivalence, section 1 of the Employment Act was, of course, designed to increase the use of secret ballots in union elections.

Underlying the policy on ballots was the belief that the silent and apathetic majority of union members were more moderate in their opinions than the small minority who regularly participated in the internal working of their trade unions. Conservatives continually saw evidence in public opinion polls, and in the pattern of voting in general elections, that trade unionists as *citizens* were ready to support moderate policies, particularly incomes policies, but that the trade union leadership often failed to reflect that moderation. Hence, for Conservatives, union leaders *must* be unrepresentative. The task for Conservatives was therefore to find a suitable vehicle for the moderate majority to express itself, and to mobilize that moderate majority. The postal ballot provided the appropriate vehicle for ensuring that unions were representative by removing the possibility of coercive influence by militant leaders and stewards. Whether the Conservatives were right or not is impossible to decide *a priori;* relevant evidence is presented below. However, it is equally plausible that trade unionists as citizens think, and behave, differently from trade unionists as trade unionists, distinguishing between national and group or personal interests (an attitude not unique to trade unionists).

The dilemmas involved in advocating the use of ballots in union elections were present, *a fortiori*, in advocating the use of ballots in strikes. On the one hand, the use of ballots might be a means of restraining union leaders from strike action, especially in unions with moderate memberships but possibly militant leaderships, as in ASTMS or AUEW (TASS). At the very least, strike ballots could delay strike action. Moreover, there was a fundamental belief that workers whose 'livelihoods were being placed in jeopardy' should express their views directly on the issues involved. On the other hand, the Donovan Commission had pointed out the considerable practical problems involved in strike ballots: their use would only be relevant in the relatively small number of official strikes; there was uncertainty over responsibility for framing the question; difficulties were inevitable in allowing for the flexibility necessary for effective collective bargaining.[19] Moreover, there was no guarantee that strike ballots would produce 'moderate' results, especially if strike ballots followed a period of less serious industrial action, which had already raised membership expectations. In the only ballot conducted under the 1971 Industrial Relations Act, on strike action over British Rail's pay offer in May 1972, a very substantial majority favoured strike action. Despite these uncertainties the prevailing Conservative view was that strike ballots ought to be encouraged.

In summary, facilitating the increased use of ballots was not the central feature of Conservative party industrial relations strategy in the 1970s; however, it was seen as one element in an overall strategy to increase individual rights, roll back the frontiers of corporatism and reduce the imbalance of power in industry. Increased use of ballots would reduce the ability of militant union leaders to distort union resources for their own (often political) ends by enabling the moderate majority to exercise more effective influence over union leaders, both through elections and through votes on specific issues, especially strikes.

Conservative Policy on Ballots

Conservative policy on ballots concerned two areas: union elections and strikes. The importance of the two areas varied throughout the 1970s, according to political and industrial preoccupations. Hence the 1971 Industrial Relations Act dealt with strike ballots, but not with union elections. Following the events of 1974, the party became more concerned with union elections, and less concerned with strike ballots. The party was concerned to stimulate long-term changes in the union leadership, and was highly aware of the practical difficulties involved in strike ballots. However, concern with strike ballots revived at the end of 1978, and attention was again focused on them in the run up to the 1979 election.

The 1971 Industrial Relations Act provided for ballots to be held in three situations: first, in connection with the formation and continuation of 'agency shop agreements' – the acceptable face of the closed shop; secondly, in connection with granting sole bargaining rights to trade union(s); thirdly, the Act granted the Secretary of State power to apply to the National Industrial Relations Court (NIRC) for a ballot either where a strike was likely to be gravely injurious to the national interest or where a strike was likely to be seriously injurious to a substantial number of workers in the industry and there were reasons for thinking that the workers involved had not been properly consulted. If the NIRC granted the Secretary of State's request the ballots were mandatory for the union concerned.[20] The provisions were not regarded as central to the Act, and were only used once, as mentioned above: they disappeared with the repeal of the 1971 Act in 1974.

The miners' dispute of 1973–4 changed Conservative priorities on balloting. The party began to take more interest in union elections, and relegated consideration of strike ballots to the back-burner; the experience of the 1972 rail strike indicated the dangers of mandatory strike ballots. The leaders of the NUM were seen as posing a fundamental challenge to Parliamentary sovereignty by refusing to accept stage III of the Government's incomes policy. Such leaders were seen as failing to reflect accurately the views of their members (although 81 per cent of miners had voted to authorize the NUM executive to organize industrial action against the NCB). As the Conservative manifesto for the February 1974 election put it, 'the best way of curbing the minority of extremists in the trade unions is for the moderate majority of union members to stand up and be counted'.[21] This could be helped by revising the 1971 Act to 'provide more effective control for the majority of union members by ensuring that they have the opportunity to elect governing bodies and national leaders of their unions by postal ballot'. Importantly, the proposals were confined to balloting for election to national office (not to lower posts, nor to strikes), the use of ballots was to be mandatory and there was no mention of public funding. As the Conservative party was defeated in the February 1974 election the policy was, of course, not implemented.

By October 1974, the Conservative party's policy on ballots had evolved a step further. Conscious of the failure of the theme of 'who governs' in the February election campaign, the Conservative party adopted a more conciliatory attitude towards the trade unions in the run up to the October election. For the first time the Conservative party put forward the notion of a public subsidy for union ballots.[22] This change had two major advantages. It indicated that the party was not solely concerned with 'union-bashing', but was genuinely attempting to extend participation in union elections. Secondly, it made the policy slightly more acceptable to some unions who might be sympathetic to ballots (for example, because of a dispersed membership) but anxious about the costs involved. Moreover, there was no statement that the use of ballots would be mandatory: they were desirable and should be encouraged, but not required.

This more cautious approach was reflected in the discussion of ballots in *The Right Approach* in October 1976. The 'commonsense' majority of union members should 'make their voices heard and their opinions felt'.[23] This would ensure that trade union leaders were 'as representative as possible'. At present the trade unions were 'imperfectly democratic'. But 'the main desire for improvement in the democratic procedures of unions must come from the members themselves'. Nevertheless, the party was 'ready to help'. It therefore proposed that public money 'should be made available for the conduct of postal ballots for union elections where these are requested'. There was therefore to be no dictation to unions on how to elect their national officials: the initiative was to come from the unions themselves, with the Government providing a helping hand. In putting forward this cautious line *The Right Approach* was following the preferences of James Prior, which were at that stage acceptable to Mrs Thatcher, who was concerned to allay any suspicions that the Conservative party was only interested in 'union-bashing'.

Conservative party policy on ballots was thus very different from the policy expressed in the manifesto of the February 1974 election. Most importantly, the emphasis was on voluntary action by trade unions, with only a very limited role envisaged for the Government. Perhaps surprisingly, support for government action on ballots was strongest amongst the left wing of the Conservative party. In his *The Ascent of Britain,* published in 1977, Peter Walker argued that trade unions would have to be forced into adopting postal ballots for the election of union officials: a permissive and voluntary scheme would be useless since the existing union leaderships would not seek to change the electoral systems which kept them in power.[24] Public funds were to pay for mandatory postal ballots in union elections. His arguments had little impact in the short term.

Conservative policy on balloting, as on industrial relations generally, changed little between the publication of *The Right Approach* in October

1976 and the end of 1978. Towards the end of 1978 Conservative leaders, especially Sir Geoffrey Howe, began to pay more public attention to the inadequacies of trade union democracy, as part of the build up to the anticipated general election. 'We must invite the electorate to demand a fundamental change in the objectives and role of Britain's trade unions.' Sir Geoffrey's overall aim was to ensure that it would be much more difficult for union leaders in future 'to continue the pursuit of socialism regardless of the wishes of their members'. In a later speech he declared: 'Union members increasingly contract out of Labour party membership. A mixed Labour and Communist union hierarchy claims to speak for a membership of whom virtually none vote Communist – barely even vote Labour any longer. Yet the questionable reality remains in the form of a union leadership pledged to maintain a failed but compliant Labour government in power.' The strategy of the party, Sir Geoffrey claimed, was not to 'alienate the union rank and file from its leadership but to shame the leadership out of its cosy relationship with Labour back into line with its members needs and aspirations'.[25] He elaborated later:

> In this debate we are addressing three questions. Does the claim of union leaders to speak for their members stand up to critical examination? Does the political partnership between union leaders and Labour politicians mean that the former can often mishear or disregard the voice of the people and continue to pursue their own generally Socialist objectives? If so how can we jointly develop a positive role for the trade unions so that they increase wealth and employment rather than reduce it?[26]

Towards the end of 1978, Conservative party policy on union balloting began to change. In October, Ford workers began a strike in defiance of the Government's '5 per cent' wage norm. Ford workers nationally had walked out when they heard the company's original wage offer. As the strike developed, increasing concern began to be expressed in the press about the way decision making was being conducted at union mass meetings. Union meetings at the beginning of November were extensively criticized in the press, when it appeared that the majorities being claimed by the union platform hierarchy in favour of continuing strike action were exaggerated. This concern was echoed by the then Labour Prime Minister in the Commons when he announced that he was not satisfied with the show of hands method of voting, and declared, much to the surprise of the Opposition Front Bench, that: 'We have to be very careful how we talk to the trade unions about legislation on these matters . . . But if the trade union movement comes forward and says that it would like to alter the system and that it would like some legislation to do this, certainly I should respond.'[27]

This declaration by Mr Callaghan caused some consternation amongst the Conservatives, suggesting that the Labour government were threatening to take over what had been identified until that time by the electorate as an exclusively Conservative policy. This posed tactical problems for the party in the run up to the general election.

At the end of December the *Financial Times* reported that the Conservatives were about to launch 'a major new initiative' over the use of secret ballots.[28] The new policy would cover strike ballots as well as union elections. The aim of this initiative was to identify the wider use of secret ballots clearly with Conservative party policies. The objective was to encourage moderation amongst union members by protecting the 'commonsense majority' from being pressured at mass meetings into supporting strike action which they would otherwise not have countenanced. This new initiative was launched by the Leader of the Opposition on London Weekend Television's 'Weekend World' programme on 7 January 1979. Mrs Thatcher said '. . . we are prepared to legislate to have free secret postal ballots for the election of union officials and for [these] to be paid for by the Government . . . [and] for any major decision which affects the livelihood of their members and of course a major strike does . . .'. Between the beginning of November and the end of December, the party adopted the policy of extending their originally limited scheme to include 'any major decision' which a union proposed to make and which affected the livelihood of union members. When pressed by Brian Walden to explain how her policy would work in practice, Mrs Thatcher said 'it might be possible to say that you should only be able to get benefits, social security benefits, as a result of a strike if it is quite clear that that strike has been taken as the result of a secret ballot . . .'. This statement was apparently made without the approval of the Shadow Cabinet. If the policy on encouraging the wider use of ballots before a strike had been genuinely one of long standing, it is highly unlikely that such a radical amendment to the basic position would have been without the approval of her Front Bench team.

The party had thus become committed to encouraging the wider use of balloting within the union movement through public subsidy. Leon Brittan, who had chaired a working party on industrial relations policy, summed up the new official position in a debate on 16 March: 'There is ample room for extending a greater measure of democracy at all levels in the trade unions, whether in relation to the election of officers or decisions about strike ballots . . .'.[29] In accordance with this policy, at the end of March the party attempted to pass provisional legislation which would 'encourage the use of secret ballots in trade union affairs' under the Ten Minute Rule. This was obviously an exercise in public relations; no Bill introduced under these provisions by an Opposition MP has any real chance of becoming law. However, what was significant was that the Shadow Cabinet clearly attached importance to the Bill. Mrs Thatcher and her senior colleagues were all present during the debate and duly voted in the lobbies, where the Bill was given a first reading by a majority of 194 to 189.

In introducing the Bill, Ray Whitney condemned the fact that the procedures under which many union leaders were elected, often for life, were undemocratic. Whitney commended the AUEW (E) for its system of postal elections, which had resulted in a 'sensible and moderate' leadership. The electoral procedures of the GMWU, however, were an example to Mr Whitney of an unsatisfactory system in which branches cast block votes. Mr Whitney did not refer to ballots before strikes at all; he confined his comments on the inadequate condition of union democracy exclusively to elections to union office. In contrast, Tom Litterick, who spoke against the Bill, was under the impression that the Conservatives wanted to legislate with pre-strike ballots specifically in mind. The Bill, for Mr Litterick and the Labour party, was 'hostile and critical' towards trade unions and reflected the 'extreme ignorance' of Mr Whitney on the whole subject.[30]

Parliament came to an end on 26 March when the Government lost a 'no confidence' debate in the Commons, and the Bill on ballots disappeared. The Conservative party's election manifesto was published early in April. Running through the manifesto was the concern for the supremacy of Parliament which had characterized policy documents since 1974. The manifesto confirmed the earlier impression that party policy on ballots was devised to achieve political as well as industrial relations objectives. In a reference to Labour's trade union legislation of 1976, the manifesto complained: 'by heaping privilege without responsibility on the trade unions, Labour has given a minority of extremists the power to abuse individual liberties and to thwart Britain's chances of success'. The manifesto referred to the fact that 'too often trade unions are dominated by a handful of extremists who do not reflect the commonsense views of most union members'. The party's main task was therefore 'to restore the health of our economic and social life by controlling inflation *and striking a fair balance between the rights and duties of the trade union movement* . . . .'[31] Encouraging the use of postal ballots was to be a major plank in securing this overall objective. The manifesto was to be basis of the 1980 Employment Act.

Throughout the 1970s Conservative policy on ballots changed substantially. During 1971–4 the party was concerned solely with strike ballots and the best method of dealing with national strike 'emergencies'; there was no policy on union elections. However, the experience of 1973–4 led the party to consider methods of ensuring that trade union leaders took account of their members' opinions. Hence the references to mandatory ballots in elections for national union office in the February 1974 manifesto; no mention was made of further proposals on strike ballots. In October 1974 the party was still concerned with elections to union offices, but wished to avoid appearing concerned solely with 'union bashing'; hence, the conciliatory tone and the proposal for public subsidies for ballots. This remained party policy until the end of 1978. The events of the winter of 1978–9 revived Conservative interest in strike ballots, and at the beginning of 1979 the party announced a new initiative on ballots, involving the use of public subsidies for ballots in all circumstances in which union members' economic interests were substantially involved.

By the 1979 general election, Conservative policy involved encouraging postal ballots 'at all levels' in trade unions, both in industrial action and in union elections. The objectives in the two areas differed. In the former, the Conservatives' objectives were primarily short term: ballots might be a means of reducing the frequency of industrial action. In the latter case, the party was concerned to change the whole political complexion of the trade union movement, to permit the large numbers of 'moderate' trade unionists to influence the political tenor of union leaderships. Doing so would have a major impact on industrial relations and on politics by leading to a more limited, and more generally legitimated, role for trade unions.

Working Paper on Support from Public Funds for Union Ballots

The Conservative party's manifesto and the speeches of the leadership during the 1979 general election campaign had unequivocally committed the party to urgent action in the area of trade union reform. But there were differences of view on the degree of urgency necessary between the Prime Minister and her Employment Secretary, James Prior. Mr Prior had always favoured a patient and pragmatic approach to the problems of industrial relations, and had envisaged holding a number of informal meetings with TUC and CBI officials. These talks would have been used as a sounding board for more structured and formal discussions later in the autumn, preparing both sides of industry (but particularly the unions) for what was to come. For the first few weeks of the new government it seemed that Mr Prior would have his way.

Mr Prior's original strategy of making a careful start along the road leading to legislation came under early attack from the group of Ministers who were particularly close to the Prime Minister and the 'market wing' of the party which she represented. The TUC's muted reaction to Sir Geoffrey Howe's first Budget appeared to convince the Prime Minister that the advantage which the Government had gained should be pressed home, and that there should be no delay in producing definite proposals for the legislation on trade unions promised in the manifesto. The Prime Minister and the Cabinet, in a reversal of Mr Prior's original policy, decided to speed up the consultation process and send the proposals to the TUC and CBI by the middle of July. Accordingly, on 9 July the Government produced three working papers on picketing, the closed shop and support from public funds for union ballots, and invited comments from interested parties on their contents.

In the Working Paper on *Support from Public Funds for Union Ballots*, the Government commented:

> There is a wider public support for more extensive use of secret ballots in unions and growing recognition within the union movement itself that secret ballots on important matters are desirable. Ballots produce greater membership involvement in decision-making and give every trade union member the opportunity to record his or her decision without others watching and taking

note. It is not practicable for every decision whatever the circumstances to be taken after a secret ballot of the membership and unions themselves must decide when ballots are appropriate. But the purpose of the legislation will be to remove major financial constraints on unions from holding important ballots and this should enable unions increasingly to employ secret ballots on important issues.[32]

The Government had thus set out its own arguments for producing these proposals (i.e. wider membership participation and freedom to express an opinion without fear of future reprisal) and the effect the forthcoming legislation was envisaged as having (i.e. more extensive use of secret ballots). The matters to be covered by the proposed scheme were listed as being: first, 'elections to full time trade union office and to the executive or other governing body of an independent trade union': secondly, 'matters involving changes in union rules'; and thirdly, 'the calling or ending of strikes'. The Working Paper also raised the question as to whether the Secretary of State should have powers to extend the scope of the scheme by Order in Council. Unions would be able to claim reimbursement of 'the reasonable postal costs of conducting a secret ballot' on any of the matters listed above. The question whether workplace as well as postal ballots should qualify for public subsidy was left open-ended in the Working Paper, although concern was expressed about the difficulties of ensuring the secrecy of workplace ballots.

The Government regarded the certification officer as the 'most appropriate person' to administer the scheme. The certification officer would need to 'satisfy himself that the relevant expenditure was reasonably incurred and that the secrecy of the ballot was properly secured.' No ballot was to qualify under the scheme if it had been held contrary to union rules.

The TUC's immediate reaction to the three Working Papers was hostile. Len Murray, TUC general secretary, described the proposals as 'a major challenge to the existing rights of workers and their unions',[33] and other union leaders such as Tom Jackson, David Basnett and Alan Fisher were equally critical. But the main targets for union hostility were the working papers dealing with picketing and the closed shop. There was very little direct comment made on the ballot proposals. The CBI responded to the working papers by stating that its members welcomed the proposals made and that they were in no doubt that changes were needed after the events of the preceding winter. The press viewed the Government's proposals on balloting as being non-controversial and harmless. According to the *Observer*: 'the proposal to provide Government finance to encourage secret ballots is at worst harmless and may do some good . . .'.[34] The *Financial Times* commented in a similar vein. Although the Government had hoped that the ballot proposals would be uncontroversial, it rapidly became clear that, for the TUC, effective opposition to the Government's proposals on picketing and the closed shop would necessitate firm rejection of the offer of public subsidy for union ballots. Any other position would have been hypocritical and untenable.

Response from Employers

The CBI's initial statement welcoming the Government's three working papers in July was followed by detailed analysis and comment in September. The CBI had submitted a lengthy memorandum to Mr Prior in June 1978, setting out its agenda for industrial relations reform. The memorandum called for legislation on picketing, the closed shop and finance for strikers' families; it did not ask for legislation on balloting. The CBI therefore naturally welcomed the Government's July 1979 proposals. The CBI's general position was that 'changes are needed to redress the present imbalance in industrial relations legislation and that urgent action is required in some cases'. The CBI endorsed the working papers on picketing and the closed shop enthusiastically: 'the papers on picketng and the closed shop are very much in line with CBI's own thinking on these subjects'. However, the CBI was lukewarm on the government's ballot proposals: 'We naturally support the idea of greater involvement of trade union members in decision making in their unions but we have reservations as to the extent to which the offer of financial assistance by government will encourage this. Nevertheless we believe that it may be helpful in certain circumstances.'[35] In the mid-1970s the CBI had not considered internal union affairs to be their concern. Hence in 1977 the CBI stated: 'Employers can and should have little to say in how a union conducts its affairs. That is a matter for the union membership, subject to certain minimum requirements laid down by Parliament'. The CBI's view had changed by the following year. In its 1978 policy statement, *Britain Means Business*, the CBI declared: 'When the actions of trade unions can so seriously affect the livelihoods of individuals, and the economy of the country, it is a matter of public policy that trade unions should be democratically accountable'.[36] The CBI's reservations about the Government's July 1979 proposals appeared to be that they would be ineffective, certainly in the short run, not that they were illegitimate.

In commenting on the details of the proposed scheme, the CBI saw 'no difficulties' in applying the scheme to internal union matters such as the election of union officers and changes in union rules. However, there were difficulties envisaged about balloting on industrial action. The CBI was concerned about who would have responsibility for drafting the question to be put to the workforce, and the timing of a ballot, which might be used merely to strengthen a negotiator's hands. Balloting on the ending of industrial action was thought to be particularly difficult; in this situation, 'balloting can result in delays and limits the discretion of union officials'. Financial assistance should be 'limited to postal ballots and to such easily identifiable items as the cost of printing and postage'. Workplace ballots ought not to be covered by the scheme because of 'the difficulty in establishing which items of expenditure may have been justified and whether the ballot has been properly conducted'.

Amongst CBI members there was little disagreement on the desirability of public financial provision for union ballots. Twenty-one organizations formally commented to CBI officials on the three working papers and fifteen on the working paper on ballots, out of a total membership of over a hundred employers' organizations. Of these fifteen replies, only the Electrical Contractors Association of Scotland opposed the idea of any financial support. The Association commented: 'We agree that unions should make every endeavour to see that their members are democratically represented and should be encouraged to do so. Whether public funds should be used for this purpose is something we would question seriously and would not lend our support to this concept at present.'[37]

This unique response to the working paper resulted from consultation with the Association's membership and, originally at least, did not appear to have been the subject of any great attention. But subsequent experience confirmed the Association's conviction that this had been the correct approach. The Association encountered major difficulties over a ballot on a new North Sea Oil Agreement covering the terms and conditions of employment of electricians, boilermakers and sheet metal workers employed in the North Sea in late 1979. The ballot result was inconclusive, and the ballot itself had taken over a month to organize. In addition, the Association was aware that there was at least a possibility that responsible union officials might be replaced by more militant officials if balloting on union elections were to become more widespread.

There was little pressure from CBI members for ballots to be made compulsory on some issues; only one respondent to the CBI's request for comments on the working paper favoured consideration to be given to this question. The Engineering Employers' Federation (EEF) was the most articulate in expressing support for the scheme's 'permissive' nature: 'It is, right, however, not to seek to compel a system of balloting, but rather to encourage the demand for wider balloting to arise voluntarily within the membership.'[38]

The EEF's thinking on ballots was far more developed than that of most other CBI members. This was because the EEF had set up an internal working party to consider the Conservative party's industrial relations policies and their implications for engineering companies before the election. The majority of the EEF working party thought that the Conservative party's policy on ballots would be a useful means of removing any excuse on the part of unions for not holding ballots. At the same time, engineering employers did not want to be seen as interfering in the domestic affairs of independent trade unions, and the ideal position would have been for unions to finance their own ballots. However, the EEF working party believed that something would be needed to 'start the ball rolling', and a public subsidy might well prove to be the necessary catalyst. This view was expressed in the Federation's own comment on the July Working Paper:

> . . . it will be necessary in due course to review the situation in the light of the extent of charge to the public which is actually incurred. In any such review it

would be desirable to have regard to a presumption that once the reasonableness of the principle of balloting is more firmly established, unions will wish to create the conditions whereby they can operate the principle without recourse to public subsidy.[39]

CBI members were fairly evenly divided on the question of whether the proposed scheme should cover non-postal (i.e. workplace) as well as postal ballots. Not surprisingly, the Building Trades Employers, faced with their unique circumstances, favoured workplace ballots coming within the scheme, as did the EEF and the Port Employers. However, a very small majority of those participating in the consultation did not favour this development, and this appears to have been the view echoed on the Industrial Relations Sub-Committee and the Employment Policy Committee of the CBI who considered the membership's representations.

The CBI's general attitude towards the Government's proposals on ballots was therefore ambivalent and unenthusiastic. The CBI did not reject the scheme, but neither was it positively in favour. Politically, it would have been unthinkable to rebuff the Government's initiative. But the CBI clearly did not attach any great importance to the proposal, nor did it envisage that it would have any significant effect on industrial relations.

The only amendment which the CBI asked the Government to consider to the scheme was that it should cover ballots on major wage offers. The CBI was concerned that the scheme proposed by the Government would only cover such ballots (if at all) if the decision whether or not to accept an employer's offer was attached to a call for strike action. In the CBI's view this would have been unnecessarily provocative. The Department of Employment, however, turned down the CBI's request on the simple ground that it would create too heavy a financial strain on the scheme's finances (although they revised the scheme in accordance with the CBI's wishes in 1982).

The British Institute of Management (BIM) was strongly in favour of the use of public money 'to encourage and facilitate secret ballots' and accepted all of the Government's proposals on the matters to be covered by the scheme. The Unquoted Companies Group (UCG), led by Sir Emmanuel Kaye, submitted detailed comments on the working paper. The Group consists of private companies, many of them large undertakings such as Lansing-Bagnall, acting together informally: it has no full time staff or central facilities. Nevertheless, the UCG is particularly close to the market wing of the Conservative government, with excellent relations with Mrs Thatcher and Sir Keith Joseph. The UCG 'fully supported' the aim of encouraging the use of secret ballots, including the use of public funds. But the Group was unhappy about the provisions of many union rule books regarding the conduct of ballots, rules which for the UCG either encouraged apathy or provided a positive disincentive to vote. The UCG was therefore opposed to the use of public funds to help finance trade union ballots unless there was a reasonable measure of public accountability for the rules governing ballot procedures. According to the UCG, legislation should require of unions that their rules make provision for the election of governing bodies and should specify the manner in which the ballots should be conducted. The UCG also recommended that legislation should provide for minimum standards in union rules relating to ballot procedures. Such views were to be echoed in the Government's policy after the 1983 General Election.

The Institute of Directors regarded the holding of secret ballots on the matters specified in the working paper as 'vital'. However, the Institute believed that postal ballots were open to abuse, and consequently favoured workplace ballots. The Institute believed that the unions themselves rather than the taxpayer should pay for ballots. In addition, there would need to be 'effective independent supervision of ballots'. In effect, the Institute of Directors disagreed with the substance of the Government's proposals, whilst favouring the Government's underlying assumptions about the value of a wider use of secret ballots.

Aims, the free enterprise organization led by Michael Ivens, commented that the Government's proposals were 'an essential step forward', but that they were only 'a first step' – 'much more has to be achieved if Britain is to become prosperous'. On the working paper on ballots, Aims rather curiously asked the Government to extend the proposals 'to deal with important union matters such as the election of union officials'. Since the Government had already proposed to include elections to full time office and to union executives within the scheme, Aims may have been asking for the election of lay union officials to be covered as well. However, Aims did not make clear exactly what they were asking the Government to do, and Patrick Mayhew, Parliamentary Under-Secretary at the Department of Employment, in his reply to Mr Ivens simply assumed that Aims were expressing support for the Government's existing proposals.

The Institute of Personnel Management was not as uncritical in its support for the Government's working papers as many other employer groups. On picketing, for example, the IPM felt that the existing law could deal with 'some of the more undesirable aspects of picketing' already, and warned against preventing employees from being able to picket their own company's head office, a proposal set out in the working paper. On balloting, the IPM told the Secretary of State that postal ballots should be confined to electing union officials and changing union rules; they were not appropriate for the calling and ending of strikes. 'In practical industrial relations it is often better to be negotiating in a flexible situation where a ballot has not locked the union into strike action and where a return to work can be achieved as speedily as possible.'[40] The IPM was opposed to the provision of public funds for workplace ballots and for the administrative costs of postal ballots. The IPM took a very similar line on ballots to that of the CBI. Internal union ballots were favoured by both organizations, but postal ballots on industrial action were considered undesirable and impractical.

The response to the Government's proposals on ballots from employers was therefore mixed, only the BIM being unreservedly in favour of all the basic proposals in the working paper. All of the other organizations which commented expressed reservations concerning some aspects of the proposals on the grounds that they involved public expenditure, infringed union independence, were impractical or would make little difference. There was definitely no universal acclaim from industry in support of the Government's new initiative on ballots; most employers favoured some features of the government's proposals, but were generally unenthusiastic.

Trade Union Response

The immediate response from the trade unions to the Government's working papers was hostile. This hostility was directed primarily against government proposals on picketing and the closed shop. On 27 July a note setting out the TUC's comments on the three working papers was circulated to all affiliated unions. The TUC complained that the working papers were 'irrelevant to the basic issues of improving industrial relations, and promoting improvements in productivity, real earnings and job and income security'. There was little attention paid to the balloting proposals; in a document comprising forty paragraphs there were only two paragraphs on ballots. The TUC commented:

> Unions would have a choice whether to apply for public funds. But if they do so they must recognize that financial help will not be given from public sources without public accountability. This would have implications for union autonomy if – as appears possible – it led to the Certification Officer developing procedures (which might need to be incorporated in unions rules) and also supervising aspects of the ballots . . . Affiliated unions would need to recognize very clearly the implications for their autonomy of accepting money from public sources.[41]

The idea of publicly funding union ballots was not rejected outright; the objection at this stage was to the threat to union independence which accepting public funds might pose.

On 22 August a TUC delegation led by Len Murray and Harry Urwin, Chairman of the Employment Policy and Organization Committee, met with James Prior and Patrick Mayhew to discuss the working papers' proposals. The TUC rejected the whole package of reforms on picketing and the closed shop put forward by the Government, and urged the Government to allow the TUC time to operate the February guidelines on the closed shop and the conduct of industrial disputes (which contained guidance on picketing). For its part the Government made clear its intention of legislating in the autumn, with or without the agreement of the unions.

This stand taken by Prior and Mayhew raised the questions of what the Government was expecting to achieve by consultation and how genuinely it was prepared to consider union requests for amendments to the working papers' proposals. The *Observer,* and some TUC officials, thought that

Mr Prior would have been wiser to challenge the TUC publicly to enforce its guidance to unions rather than to produce immediate plans for legislation.[42] However, the Government was too deeply committed politically to trade union reform to permit Mr Prior even to contemplate using purely voluntary methods in the pursuit of the manifesto commitments. These commitments were also too entrenched to permit any genuine negotiation with the unions; for example, there could be no question of Prior dropping his proposals on the closed shop in return for tougher TUC action on picketing. Moreover, it would have been difficult for Mr Prior to have moved towards the TUC position on union reform without seriously offending the employers. There was therefore little prospect from the beginning of the consultation process that the Government would be persuaded by the TUC to change its proposals significantly.

At the August meeting between the TUC and Mr Prior, the TUC had asked the Government to elaborate on their proposals for union ballots. Speaking at the TUC Annual Congress two weeks later, Harry Urwin claimed that the Government had expressed at this meeting a willingness to drop ballots on strikes from their proposed legislation.[43] This made the TUC unclear as to the Government's objectives, since the Government did not appear to have finalized any definite policy at all. The TUC was therefore prepared to adopt a policy of 'wait and see' on ballot proposals, whilst unequivocally opposing the Government's other proposals.

The publication of the working papers also produced an immediate hostile response from individual unions. A motion on the preliminary agenda for the TUC Congress in the name of UCATT called upon the General Council to 'withdraw from all discussions with the Government based on their proposals as published'. However, this motion failed to reach the final agenda, as TUC leaders were not prepared to withdraw from all contacts with Ministers at that stage. Instead of the UCATT resolution, the TUC agreed without any dissension to 'resist vigorously fundamental attacks on trade union rights by a campaign mobilizing the resources and membership of the entire trade union movement'. Again, the motion concentrated heavily on the proposals concerning the closed shop and picketing; the only reference to the Government's policy on union ballots was the statement that: 'Congress rejects . . . any attempt by the Government to interfere with the internal democratic procedures of individual trade unions'.[44] In moving the resolution, Joe Wade (NGA) condemned the Working Papers as 'an insidious and calculated attempt by the Government to undermine and interfere in the internal and democratic process of trade unions'. But none of the other speakers referred to the balloting proposals. The TUC's stand on the Government's policy on ballots was thus uncertain, in part because the TUC was uncertain of the Government's intentions.

The first opinion polls on the Government's working papers were published in September. Conducted by Gallup, the findings established that trade unionists approved of Government plans to reform the law, with substantial majorities supporting the main proposals. There was overwhelming support for the proposal that there should be no industrial action taken without a secret ballot of the workforce (a proposal not being put forward by the Government).[45] On the question of whether or not public money should be used to encourage the use of secret ballots there was a marked indifference, and as many as 42 per cent positively disapproved.

With the consultation exercise completed by the end of October, the Government began the process of drafting legislation. The two sides of industry had been predictably divided in their response to the working papers on the closed shop and picketing; but on the proposals for the public funding of ballots there had been a very low-key reaction. Employers generally supported the Government's intentions, but were unenthusiastic about the details of the scheme and dismissive of its likely practical effects. The TUC was probably suspicious of the Government's intentions and worried about the autonomy of unions who might accept public money; but the policy was to wait and see exactly what the Government had in mind for the forthcoming Bill.

THE LEGISLATIVE PROCESS

The Employment Bill was published early in December 1979. Clause 1 of the Bill contained the Government's proposals on ballots. It gave the Secretary of State powers to draw up regulations to establish a scheme which was to be administered by the certification officer, providing for payments towards expenditure incurred by independent trade unions in conducting specified secret ballots. The Secretary of State also had the power to extend the scope of the scheme by further regulations.

Clause 1 provided that the Secretary of State 'may by regulations make a scheme providing for payments by the Certification Officer towards expenditure incurred by independent trade unions in respect of ballots'. The purposes for which ballots could be funded related to:

(a) obtaining a decision or ascertaining the views of members of a trade union as to the calling or ending of a strike or other industrial action;
(b) electing a person to the committee of management of a trade union or, if the union does not have a committee of management, to the body exercising the functions of a committee of management;
(c) electing a person to any post which he will hold as an employee of a trade union;
(d) amending the rules of a trade union;
(e) obtaining a decision in accordance with the Trade Union (Amalgamations, etc.) Act 1964 on a resolution to approve an instrument of amalgamation or transfer;

and such other purposes as the Secretary of State may by order specify.

Funds were to be made available only where 'the ballot is so conducted as to secure, so far as reasonably practicable, that those voting may do so in secret'. Detailed regulations were to be promulgated by statutory instruments.

The clause thus clearly followed the details contained in the working paper. There were, however, a number of changes made from the original July proposals. First, the matters to be covered by the scheme had been extended to cover ballots on amalgamations and mergers between unions. This had been a surprise omission from the original proposals as ballots (although not postal ballots) were legally mandatory for union amalgamations under the Trade Unions (Amalgamations, etc.) Act 1964. Secondly, clause 1 (3) (a) referred to ballots on 'the calling or ending of a strike or other industrial action'. The working paper had confined itself to ballots on the calling or ending of strikes; there had been no mention of ballots on other forms of industrial action. It would appear that the initiative to extend the scheme in this way had come from the EEF, which had been involved in a lengthy dispute with the CSEU during the summer of 1979. The dispute had begun with a national overtime ban which had caused considerable disruption for employers. In the EEF's submissions to the Government on the working paper, it had specifically called for the scheme to cover 'other industrial action of a significant character', using as an example a national overtime ban. In responding to the EEF's request the Government might well have been hoping to make a gesture of goodwill towards them, as they had failed to meet EEF fears concerning legislation on the closed shop.

Thirdly, the Bill specified carefully which elections to union office would be covered by the scheme. The working paper had referred to elections 'to full-time trade union office' as being an area which the Government intended to bring within the proposals for public subsidy. As it stood, this phase could be interpreted as including those union officers who performed their union duties on a full-time basis whilst remaining employees of their firms; many convenors and shop stewards fell into this category. The Bill, however, excluded such elections from the scheme, as clause 1 (3) (c) referred to 'electing a person to any post which he will hold as an employee of a trade union'. This confined the operation of the proposed scheme to a much narrower band of elections than originally envisaged in the working paper. Elections to full-time 'lay' positions within unions would thus not qualify for public subsidy unless these fell within clause 1 (3) (b), which was concerned with executive committee elections. The Government had not received any requests from any commenting organization to limit the scope of the scheme in this way. This important change may have been made accidentally, as the result of a mistake in the drafting of the clause; alternatively, it might have been deliberately introduced as a means of limiting the burden of the scheme on the Exchequer. As events were to turn out, the former explanation turned out to be the correct one.

Two issues which had specifically been left open in the working paper and on which comments had been invited were whether workplace ballots should qualify for a reimbursement from public funds, and whether the

Secretary of State should have power to extend the scheme by his own powers. The second question was resolved without equivocation: clause 1 (3) gave the Minister such powers. However, on the former question, the clause was unclear whether or not postal ballots alone would qualify for public subsidy; in fact, the clause merely referred to 'ballots' and did not distinguish between any particular type of ballot at all. Thus, in theory, provided the ballot satisfied the conditions of clause 1 (5) it would make no difference whether the ballot had been conducted at the workplace or distributed and returned by post. The Government thus appeared to provide for workplace as well as postal ballots, provided that workplace ballots were organized to provide for as much secrecy as was 'reasonably practicable'.

The Bill had its second reading in the House of Commons on 17 December.[46] In introducing his Bill, the Secretary of State referred to an Early Day Motion drawn up by Labour back-benchers during the last session of the previous Parliament. In an attempt to thwart any Opposition criticism of clause 1, Mr Prior quoted the motion in full: 'That this House in the interests of maximum democratic participation urges the Government to introduce legislation to ensure the provision of financial aid for postal ballots in trade union elections.' Clause 1 clearly went beyond the scope of this Early Day Motion, in that it proposed financial aid for a much wider range of ballots, although the reference was a useful Parliamentary ploy. Mr Prior spent little time on clause 1 in his speech, and his remarks were very modest. Clause 1 would not lead to the immediate adoption of secret postal ballots by all trade unions, but it would remove the financial obstacles to the holding of postal ballots.

Mr Prior clearly expected clause 1 to be completely non-controversial, and did not envisage any serious Parliamentary argument. This assessment was largely accurate in terms of party political controversy. Eric Varley, Shadow Employment Secretary, passed quickly over clause 1 in his concern to criticize the clauses on picketing and the closed shop, and merely remarked that he had no great objection to ballots. The only hint of strong opposition to clause 1 came from Labour back-benchers, Eric Heffer and Norman Hogg. Heffer saw the balloting provisions proposed in the Bill as the first step towards something more than state subsidies for balloting, i.e. the beginning of a move by the Government to introduce compulsory balloting. On repealing the Bill, however, Mr Heffer did say that 'any decent parts that may emerge from it may be incorporated in future legislation on the basis of experience'. This would appear to have been a reference to clause 1, as there was nothing else in the Bill at this stage (the clause on antenatal rights was only introduced in committee) which would have appealed to the Labour left wing. According to Norman Hogg: 'The suggestion that unions are undemocratic, that they do not follow true trade union practices . . . is unfair. There is no case for the use of public money for this purpose. There is no demand from trade unions that such money should be used for the purpose. There is no public demand that public money be spent in such a way . . .'

The Bill was relatively warmly received by the Liberal party. Cyril Smith thought that 'on the whole it is a good Bill'. Although he and the Liberals would object to compulsory ballots, 'as the clause is entirely voluntary, I cannot see any reason for anyone to take objection'.

Early in January 1980, the TUC published its 'Commentary on the Employment Bill'. On clause 1 the TUC complained that the scheme 'will apply to a wider range of ballots than was envisaged by the original working paper'. The TUC also envisaged that 'workplace ballots will qualify as well as postal ballots' (because the clause deliberately left the question open-ended). The inclusion of ballots on amalgamations and mergers was regarded as 'particularly important', but was seen as 'the carrot to the trade union movement to gain acceptance'. The basic TUC position on the clause remained the same as in July: 'The implications of such a scheme for the autonomy of unions which accept reimbursement for ballots from public funds will not become fully clear until the rules and details covering the scheme are issued, but it is clear that public funds cannot be handed over to unions without the acceptance by unions of some degree of public accountability'. The basis of TUC concern over clause 1 was thus the threat to union independence.

As soon as the Bill was published, it became clear that clause 1 would become a central feature of TUC opposition to the legislation, as it was the only part of the Bill which actually gave the trade unions the ability to exercise discretion, whether or not to take up the offer of public funds. The rest of the Bill made amendments to the existing law which would have immediate effects on unions and workers, irrespective of whether they accepted those changes. Thus clause 1 presented the TUC with the opportunity of 'making a stand' against the entire package of legislation which the Government was carrying through.

On the day before Standing Committee A was due to begin its deliberations on clause 1, the TUC held a special one day conference on the Bill which was attended by over 200 leaders from 73 affiliated unions. The conference decided that unions should be 'strongly advised' not to apply for public money under clause 1, and endorsed other plans to intensify the campaign against the Bill. David Basnett, chairman of the TUC's Economic Committee, took an early and prominent role in shaping Congress' policy on clause 1. In a letter to Len Murray in January 1980, Mr Basnett wrote about clause 1:

> It is a divisive provision designed to attract credibility to the totality of the Employment Bill by Unions taking advantage of the financial incentives it applies. In this sense it is analagous to the argument about the attractions of registration under the Industrial Relations Act which at first threatened to split the union movement. The provision of the finance will be subject to regulations and a possible code of practice which in effect will give the Certification Officer control over the conduct and content of ballots. This

represents the thin end of a very substantial wedge. There is a very serious danger that if a significant number of unions in a significant number of instances take adantage of the financial provisions then the Government will go a stage further and make such ballots mandatory in certain circumstances. This would represent a major incursion into trade union autonomy.[47]

Mr Basnett's role in forcing through a tough line on clause 1 in General Council was to be crucial. The only dissident voice at the special conference was that of Frank Chappell, general secretary of the EETPU. Chappell warned the conference that it could not ignore opinion polls, which showed a large measure of support for the Government's proposals. This early disagreement between Mr Basnett and Mr Chappell over what strategy to adopt towards the Bill was to increase as the months went by.

When the Bill came before the Standing Committee on 24 January, there was a major question mark hanging over the possible value of clause 1 as a result of TUC opposition. From the beginning of the committee discussion it seemed that the Labour Opposition was not entirely coherent in their position on clause 1. For example, John Evans, an Opposition whip, commented that 'we have not accepted even the principle of the ballot system at this moment.'[48] Giles Radice, in contrast, remarked that 'I am generally in favour of the idea of ballots and of encouraging them', although he went on to say that they were no panacea.[49] John Evans summed up the initial debate on the clause by stating that the Opposition viewed the clause 'not with hostility but with suspicion because of the whole context in which it appears in the Bill'.[50]

The Government used the committee stage to clear up one of the ambiguities and misunderstandings caused by the clause's wording: whether workplace ballots were to be covered by the scheme. In background notes on the clause provided for the committee's use, the Government stated that it intended 'that the regulations will provide only for [postal] ballots to be covered initially with power to bring in non-postal ballots later'. The intention was to begin the scheme by directing funds to where they were most needed; postal ballots were regarded as being much more expensive than workplace ballots and consequently needed immediate financing. Workplace ballots could be included at a later stage. In addition, another reason Mr Mayhew offered for this decision to exclude workplace ballots, at least initially, was that 'we are entering unchartered waters [and] for that reason we think it right to begin in a modest and limited way, and see how we get on'.[51]

The first amendment put down in committee by the Opposition was to impose on the Secretary of State a duty to involve ACAS in the preparation of the scheme by requiring him to make the necessary regulations only after consultation with the Service. Mr Mayhew rejected this amendment on the ground that the Government 'intends to consult ACAS, but not only ACAS'.[52] Not surprisingly, the Opposition amendment was defeated. However, Labour succeeded in extending the ambit of clause 1 (3) (c) by substituting 'office-holder' for 'employee'. Mr Mayhew accepted Labour's amendment on the grounds that 'there can be a strong case made for the provisions of the Bill to be extended to the election of shop stewards'.[53] In due course the Government introduced an amendment along these lines in the Commons. Labour also sought to delete from the clause the Secretary of State's power to extend the scheme by issuing further regulations, and to incorporate explicitly workplace ballots into the clause, but without success. Despite Labour's declared suspicion concerning the Government's intentions, clause 1 was accepted as forming part of the Bill without a vote being forced in the committee. Those fears were that the Government would, in the words of John Grant, 'be tempted towards compulsory ballots' if clause 1 did not produce the expected results, the expected results taking the form of a substantial increase in the use of secret postal ballots by trade unions: his fears were to be substantially justified.[54]

Clause 1 returned to the House of Commons for the report stage of the Bill on 20 March. Since the Bill's publication in December there had been growing unease on the right wing of the Conservative party that the Bill was too 'wet', particularly on the closed shop and picketing. The steel strike in January, especially the ISTC's decision to call out private sector steel workers without holding a ballot, focused attention on clause 1. For many Conservatives in Parliament this was intolerable, particularly as media attention focused on the reluctance of the private sector workers to participate in the strike. At the beginning of February an Early Day Motion in the name of Tony Marlowe was put down and signed by 93 Conservative back-benchers:

> That in the opinion of this House the current state of industrial law gives rise to industrial anarchy whereby any union is legally entitled through coercion and intimidation to threaten the economic well-being of the nation, and being anxious to protect the right to work of hundreds of thousands of trade unionists and others unwillingly involved in strikes over which they have not been consulted and the viability of countless firms who while not party to the dispute are currently being threatened and remembering the Conservative Party commitment at the general election calls upon Her Majesty's Government in accordance with overwhelming public demand to introduce immediate legislation to restore industrial equity.[55]

The motion called for action to curtail union immunities for organizing industrial action, and for legislation to ensure that workers asked to participate in strikes had the right to be consulted before any decisions were taken. This motion marked the beginning of a right-wing rebellion against major aspects of the Bill which was to be launched at the report stage. Another Early Day Motion, this time in the name of John Browne and Cyril Smith, was put down on 21 February.[56] This urged the Government: 'to ensure that when 15 per cent or more of members of a trade union demand a secret ballot before strike action is taken, their union shall be obliged to comply with their demands'. This motion attracted the signature of 103 MPs.

In their disquiet over the entirely voluntary nature of clause 1, Conservative MPs found considerable sympathy from the Institute of Directors, led by Walter Goldsmith. The Institute had taken a somewhat ambiguous initial view of clause 1, favouring the wider use of ballots but not wishing to see this supported by the tax payer. By the time the Bill reached the report stage the Institute wanted to see the clause amended so as to provide that ballots could be required in certain circumstances, removing the option when to hold ballots from union leaders. Instead, the Institute wanted ballots to be 'triggered' whenever a defined percentage of eligible union members requested it.

A number of back-benchers prepared amendments to clause 1 along these lines, including John Browne, the newly elected Member for Winchester, Robert Dunne and Michael Colvin. Mr Browne's amendment was drawn up in close association with Christopher Bailey, who had bitterly fought the last Labour government's plans to nationalize his ship repair company in Bristol and had, as a result, become a folk hero in the Conservative party.

Mr Browne and Mr Bailey had sought the advice and the backing of the CBI for their clause, but support was not forthcoming. This lack of support was hardly surprising, since the CBI was unenthusiastic about clause 1. The CBI's discussion document on the trade unions published in February 1980 as part of the work of the Jarratt Balance of Power Steering Group correctly identified a major dilemma in advocating extended use of ballots: trade unions can be too powerful *vis-à-vis* employers but 'weak and ineffectual' in relation to their own members.[57] The CBI clearly wanted to weaken the power of unions *vis-à-vis* employers, without weakening the authority of union officials to keep their members 'in line'. The CBI complained that 'the confidence and influence of [union] officials has been undermined by the drift in policy in many unions towards devolving power to the shop floor . . . power has shifted to such an extent that officials are increasingly reluctant or unable to assert themselves'. And most significantly, the CBI document went on to state: 'with the decline of the official the most stable element in a union's dealings with management has been seriously eroded'.[58] The CBI saw a 'danger' in all decisions 'having to be made by the rank-and-file'; such devolution became 'anarchic'.[59] The imposition by law of union rules on ballots needed 'detailed examination'.[60] In view of this it is hardly surprising that the CBI declined to support Browne's amendment.

However, the Jarratt Committee was not simply sceptical of the value of ballots; it specifically rejected balloting as a means of unions choosing their officials. 'It would be preferable for unions to appoint executive officials to salaried posts rather than to provide for their election for a fixed period only.' The CBI considered that this reduction in democracy would be 'more apparent than real', and 'more than outweighed by the increased authority of officials no longer required to satisfy a fickle electorate and by the benefits of continuity and experience'.[61] Even ballots before strike action came in for a measure of scepticism from the CBI, who argued that they should be used sparingly and 'only follow joint presentation on the points at issue'.[62]

There was thus a shift in CBI opinion against the policy of encouraging an extension in the use of secret ballots, which contrasted with the polite indifference the previous year. The CBI did not attempt to reconcile the potential contradiction in the CBI's overall policy of strengthening the authority of union officers over their own members and eliminating the closed shop; the closed shop was an obvious major weapon in the hands of union officials concerned to maintain discipline. As on other issues, the CBI was following a 'small firms' approach. At one level this is surprising in view of the dominance of large firms and employers' organizations on the major Employment Policy Committee. However, the CBI's concern to protect and promote vigorously a small firm's viewpoint was the result of an awareness that the CBI needed to expand recruitment, and most of their recruitment activity was in the small firms area. Moreover, the CBI Small Firms Council maintained a high profile in the CBI's inner councils, reminding the policy committees of its views and expectations. CBI officials were also conscious of the need to refer to the interests of small firms in their committee papers and in their dealings with Government officials. The effect of this activity was an industrial relations policy orientated towards small firms which quite often upset the larger interest groups amongst the membership. The CBI, in this respect, paralleled experience in the Conservative party.

All the back-bench amendments to clause 1 were concerned with the question of strike ballots. There was no right-wing attempt to make ballots compulsory in elections to union office, nor to give union members the right to hold a ballot in union elections if they wanted one. Mr Browne's amendment would have given trade union members the right to demand that a strike ballot be held.[63] As Mr Browne emphasized, this was 'not the same as a mandatory ballot' imposed on the union by an outside body. The purpose of putting down the amendment was, he said, 'to persuade the Secretary of State to accept the principle of a secret ballot triggered by a minority of union members'. This amendment would 're-introduce democracy for workers within their unions regarding industrial action'. Finally, the proposed new clause could provide 'invaluable experience for the future . . . on which to base subsequent legislation for a mandatory secret ballot'. The proposal would 'at best prevent some strikes and shorten others'. These comments, particularly the reference to future legislation, served to re-emphasize to Labour MPs and the TUC the pressures which existed within the Government for the imposition of compulsory ballots.

The back-bench amendments had powerful political support. George Gardiner, who took the leading role behind the scenes in marshalling support for the amendments, commented that there were 'Ministers who wish all power to our elbows', and that for 'every one Conservative Member in the Aye Lobby, there will be at least two outside wishing that

they were passing through it'.[64] Conservatives speaking in favour of the
amendments also quoted the authority of the Conservative Trade Unionists National Council which had called for trade unionists to have the right
to ballot before strikes were called. There was also public support for the
amendments. Sir Leonard Neal wrote to *The Times* on 31 March in support
of the attempts to amend clause 1, and *The Times* recommended
Conservatives to support Mr Browne's amendments in its Leader of 22
April.[65] On the other hand, *The Daily Telegraph* was opposed to the
Browne amendment, on the grounds of impracticability, and Anthony
Frodsham, director-general of the EEF, argued that Mr Browne's amendment 'may in practice worsen rather than improve industrial relations', and
urged MPs to reject it.[66] Goldsmith claimed that businessmen attached the
highest priority to stiffening clause 1 along the lines proposed by Colvin,
whose amendment, prepared in conjunction with the Institute, provided
for mandatory secret ballots on strikes.[67]

In his reply to the debate on the report stage Mr Prior played down the
importance of strike ballots, stressing instead the importance of promoting
secret ballots for union office. He rejected the amendments on three
grounds: their failure to deal with unofficial disputes, the possibility of
extremist minorities undermining moderate leaders and the difficulties of
enforcement. The Government, he said, were hoping to encourage the
voluntary extension of balloting rather than impose 'rigid procedures on
unions by law'.[68] The Secretary of State refused to be drawn into
committing himself to future legislation, although he was already committed to publishing a future Green Paper on trade union immunities.

Mr Prior's speech caused considerable animosity amongst some of his
back-benchers. John Gorst reminded the Secretary of State that 'we were
elected on Tory votes to achieve trade union reform, not to resist it on
Labour votes'.[69] And George Gardiner told Epping Forest Conservatives
in a speech two days after the debate, that if the Green Paper could form
the basis of further legislation such a Bill would 'unite the Conservative
party instead of dividing it'.[70]

The Liberals were split on whether to back the amendments. Cyril
Smith, their employment spokesman, had supported Mr Browne's new
clause on the basis that it 'has some respect for the individual within a trade
union' and was thus in tune with Liberal philosophy on the protection of
minorities. However, Mr Smith was unable to carry his party with him;
Mr Freud and Mr Ross voted against the amendments and five others
abstained, apparently on the basis that they could not bring themselves to
support an amendment which originated on the right wing of the
Conservative party.[71]

Labour MPs regarded the debate as a non-event. Ian Mikardo thought
the debate was 'silly' and Ron Leighton that it was 'nonsensical', and the
least important debate the House would have on the Bill.[72]

The amendments were lost by a very large majority, 491 to 48. None the
less, the length of the debate, the size of the minority and the strength of

feeling expressed, indicated that a large number of Conservatives were unhappy about the Employment Bill and Mr Prior's handling of its passage through Parliament.

After the vote had taken place, there were many rumours circulating within the Conservative party over the possible involvement of the Prime Minister in the revolt. Left-wing Conservatives were convinced that Mrs Thatcher had given unofficial approval to the rebellion, and pointed to the apparent lack of enthusiasm with which the whips had attempted to forestall votes being cast against the Government. Added credence was given to these rumours by the fact that the rebellion's organizer, George Gardiner, was himself well known as a close confidant and supporter of the Prime Minister. Mrs Thatcher voted against the amendments, but this did not allay suspicion that she had little confidence in her Secretary of State's policies.

After these debates on clause 1, the Government moved the amendments it had promised at committee stage to widen the range of union elections which would qualify for public subsidy. The amendments replaced old sub-clauses 1 (3) (b) and (c) with new clauses (b) and (c). The new clauses read:

(b) carrying out an election provided for by the rules of a trade union:
(c) electing a worker who is a member of a trade union to be a representative of other members also employed by his employer.

The Government had thus dropped from the clause the rather obscure reference to a 'committee of management' of a trade union, a term which had threatened to cause considerable confusion when applied to the varied committee structures to be found within the union movement. New sub-clause 1 (3) (c) was clearly intended to cover the election of shop stewards.

Labour peers took the balloting proposals more seriously than their colleagues in the House of Commons, and opposed them (instead of abstaining, as Labour had done in the votes on the amendments in the Commons). The most significant debate on the clause in the House of Lords took place on 3 June during the first day of the Bill's committee stage. Labour opposed clause 1 forming part of the Employment Bill at all. Lord McCarthy opposed the clause on three grounds.[73] First, that it was included in the particular Bill before the committee: 'a Bill which the overwhelming majority of trade unions believe is an anti-trade union Bill, so that provisions which might be acceptable . . . are bound to be regarded suspiciously when they come as a trailer at the beginning of a Bill of this kind'. Labour, he said, were also unhappy about the power the clause proposed to confer on the Secretary of State to extend the scheme to cover 'such other purposes' as he might specify by order. Lord McCarthy felt that the clause was 'an invitation to drag trade union democratic processes into an endless series of legal wrangles', due to its somewhat vague and imprecise wording. Finally, Lord McCarthy believed that legislation on ballots was not needed because existing trade union practice, 'for all its weaknesses and imperfections, is the most systematic and consistent way of consulting more people than any other institution we have in this country'. The proposals might actually cause harm, by encouraging dissident groups to ask the Secretary of State to 'help them to disrupt union government'. Labour's attempt to vote down the clause failed by 155 to 72.

The Labour party thus followed different tactics in the Lords and Commons. One possible explanation for the decision to oppose clause 1 in the Lords may have been the fact that the Bill was very close to completing its final stages in Parliament: the committee stage in the Lords was virtually the last opportunity for Labour to amend the Bill. For Labour's leaders in the Lords, voting against the clause in committee was the only way they could express their dissatisfaction with the Government's failure to make the drafting concessions they had asked for. But by voting against clause 1 Labour gave valuable political ammunition to the Conservatives who could now claim Labour were divided over their views on union ballots and, better still, that Labour were against the 'spread of democracy' within the trade union movement.

The attempt in the Commons to widen clause 1 to make provision for a 'triggering ballot' was repeated in the Lords. Lord Colville of Culross moved an amendment similar to that of Michael Colvin and, like Michael Colvin, was briefed and supported by the Institute of Directors. Lord Colville's amendment was supported by Lords Spens and Orr-Ewing, who had formed a committee with other peers to 'toughen' up certain parts of the Bill. This time, however, there was no division on the amendment – Lord Gowrie substantially repeated Mr Prior's speech to Browne's amendment in April, and Colville withdrew his new Clause. The Bill received the Royal Assent on 1 August 1980.

Workplace Ballots

Although the phrasing of clause 1 of the Employment Bill did not exclude workplace ballots, the Government stated that funds would be restricted to postal ballots in the initial stages of the scheme. Following this guidance, the certification officer interpreted his remit as covering postal ballots only, postal ballots being the most effective way of meeting the statutory requirement of ensuring secrecy as far as 'reasonably practical'. As shown below see p. 176, applications for funds by some non-TUC organizations were rejected on the grounds of failure to use the postal services. However, there was extensive feeling within the Conservative party, and amongst some groups of employers' spokesmen, that workplace balloting was desirable, both for union elections and, more particularly, for industrial action. Workplace ballots were seen as a practical and speedy alternative to postal ballots on industrial action, and would be an effective method of reducing the emotional pressures generated by mass meetings on strike decisions. The dangers of emotional pressures leading to ill-considered strike action would be reduced even more if the ballot arrangements were made by employers, especially if employers were able to influence the form of the questions asked.

Public funds for workplace ballots were already permitted in principle under the terms of the Employment Bill, on the same terms as for postal ballots: the subsequent practical restriction to postal ballots was based upon the regulations drawn up as a Statutory Instrument on the basis of the delegated authority provided by the Act. However, there was some feeling that the Bill itself, as originally drafted, did not give sufficient encouragement to workplace ballots, a feeling justified by the restrictive regulations subsequently promulgated. Lord Robens, being familiar with workplace balloting in the coal mining industry as a former chairman of the NCB, took the initiative in January 1980 in proposing to the Secretary of State that the Bill should include a provision obliging employers to provide facilities for secret ballots at the place of work in working time at the request of recognized trade unions. In February the CBI's Employment Policy Committee decided to support the idea, despite major reservations, especially about the practicality of the proposals. The CBI officials who favoured the scheme argued that workplace ballots were easier, quicker, and cheaper than postal ballots; that the proposal would discourage decisions on important matters being taken at meetings outside company premises, when moderates might be reluctant to express dissent; that the existence of a statutory right to hold secret workplace ballots would bring pressure to bear on trade unions to use it; that imposing an obligation on employers would be popular with the Government, which could claim that it was being even-handed between employers and trade unions; and that employers would be encouraged to cooperate in the general balloting scheme if it were made clear that ballots on employers' premises were being encouraged. On the other hand, opponents argued that such an obligation could not be reconciled with the Government's expressed intention of reducing the legislative load on employers; that workplace ballots already required the employer's permission, and allowed them to exercise as much influence where they occurred as they would be able to under the new proposal; and that in any case postal ballots might be preferable in some instances, since they would allow employees to consider the issues in a domestic rather than industrial setting, and therefore be less susceptible to influence from stewards and workmates.

The CBI proposed the inclusion of the 'Robens clause' at a meeting with the Secretary of State on 23 March. The Secretary of State accepted the proposal and subsequently introduced an amendment to the Bill at the committee stage in the Lords (3 June): the proposal became a new section 2 to the clause. Although employers were obliged to provide facilities for ballots, they were not obliged to provide employees with paid time off to vote or to attend meetings called to discuss issues related to the vote. In an earlier speech, to the 1976 Conservative party conference, Mr Prior had floated the possibility of encouraging ballots by placing an obligation on employers to provide time off for employees to vote in union elections.[74] However, such a proposal would have been very unpopular with employers, including the CBI, and was therefore not advanced in the discussions. Labour did not divide the committee on the amendment, and the new clause was subsequently endorsed without division in the Commons.

Under the Act, employers are required, so far as is reasonably practical, to permit the use of premises for balloting when requested to do so by a recognized union, and when the ballot is for the purposes specified in the Act. The provision does not apply to employers employing twenty or fewer workers (section 2). As in the section relating to public funds, the ballots are to be as secret as 'reasonably practical'. If the employer refuses to make the premises available, the recognized union can complain to an industrial tribunal, which may award compensation (for example, to cover the expense of balloting elsewhere) to the union if the complaint is upheld. The clause could give rise to major legal difficulties: what is a recognized trade union for this purpose? What is 'reasonably practical'? What would be appropriate compensation? However, the provision has not led to any serious difficulties since it has not been operated: workplace ballots have been organized since the Act, as before, by agreement between employers and the relevant unions.

The specific provisions of section 2 of the Employment Act have had limited effect. However, the issues raised in the discussions leading up to the amendments were, and are, of major importance. The major issue relates to the role of employers and unions in workplace representation. Some of the support amongst employers for workplace ballots was based upon the premiss that such ballots would be organized by employers, as at British Leyland (BL). This view was reflected in the suggestion in the 1983 Green Paper that public funds might be made available for employer-organized ballots on the relevant issues, perhaps where unions refused to hold ballots. Alternatively, employers might be permitted to trigger ballots of members in dispute.[75] The Government has stated its view that employer ballots are desirable, as a 'good industrial relations practice'.[76] However, there has been no statutory encouragement to employer organized ballots, and the suggestion that public funds might be made available has not been proceeded with to date (November 1983). The statement on 'Proposals for Legislation on Democracy in Trade Unions' of 12 July 1983 contained no reference to the proposal, despite the favourable reference in the earlier Green Paper.

TUC Reaction to Ballot Proposals of Employment Bill

As shown earlier, the TUC expressed strong opposition to the Government's working papers published in July 1979. This hostility was reinforced by debates on the Government proposals at the 1979 Congress. Similar feelings were expressed at a special one-day conference on the Employment Bill, held in London in January 1980. Union opposition to the proposed legislation on picketing and the closed shop was unanimous and clear cut. However, the position on clause 1 was more complex: two important unions, the AUEW(E) and the EETPU, made extensive use of postal ballots, were concerned about the expense involved and were seriously considering applying for funds. Hence the TUC could not simply prohibit unions from applying for funds upon pain of expulsion from the TUC: the unions concerned were too important. The TUC gradually moved towards a policy of indicating to affiliated unions that they should have nothing to do with the Government scheme, without specifying what the penalties would be for failing to comply.

The special conference on the Employment Bill decided to 'strongly advise' affiliated unions against making use of clause 1. Although the conference had no constitutional standing, it indicated the tenor of union feeling in general. Following the conference, TUC officials suggested to the General Council's Employment Policy and Organization Committee at its February meeting that the committee should recommend the General Council to 'advise' unions not to apply for public funds under clause 1. This recommendation turned out to be unacceptable. Leading the pressure for a firmer line was Ken Gill, Communist general secretary of AUEW(TASS). Mr Gill was anxious for the TUC to adopt a tough line on clause 1 partly because any climate which encouraged a more extensive use of postal ballots on union elections might threaten his position in TASS (whereby the general secretary is appointed not elected) and partly in order to keep the TUC opposition to the Bill as firm as possible in order to 'kill it off' in the long run: in addition, AUEW(TASS)'s relations with the AUEW(E) were sour, and the union was not averse to making difficulties for the AUEW(E). Gill and Basnett united at the March General Council meeting in persuading the Council to recommend that unions 'should not' make use of clause 1 at all. This policy was opposed by the Engineering Section of the AUEW as well as by Frank Chappell's EETPU (who had opposed the policy at the January conference). The March decision represented a compromise, for it deliberately left open the question of how the Council should react to those unions which decided to ignore official TUC policy and accept public funds under clause 1. If the AUEW(E) and EETPU maintained their policy of using clause 1, the General Council would clearly have to make very difficult decisions regarding disciplinary action and possible suspension in the future: the problems posed by failure to de-register following the 1971 Industrial Relations Act would reappear in a more acute if more limited form.

Both the AUEW(E) and the EETPU kept to their declared positions. On 1 May 1980 the national committee of the AUEW(E) rejected by 27 votes to 24 a motion instructing the executive council 'not to become engaged in any agreement with the Government for state assistance in the conduct of all or any trade union ballots'. In a television interview in June Gavin Laird, a leading member of the AUEW(E)'s executive council, indicated that the union might also make use of clause 1 in respect of strike ballots as well. Frank Chappell in the meantime had repeatedly emphasized that his union would be making use of clause 1 when it became law.

The possibility that such a move by the two unions would lead to expulsion was consistently played down by TUC officials. Murray himself rejected the argument that making use of clause 1 would be akin to registering under the Industrial Relations Act. The General Council had refrained from issuing an *instruction* to affiliated unions on clause 1, which meant that expulsion was extremely unlikely for unions which might accept public funds under the clause. However, the possibility that expulsion might face the AUEW(E) and the EETPU increased when both unions became involved in a dispute with the GMWU over the possible use of 'blacklegs' during a dispute at the Isle of Grain power station in June. The AUEW(E) and EETPU rejected an instruction from the General Council to accept a peace formula, further exposing the two unions to general union hostility.

Divisions in the Labour movement increased further when Eric Varley, Labour's employment spokesman, commented that Labour 'never had the view that the Government was going to impose conditions' in respect of money paid out under clause 1. He emphasized that trade unions had no difficulty in accepting public money through the TUC to finance education and training, and he could not see any objection in principle to doing so for ballots. This angered TUC officials. The TUC rejected such an analogy; money received for educational purposes had no 'strings' attached to it, unlike clause 1. The offer of public money under clause 1 was, in the TUC's view, linked to the Conservative equation that 'mass participation = moderation' and that the present hierarchy in unions was unrepresentative. Clause 1 was telling the unions how they should make their decisions, and that their existing policies were unrepresentative because of defective democratic procedures.

Despite differences of view amongst TUC unions, the General Council policy adopted in March 1980 has remained in being. In an amendment to a motion from the AUEW(F), the Bakers proposed that any union taking advantage of clause 1 should be expelled from the TUC: as a union using postal ballots, the Bakers could not be accused of making ideological stands at the expense of others.[77] However, the original AUEW(F) motion was itself withdrawn, and the Bakers' amendment was withdrawn with it: Congress did not discuss what the TUC should do if unions sought funds under clause 1. In October 1980, when the Government scheme came into effect, the General Council reaffirmed its policy that affiliated unions should have nothing to do with the scheme. The policy was accepted, even by the AUEW(E) and the EETPU (see p. 173).

In summary: The Employment Act 1980 did not generate the political controversy of the 1971 Industrial Relations Act. The Conservative party had won a substantial electoral victory, the Labour party was preoccupied with internal controversy, the trade union movement was weakened by unemployment, industrial relations legislation had become familiar throughout the decade and the Act itself was more cautious than the 1971 Industrial Relations Act. Furthermore, Parliamentary attention was focused on the provisions for restrictions on picketing, secondary action and the closed shop: the balloting provisions were less contentious. Clause 1 produced a controlled rebellion amongst Conservative back-benchers, which served to give notice to Mr Prior that many members of the party were sceptical of the gradualist approach to industrial relations reform he was following, but the symbolism of rebellion was more important than the substance. Legislation to encourage the use of ballots was seen by Conservatives as helpful, and in the long term important in changing the political complexion of trade unions – but not central in the short term.

The external reaction to the balloting proposals was also muted. The proposals were generally welcomed by employers, although there were disagreements over details; the CBI had mixed feelings about the clauses, and the Institute of Directors felt that the legislation did not go far enough. The Institute favoured greater encouragement to minorities to be able to call for ballots on union policies. In the House of Commons the Labour party abstained on the balloting proposals, regarding them as irrelevant, whilst the Labour peers opposed the clauses, although this may have indicated confusion and crossed lines rather than political divisions. The trade union movement generally opposed the proposals, although two major unions, the EETPU and the AUEW(E), favoured them and other unions did not regard the proposals as of immediate importance: restrictions on picketing and the closed shop were more important. Nevertheless, the TUC asked unions not to utilize the scheme, and TUC unions refused to ask for money under the scheme established even where they were entitled to do so.

CONSERVATIVE POLICY ON BALLOTS AFTER 1980 EMPLOYMENT ACT

The provisions of the Employment Act 1980 did not become effective immediately on the Act receiving the Royal Assent on 1 August since the legislation provided for the major clauses to come into effect when the Secretary of State so ordered. However, the ballot proposals were implemented before the remaining clauses. As early as May the Government had been consulting on the regulations which would give the legislation statutory effect. The Statutory Instrument establishing the scheme was made on 18 August, laid before the House on 8 September and came into effect on 1 October 1980 (Statutory Instrument 1980/1252). As shown in chapter 4, the scheme had only limited impact: TUC-affiliated unions did not seek reimbursement, even where the unions used secret ballots and would have found the money useful to cover the heavy expenditure involved. Whether the Government would have considered further legislation if the legislation had been an immediate success, it is impossible to say. As it was not an immediate success, ballots remained on the political agenda after the passage of the 1980 Act.

The scheme established under the Act was substantially extended in 1982, making it possible for funds to be made available for ballots on employers' offers (see p. 171). More importantly, the possibility of applying further pressure on trade unions to extend the use of ballots remained.

Prior was reluctant to introduce further legislation on industrial relations following the 1980 Act, believing that caution was necessary in approaching industrial relations and that further legislation was likely to cause harm with uncertain benefits. However, he was replaced as Secretary of State for Employment in September 1981, and transferred to Secretary of State for Northern Ireland: his junior ministers were transferred at the same time. The new Secretary of State, Mr Norman Tebbit, was less inhibited in his approach to legislation, believing that further legislation was politically desirable, industrially beneficial and practically possible. Mr Prior was reluctantly persuaded to prepare a Green Paper on *Trade Union Immunities* in January 1981, and the paper itself was notably inconclusive. Mr Tebbit approached a similar task with more enthusiasm, publishing a more decisive Green Paper on *Democracy in Trade Unions* in January 1983. Both Green Papers discussed the issue of ballots, the 1981 paper in relation to strikes, the 1983 paper in relation to union elections and to strikes: there was no legislation on ballots in the 1982 Employment Act.

The discussion of ballots in the January 1981 Green Paper naturally reflected the views of the Front Bench in the spring of 1980. The relevant section concluded: 'The Government would welcome views on the practicalities and balance of advantage of making secret ballots compulsory and on what further steps might be taken to encourage their voluntary use.'[78] However, the emphasis of the discussion was strongly on the inappropriateness of requiring secret ballots before strike action: the Donovan Commission had rejected them; North American experience indicated that they were likely to result in majorities for strike action; arrangements for calling off strikes became more difficult; and there were practical difficulties surrounding the drawing up of the ballot paper.[79] More positively, the Green Paper discussed means of encouraging the use of ballots, especially through provisions for allowing union members to trigger ballots in specific circumstances. However, there were major difficulties even with this approach: it might make 'responsible' union leadership more difficult. How would the threshold be determined? Would there be immunities whilst the ballot was being conducted? If the 'triggering' system required oversight it would incur the same criticisms from trade unionists of outside interference as a mandatory system. In general, the Green Paper was discouraging about the desirability of legislation to promote secret ballots on strikes, either mandatory or voluntary. Although the use of ballots in union elections was mentioned, there was no extended discussion.[80] In these circumstances it is hardly surprising that there was no mention of ballots in the 1982 Employment Act.

The issue, however, had not disappeared: it reappeared more strongly in 1983. The January 1983 Green Paper, *Democracy in Trade Unions*, was concerned with two issues: the political levy and ballots. The 1983 Green Paper, unlike that of 1981, started from the assumption that further legislation on industrial relations (or more specifically trade unions) was necessary: attention was focused upon the 'what' and 'how', rather than the 'whether'. The discussion of union elections concluded: 'This chapter has identified the need for the reform of trade union election procedures to ensure that the leadership is more representative of the members. It is clear that few trade unions have taken the initiative in bringing about democratic reform, and the Government has reluctantly come to the conclusion that some legislative intervention is necessary.'[81] There was less conviction on the desirability of legislation on strike ballots, the relevant section concluding: 'The Government would welcome views on this analysis of compulsory strike ballots and on the possibilities for encouraging the use of such ballots by both trade unions and employers.'[82]

Legislation to extend the use of ballots in elections to union office was both desirable and practicable. It was desirable because trade unions had not taken the necessary measures themselves:

> With a few notable exceptions trade unions have made few or painfully slow attempts to reform their internal affairs and electoral practices in ways which can attract general public confidence in them. The Government therefore believes that the time has now come for legislation to assist this process forward. Voluntary reform is still the desired aim and most desirable means . . . But without legislation it is clear that the impetus to reform will continue to be lacking.[83]

It was practicable because trade unions had accepted the principle of requiring secret ballots in relation to 'political objects' (Trade Union Act 1913), amalgamations [Trade Union (Amalgamations, etc.) Act 1964] and statutory recognition (Employment Protection Act 1975). The Government recognized that a number of major issues required resolution: the precise method of voting, the role of indirect elections, the treatment of full-time officers (union civil servants?), the electoral arrangements and the scope of offices to be covered by the legislation. It was similarly recognized that there were difficulties over legislative strategies: should legislation be mandatory, requiring specific standards, require unions to seek approval for their electoral rules, without laying down precise requirements, or provide means for union members to take action if they believed that unions were not conducting their electoral affairs appropriately. Finally, the issue of appropriate sanctions was faced: fines for contempt of court, loss of fiscal privileges (notably the right to tax relief on expenditure on provident benefits) or loss of immunities.

The Government believed that ballots on strikes were as desirable as ballots for union elections: 'the argument of principle for strike ballots is . . . simple and unanswerable'.[84] However, it was not convinced that legislation requiring strike ballots was practicable. Mandatory strike ballots were not widely supported because they would simply encourage unofficial strikes or industrial action short of strike action. Triggered strike ballots posed major practical difficulties, and might in any case simply result in reaffirmation of loyalty to union leaders. As a much less ambitious, and less contentious, alternative, the Government simply suggested that employers should be able to call upon public funds to carry out ballots where unions refused to ballot their members.

Following their victory in the June 1983 general election, the Conservative party placed trade union reform at the centre of its legislative programme for 1983–4. In July the Government published its 'Proposals for Legislation on Democracy in Trade Unions'.[85] The proposals covered three areas: trade union elections, strike ballots and the political levy. The proposals were based upon the policies discussed in the January 1983 Green Paper. The legislation proposed would require elections to union executives (misleadingly designated as governing bodies, a term more accurately used of annual conference, the usual sovereign body) to be by secret ballot. All union members must have 'an equal and unrestricted opportunity to vote'. Unexpectedly, in view of the limited previous discussion of the issue, unions were to be required to provide that all members should be able to vote directly for members of the governing body. On strike ballots, the legislation proposed will require unions to hold secret ballots before calling official strikes, or forfeit immunity in tort. The legislation will also provide for affirmative ballots on union political funds every ten years. The Secretary of State offered to consult with the TUC on means of ensuring that union members 'are freely and effectively able to decide for themselves' on whether or not to pay the political levy – in other words, how to phase out the practice of 'contracting out'.

The July proposals were incorporated in a Trade Union Bill, published on 26 October 1983.[86] The Bill covered three issues: election to union executive committees, strike ballots, and the political levy. The Bill proposed that all voting members on union executives, including the president and general secretary where they have been voting rights, should be subject to periodic re-election at least once every five years. Such elections should be by secret ballot, as far as 'reasonably practicable'. Elections must be directly by the union members, unless union rules define special occupational, geographical, or sectional constituencies; indirect elections are not acceptable. Aggrieved union members are entitled to apply to the High Court for a declaration that a union has not complied with the legislation, and the High Court is empowered to impose requirements on a union subject to a time limit of not less than six months; union members are entitled to undertake enforcement proceedings where unions fail to comply in the time period. On strike ballots, the Bill removes union immunities from tort actions where a union 'authorizes or endorses' strikes or other industrial action without the holding of a ballot, preferably secret, of the members affected; union members not directly involved in the industrial action are not entitled to vote. The Bill also provides for periodic ballots, at least every ten years, on union political funds.

The legislative changes proposed have major implications for union structure, government and negotiating practices. As shown in chapters 2 and 3, union rule books will require major revisions before unions will be able to meet the statutory requirements on union elections. The range of offices covered by the 1983 Bill is limited, covering the executive committee and including presidents and general secretaries only when they have a vote on the union executive committee, unlike the 1980 Employment Act. However, the organizational changes required to provide for direct elections to executive committees are considerable. Even unions regarded as democratic in conventional terms would need to revise their rule books extensively.

Although the organizational consequences of the legislation could be major, the Government has avoided assuming any long-term role in its enforcement. Hence the initiative for undertaking proceedings against unions failing to reform procedures to accord with the legislation will rest with members of the unions concerned. A union member, or group of members, will be able to apply to the courts for a declaration that their union had failed to comply with the statutory requirements in a particular election. The union would be given a specified period of not less than six months to carry out its statutory duty, and if it failed to do so could be subject to contempt proceedings. The Government has similarly maintained its distance from industrial relations practices in the proposals relating to strike ballots. The initiative for undertaking legal proceedings against the unions lies with the employers damaged by strike: unions will lose the protection of 'the golden formula' if sued for breach of contract unless strikes have been called in the approved manner.[87] The Government is thus proposing major changes in 'the rules of the game', but attempting to avoid becoming a long-term participant.

CONCLUSION

Like other, more contentious, aspects of Conservative industrial relations policy, the policy on ballots was developed in response to both political and industrial relations pressures. There was wide political support for ballots – in the Labour party and amongst trade unionists as well as Conservative politicians: it was difficult to oppose the principle of the secret ballot. Legislation on ballots was therefore capable of being presented as a measure facilitating increased democracy in trade unions and as such opposed only by union leaders anxious to retain their posts when they failed to represent their members' interests. It was therefore hoped that clause 1 of the 1980 Employment Act would help to reassure trade unionists that the Government was not simply introducing anti-trade union legislation. In view of the proposals on picketing and the closed shop, the hope was always faint: this faint hope was destroyed by the opposition of right-wing Conservatives and the subsequent Commons debate on the ballot proposals.

To summarize the Conservative analysis: no one could oppose the extended use of ballots; at the same time they promised to increase the role of 'moderate' opinion in the trade union movement. Opinion polls indicated that substantial numbers of the electorate, including trade union members, believed that trade unions had too much power. The number of respondents agreeing that trade unions had too much power varied, but never fell below 66 per cent. The 1979 general election confirmed this view: substantial numbers of trade unionists supported the Conservative party, despite the party's known views on trade unions. Increased membership participation in union elections and, more contentiously, increased rank-and-file involvement in strike decisions, were likely to result in more moderate outcomes. This would reduce the level of conflict indirectly, through reducing the chances of militants being elected to office, and might reduce the level of conflict directly, through votes against strike action. Even if strike ballots usually reinforced executive recommendations to strike, knowledge that strike recommendations had to be put to ballot might engender caution. The increased use of ballots was thus likely to appeal especially to Conservatives who wished to reduce the role of union militants.

Ballots in trade unions were therefore desirable: even unions themselves were making increased use of them, although more in elections than in strikes (see chapters 2 and 3). The dilemma for the Conservative party concerned the extent to which legislation should require the use of ballots in specified circumstances, or rely upon unions introducing them themselves, as they perceived them necessary. The disadvantages of requiring ballots were well known: most importantly, the Government would be interfering in the internal operations of trade unions, and considerable opposition could be expected. Unions might refuse to carry out mandatory ballots themselves, and refuse to assist in ballots carried out by others; at the very least, they might attempt to undermine the balloting process. These dangers were especially likely if ballots on strike action were made mandatory. On the other hand, the pace of introducing ballots was slow: few unions were following the example of the AUEW(E) or the NUM. Even the 1983 Green Paper indicated a preference for voluntary reform; but the same document indicated the Government's exasperation at the slow pace of change and its intention to hasten the process, at least with regard to union elections. This intention was realized in the 1983–4 session of Parliament.

Different politicians had different priorities. Mr Prior's major objective was the gradual transformation of union leadership, towards an industrially moderate, and possibly even politically non-Labour (if not Conservative), leadership. As with the Prime Minister's overall economic strategy, success could only be achieved over a decade, not overnight – if at all. The extension of strike ballots might have more spectacular effects in particular circumstances, but was less important in the long run. Other politicians attached more importance to extending the use of strike ballots, believing that they provided the means for moderate 'ordinary' members of unions to discipline militant union leaders. However, the major attention was focused on the extension of ballots in elections to union office.

The impact of the balloting provisions of the 1980 Employment Act on industrial relations was limited: the availability of public money did not encourage unions which did not use ballots to do so, and TUC unions which already used ballots did not apply for money under the scheme. Anticipating this outcome, some Labour politicians described section 1 of the Act as irrelevant, either because electoral mechanisms were themselves unimportant or because unions already made extensive use of ballots. However, this disregard was politically short-sighted. The trade union movement was not sufficiently popular to be able to expect that its reassurances on its own democratic procedures would be accepted at face value: trade union reform was popular precisely because of public disquiet, which was only likely to be reinforced by Labour MPs expressing union complacency. More specifically, union failure to take up public funds obviously paved the way for firmer measures. If unions reformed their procedures to be eligible for money under the scheme, the Conservative objective of increased use of ballots was achieved; if they did not do so, the case for mandatory ballots was immeasurably strengthened – voluntarism had failed.

2 The Role of Ballots in Union Elections

In 1976 the Conservative party claimed that '. . . trade unions are imperfectly democratic'.[1] Their views had not changed seven years later, in 1983, despite their attempts to reform unions by offering to subsidize postal ballots for certain union elections; the 1983 Green paper *Democracy in Trade Unions* indicated Conservative scepticism about union democracy and in particular their '. . . concern about the electoral arrangements of trade unions'.[2] In order to examine the grounds for this anxiety and the effect of Conservative action to reform trade union electoral methods, it is necessary to set Conservative proposals and actions within the context of union behaviour. This involves surveying union rules covering those elections open to a state subsidy under the 1980 Employment Act and associated regulations, before turning to examine unions' actual electoral practices in a number of case studies.

This chapter will therefore begin by examining the formal provisions relating to electoral procedures contained in union rule books, which reveal a broad contrast between two types of union office, with differing provisions for selection: the 'professional', which is frequently, but not invariably, appointed (e.g. general secretary, full-time officers), and the 'representative' (e.g. president/chairman, executive committee), which is almost invariably elected. The introduction of ballots would therefore have different effects on different offices. The chapter will then focus on union electoral practices, distinguishing between unions according to their 'primary' balloting method: postal, branch or workplace ballot. Six unions using postal ballots are examined: the AUEW(E), EETPU, FTAT, Bakers, NUS and Equity. Five unions using branch ballots are also examined, two using individual counts (TGWU and ASTMS) and three employing block voting systems (GMWU, NUR and POEU). Finally, the system of workplace ballots used by the CPSA and NUM is examined. The chapter concludes by focusing upon four major areas: the methods used to choose officers; the circumstances under which electoral procedures are changed; the effect of ballots on the electoral process (turnout, secrecy and malpractice); and the effect of balloting on electoral outcomes. As the chapter shows in detail, the introduction of balloting or the revision of balloting arrangements to meet statutorily prescribed principles will have major and differing effects on different unions.

ELECTORAL PROCEDURES IN UNION RULE BOOKS

The elections covered by the 1980 Employment Act and 'The Funds for Trade Union Ballots Regulations 1980'[3] include the individual positions of president, chairman, secretary or treasurer and 'any position which the person elected will hold as an employee of the trade union'.[4] This latter provision refers to the ordinary full-time official. In addition, the executive committee was included in the scheme. Hence, all the major national posts normally found in unions were covered by the legislation, but the subsidy did not extend to the annual or biennial conference which unions usually hold to determine policy. In July 1983 the Conservatives published further proposals for legislation to ensure that union executives were elected by secret ballot in which members had an 'equal and unrestricted opportunity to vote'.[5] This paper appeared to suggest that any secret ballot held at a convenient time and place would be acceptable as a democratic method.

Although union rule books are more explicit in respect of methods for choosing leaders than in respect of methods for reference back of agreements and strikes, there are still difficulties in identifying the specific role that ballots play in the electoral process. In some unions (e.g. the GMWU) the executive committee is composed of members chosen by more than one method of selection.[6] Other unions occasionally give their executive or local committees discretion regarding the details of the balloting system (e.g. the CPSA). Further, some unions employ both elected and appointed full-time officials (e.g. the NUS). Thus the codification of rules which are sometimes imprecise and open to a number of qualifications raises interpretative problems. Where it was difficult to classify a union's electoral procedures in the critical area of membership election, the tendency was to exclude rather than include it in the category of those unions choosing their leader by a vote of the membership. Hence the survey will understate, rather than overstate, the degree to which union members are directly involved in elections. However, the need to allocate somewhat arbitrarily a small number of unions with very complex or less than specific rules to certain categories should not materially detract from the general conclusions drawn from the survey

The survey covered 103 rule books of unions affiliated to the TUC in 1980.[7] They represented 12,127,205 members out of a total TUC membership of 12,172,508. The unions which supplied the rule books were asked for the most recent copies and hence the rules analysed generally represent the position in the late 1970s: in a small number of instances rule changes have occurred since our research, particularly following amalgamations.

The methods of choosing union leaders will be examined in the following order: general secretary, president/chairman, treasurer, ordinary full-time officers and executive committee. This order reflects the relative importance of the first four posts in the majority of unions, before turning to consider the executive which carries responsibility for managing the union and applying policy between meetings of the union conference.

Finally, the type (manual/non-manual, craft or craft origins) and size of the unions surveyed will be briefly examined in respect of each of the leadership positions and committees listed. This will make it possible to examine the relationship between the occupational base or origin of the union and its existing methods for choosing leaders. Comment on the possible causal relationship between union size and systems of selection will be made where it appears relevant. However, this latter relationship will not be stressed, for many of the unions studied adopted their present general system of choosing leaders when their size was significantly different from that recorded in the 1980s. For instance, the TGWU had 292,460 members in 1922 when it adopted its present system of government,[8] the AUEW moved to an elected full-time executive and election of ordinary full-time officers in 1892 when it had 70,000 members[9] and the GMWU had 241,000 members in the early 1930s when it established its system of appointment and confirmatory elections for full-time officials.[10]

General Secretary

General secretaries are the most senior full-time officials for the majority of unions in the survey, although exceptions to this general rule include both the NUM and the AUEW(E) in which the president has at least equal status. Table 2.1 shows the distribution of unions by the method of choosing their general secretary, and table 2.2 the method of conducting the election in the 51 unions opting to elect by a membership vote. Hence 51 unions elect their general secretary by a vote of the membership. Although these unions only account for 51 per cent of those unions surveyed, they represent 7,821,500 members or 64 per cent of the TUC's membership. Eight unions in this group in 1980 use a full postal and none a half postal ballot. In a full postal ballot the paper is distributed to the member's home address and returned by post; in a half postal ballot it is returned by post but distributed by some other method, for example, the branch secretary may distribute it by hand. The spread of voting methods across the unions choosing the general secretary by a vote of the membership reveals that no one method predominates.

The second largest group of unions (*n* = 32) prefer their executive committee to choose the general secretary. In some of these unions the conference is called upon to ratify the executive choice. Of the 14 unions electing their general secretary at conference, without the prior involvement of the executive, 5 use a ballot vote, 2 a show of hands, and 6 do not specify the voting method.

TABLE 2.1   Method of choosing general secretary

Method	No. of unions	% of total
Election by whole membership	51	50
Election by conference delegates	14	14
Election by executive committee	32	31
Other method	2	2
Not specified	4	4

TABLE 2.2   Method of electing general secretary by membership vote

Method	No. of unions	% of those electing
Full postal ballot	8	16
Half postal ballot	0	0
Ballot (branch meeting)	8	16
Show of hands (branch meeting)	3	6
Ballot (general meeting)	2	4
Show of hands (general meeting)	3	6
Other ballot	12	24
Discretion as to any of above	2	4
Not specified	13	26

Fourteen unions also require candidates for general secretary to be vetted by the executive or to take an examination before contesting the election. Canvassing is forbidden in 13 rule books, and election addresses are expressly permitted by 15 unions. In direct contrast to the president/chairman and executive elections, only 57 unions require candidates for the post of general secretary by rule to be existing members of the union. This reflects the view held by many unions, particularly those with a non-manual membership, that the general secretary is the specialist senior civil servant working under the executives' direction. This view of the job also influences the tenure given to the general secretary: 81 unions do not require their general secretaries, once chosen, to submit themselves to further tests or elections, but normally permit them to hold their jobs until retirement or at the pleasure of the executive and/or members. In the 22 unions requiring the general secretary to stand for re-election, the most common tenure is five years, as shown in table 2.3.

There is a clear division between manual and non-manual unions in the method of choosing general secretaries. Even given the problems of determining what is or is not a manual and non-manual worker,[11] (for example, were we correct to define The Prison Officers' Association as a manual workers' union?), there can be no doubt that the non-manual unions surveyed reveal a marked antipathy to electing their general secretary by a vote of the membership. Only 3 non-manual unions choose their general secretary in this manner. This represents 8 per cent of the total non-manual unions surveyed. In contrast, 76 per cent of the manual unions in the survey elect their general secretary by a vote of the

TABLE 2.3   Periodic re-election of general secretaries

Length of tenure (years)	No. of unions	% of those with periodic re-selection
1	4	18
2	2	9
3	5	23
4	2	9
5	8	36
6	1	5

membership. All but 4 of the 26 unions identified as craft or with craft origins elect their general secretary by a vote of the membership. Hence, it is not surprising that the 8 unions using a full postal ballot are all manual worker unions and that 6 are craft or had craft origins. Six of the 8 unions are also in the TUC's engineering and building groups.

There is less of a relationship than might be expected between union size and the method of choosing the general secretary. Table 2.4 gives the dispersal of unions analysed by size in respect of the main means of choosing the general secretary. This shows that the size of unions employing the same method for choosing their general secretaries varies widely. For example, the Society of Shuttlemakers with 110 members and the TGWU with 2,086,281, in 1980, both hold membership votes to elect their general secretaries.

TABLE 2.4   Size of union and method used for choosing general secretary

Union size	Election by whole membership	Election by conference delegates	Election by executive committee
1 – 1000	10	1	—
1001 - 10,000	9	4	8
10,001 – 50,000	10	7	12
50,001 – 100,000	8	2	2
100,001 – 500,000	11	—	8
500,001 +	3	—	2
Total	51	14	32

Nor are specific methods of election neatly confined to any one size of union (table 2.5). For example, the AUEW(E) had a membership of 1,217,760 in 1980 compared with the EETPU, 420,000, the NSMM, 50,369 and the NU Scalemakers, 1,937; yet all four have rules requiring the use of postal ballots in the election of general secretaries. Not surprisingly, those unions which use a general meeting of all the members to elect the general secretary tend, given the difficulties of convening such meetings, to be among the smallest unions in the survey.

TABLE 2.5   Size of union and method of conducting membership election of general secretary (24 not specified)

Union size	Full postal ballot	Half postal ballot	Ballot (branch meeting)	Show of hands (branch meeting)	Discretion as to 1–4	Ballot (AGM)	Show of hands (AGM)
1 – 1001	1	—	—	—	—	—	3
1001 – 10,000	1	—	3	—	—	2	—
10,001 – 50,000	2	—	1	—	—	—	—
50,001 – 100,000	2	—	2	—	—	—	—
100,001 – 500,000	1	1	2	3	—	—	—
500,001 +	1	—	—	—	2	—	—
Total	8	1	8	3	2	2	2

President/Chairman

The office of president/chairman is normally of lower status than that of general secretary, and the incumbent often performs quite different functions. This difference in status and function affects the methods used for choosing the president/chairman, as given in tables 2.6 and 2.7.

The 37 unions choosing their president/chairman by a vote of the membership represent 37 per cent of the unions in the survey and 4,820,270 members, or 40 per cent of the TUC's membership. Of the unions electing their president/chairman by a membership vote, 4 use a full postal

TABLE 2.6   Method of choosing president/chairman

Method	No. of unions	% of total
Election by whole membership	37	37
Election by conference delegates	41	40
Election by executive committee	23	23
Election by other national committee	1	1

TABLE 2.7   Method of electing president/chairman by membership vote

Method	No. of unions	% of those electing
Full postal ballot	4	11
Half postal ballot	6	16
Ballot (branch meeting)	14	38
Show of hands (branch meeting)	1	3
Ballot (general meeting)	2	5
Show of hands (general meeting)	4	11
Not specified	6	16

and 6 a half postal ballot. This group represents almost a third of the unions electing their president by a membership vote, but it is not as large as the 38 per cent or 14 unions voting at the branch where 13 of the 14 opt for a ballot.

The most common method used for choosing the president/chairman is by a vote of conference delegates, as shown in table 2.6. Forty-one unions opt for this method and a further 23 give their executive the responsibility for choosing the president/chairman. In some unions the delegation of responsibility to the conference or executive would appear a logical decision, as the main function of the person chosen is sometimes to do little more than chair the conference and in some instances executive meetings. In a large majority of unions (71 per cent of those surveyed), the president/chairman holds office for two years or less, and 92 presidents/chairmen face election every five years or less. Also, 84 per cent of presidents/chairmen are, by rule, lay members, although they may in practice spend a considerable amount of time on union business.[12]

The president/chairman is by rule full-time in 10 unions.[13] These unions all have over 10,000 members. Six of the 10 full time presidents/chairmen do not, unlike the great majority of their colleagues in other unions-stand for re-election but hold office for life or until retirement. However, in all of the unions surveyed the candidate for president/chairman has to be an existing member of the union.

Thus, the president/chairman is normally a lay member, is elected in a different way from the general secretary and performs a different role. The president/chairman emerges from the ranks of the activists and is hence not presumed to have the expertise of many of the appointed general secretaries. He represents the lay members' interests, chairs the formal meetings and conferences, and may be called on to interpret and safeguard the rules. However, in contrast the full-time president/chairman in a minority of unions, including the AUEW(E) and the NUM, while also performing these functions, is a much more influential figure in the day-to-day running of the union.

There are no easily definable common features distinguishing those unions which do or do not elect their president/chairman by a vote of the membership. The 24 manual worker unions using the membership election method account for 38 per cent of the total manual worker unions in the survey compared with 34 per cent of all non-manual unions electing their president/chairman by the same method. The 11 craft unions opting for election by membership account for 42 per cent of all such unions in the survey. As table 2.8 indicates, the three main methods of selection are used by unions of all sizes. An examination of methods used by unions electing by membership vote also reveals a wide range of voting systems across the 37 unions concerned, except that the smaller unions again monopolize the use of the annual general meeting (table 2.9).

The 11 unions choosing to operate a full or half postal ballot are dispersed across all the categories of size given in table 2.8. The four

TABLE 2.8   Size of union and method of electing president/chairman

Union size	Election by executive committee	Election by conference	Election by membership
1 – 1000	4	2	5
1001 – 10,000	5	6	11
10,001 – 50,000	6	19	5
50,001 – 100,000	1	7	5
100,001 – 500,000	5	6	9
500,001 +	2	1	2
Total	23	41	37

unions using full postal ballots ranged from the AUEW(E) with 1,217,760 members through the Educational Institute of Scotland[14] with 48,479, the National Union of Scalemakers with 1,937 to the Military and Orchestral Musical Instrument Makers Trade Society with 226 members. There are, therefore, no obvious features common to unions adopting similar methods for the choice of president/chairman. However, in respect of election by the membership, the proportion of craft unions is higher than that of manual or non-manual unions, and unions in the TUC's engineering group are well represented.

TABLE 2.9   Size of union and method of conducting membership vote of president/chairman (6 not specified)

Union size	Full postal ballot	Half postal ballot	Ballot (branch meeting)	Show of hands (branch meeting)	Ballot (AGM)	Show of hands (AGM)
1 – 1000	1	—	—	—	—	3
1001 – 10,000	1	3	3	—	2	1
10,001 – 50,000	1	1	3	—	—	—
50,000 – 100,000	—	1	3	—	—	—
100,001 – 500,000	—	2	3	1	—	—
500,001 +	1	—	1	—	—	—
Total	4	7	13	1	2	4

Treasurer

The treasurer is of considerably less importance in most unions than the general secretary and the president/chairman. Two of the exceptions are the POEU and the CPSA where the treasurer is full time and holds a senior position below that of general secretary. It is more usual, however, for the post of treasurer either not to be indentified in rule (25 unions) or to be held as a second job by the general secretary (25 unions). Hence almost

TABLE 2.10   Method of choosing treasurer

Method	No. of unions	% of total
Election by whole membership	20	20
Election by conference delegates	16	16
Election by executive committee	17	17

TABLE 2.11   Method of electing treasurer by membership vote

Method	No. of unions	% of those electing
Full postal ballot	2	10
Half postal ballot	4	20
Ballot (branch meeting)	3	15
Show of hands (branch meeting)	1	5
Ballot (general meeting)	4	20
Not specified	6	30

half of the unions surveyed do not provide for the election or appointment of a national treasurer as a separate post.

In the 53 unions identified as maintaining the separate post of treasurer, the most common method of filling the position is by a vote of the membership (table 2.10). The 20 unions electing their treasurer by a vote of the membership employ a wide variety of methods (table 2.11). The small number of unions using a postal balloting system includes the NUS, where the treasurer's post is held jointly with that of assistant general secretary. The other 5 unions are the National Union of Domestic Appliance and General Metal Workers, the NUT, NATFHE, FDA and the Military and Orchestral Trade Society. Only 15 of the treasurers are designated fulltime in rule and 33 are required to stand for re-election. Although the post is important because of unions' needs for financial security, it normally carries no great weight constitutionally and is not generally in the same category of jobs as general secretary and president/chairman.

Full-time Officials

Full-time officials are defined here as those officials employed full time by the unions but not elected to the post of general secretary, president/chairman or treasurer. The great majority of unions ($n = 85$) acknowledge in their rules the existence of full-time officials. There are, however, particular difficulties in attempting to aggregate union rules in respect of these officials. Some unions, for example, the NUS, elect some officials and appoint others. Yet other unions appoint officials initially on a probationary basis before confirming them in their posts through an election which is open to competition from other members; the GMWU operate in this manner. Further, the NUM, which in practice elects its officials, does not include in its own rules a definition of the relevant electoral method. It prefers to leave the federated areas considerable discretion to choose their own method. Thus, although most areas rely on the traditional pithead ballot, the Northumberland area uses a postal ballot. In dealing with these and other variations, unions have been classified according to their national rules and whether or not they elect all or some of their officials in the first instance. Thus, the NUM and the GMWU have been placed in the category 'Not specified', but the NUS is included in the column 'Election by membership'. The details of electoral methods are given in tables 2.12 and 2.13.

The 18 unions which appear from their rules to have no full-time officials are not surprisingly the smallest unions. The 21 unions choosing their full-time officials by a vote of the membership represent 3,013,142 members or 25 per cent of the TUC's membership. But, as table 2.12 shows, a much larger group of unions, 50 in total, gives the responsibility for choosing their full-time officials to their executive committees. This figure represents 59 per cent of those unions which actually employ full-time officials. In 10 cases the selection of full-time officers has to be confirmed by some other authority in the unions.

TABLE 2.12   Method of choosing full-time officials[a]

Method	No. of unions	% of total
Election by membership in relevant division, etc.	21	20
Election by conference delegates	3	3
Election by executive committee	50	47
Combination of methods	6	6
Some other method	1	1
No full-time officers (apart from general secretary, etc.)	18	17
Not specified	8	7

Note:
[a] Four unions appear twice, in both 'Election by membership' and a 'Combination of methods'.

TABLE 2.13   Method of electing full-time officials by membership vote

Method	No. of unions	% of those electing
Full postal ballot	5	24
Half postal ballot	0	0
Ballot (branch meeting)	7	33
Show of hands (branch meeting)	2	10
Ballot (general meeting)	1	5
Other ballot	6	29

Table 2.13 reveals, yet again, that there is no uniformity regarding the appropriate method of election among unions choosing their full-time officers by a vote of the membership. Although 5 unions operate a postal ballot, 9 prefer to elect their officials at the branch. Hence only 6 per cent of unions with full-time officials use a postal ballot for their election.

In many unions there are a number of similarities between the method used for choosing full-time officials and that for choosing general secretaries. In 50 cases, for example, the full-time official needs to be an existing member of the union; in the choice of general secretaries the figure is 57. Moreover, in a number of elections the candidates have to be vetted or tested on their knowledge of the union before proceeding to election or selection. Similarly, only a small minority of unions ($n = 10$) subject their full-time officials to re-election, in marked contrast to the position of president/chairman (table 2.14). Once confirmed, full-time officials therefore generally hold their jobs until retirement, unless they commit some misdemeanour for which they may be dismissed. Like the general secretary, they are a source of expert advice, accepting and working under the policies as interpreted by the executive committee.

TABLE 2.14   Periodic re-election of full-time officials

Length of tenure (years)	No. of unions
3	3
4	1
5	5
6	1

The similarities between the majority of general secretaries and full-time officials do not end at the method of selection or function. In both cases there is a sharp distinction between manual and non-manual unions in their methods of choosing full-time officials. All the unions electing their officials by a vote of the membership are manual worker unions.[15] Hence it follows that all 5 using postal ballots are also manual unions. Twelve of the unions electing their officials are also craft or have craft origins. The 21 manual unions represent 62 per cent of those manual unions identified by rule as having full-time officials. In contrast, all the non-manual unions choose their full-time officials by some other method. However, the non-manual unions do not have one commonly preferred method of selecting their officials, although the majority (69 per cent) give the job to their executive committee.

Election of officials by a membership vote is not linked to size (tables 2.15 and 2.16). Unions of different sizes operate the two main systems of election by the membership and by the executive. For example, the largest union, the TGWU, uses its executive, and the second largest the AUEW(E) elects by membership, while the third largest, the GMWU, uses a combination of both systems and gives its regions some discretion in certain appointments. Out of the 21 unions electing their officials by a membership vote, the 5 operating a postal ballot represented in 1980, 1,444,432, or 12 per cent of the total membership surveyed: the NUS, AUEW(E), NSMM, FTAT and Bakers.

TABLE 2.15   Size of union and method of electing full-time officials (5 not specified)

Union size	Election by whole membership	Election by conference delegates	Election by executive committee	No other full-time officers	Other method	Combination of 1–3
1 – 1000	—	—	—	11	—	—
1001 – 10,000	2	—	12	5	—	—
10,001 – 50,000	6	2	18	2	—	2
50,001 – 100,000	6	1	5	—	—	1
100,001 – 500,000	6	—	12	—	1	3
500,001 +	1	—	3	—	—	—
Total	21	3	50	18	1	6

TABLE 2.16   Size of union and method of conducting membership election of full-time officials

Union size	Full postal ballot	Half postal ballot	Ballot (branch meeting)	Show of hands (branch meeting)	Ballot (AGM)	Other ballot
1 – 1000	—	—	—	—	—	—
1001 – 10,000	—	—	1	—	1	—
10,001 – 50,000	2	—	1	—	—	3
50,001 – 100,000	2	—	2	—	—	2
100,001 – 500,000	—	—	3	2	—	1
500,001 +	1	—	—	—	—	—
Total	5	0	7	2	1	6

Executive Committee

Unions' executive committees are normally responsible in the constitution for governing the union between policy making conferences. However, their role is not normally as passive in the field of policy-making as this suggests. They do, with the general secretary, often promote policy and manage the conference. As tables 2.17 and 2.18 show, they are that part of a union's national hierarchy which is most frequently directly accountable to the membership through election, and most likely to be elected by postal ballots.

TABLE 2.17   Method of choosing executive committee[a]

Method	No. of unions	% of total
Election by whole membership	65	60
Election by conference delegates	22	20
Election by other national committee	3	3
Election by local committee	12	11
Combination of methods	7	6

Note:
[a]Six unions appear twice. They appear under the heading of 'Election by whole membership' and in other columns because at least some of their ordinary executive members are elected by a vote of the membership. Hence 59 unions had all of their executive elected by the membership.

TABLE 2.18   Method of electing executive committee by membership vote

Method	No. of unions	% of those electing
Full postal ballot	9	14
Half postal ballot	6	9
Ballot (branch meeting)	13	20
Show of hands (branch meeting)	4	6
Ballot (general meeting)	1	2
Show of hands (general meeting)	4	6
Other ballot method	11	17
Discretion in balloting method[a]	2	3
Not specified	14	22

Note:
[a] The discretion lay with the local committee in both cases.

The 65 unions using a membership vote to elect their executives accounted in 1980 for 61 per cent of the TUC's membership. Among this group, 9 unions use a full postal and 6 a half postal ballot. This represents the largest number of unions using postal ballots in any of the elections discussed, and accounts for 2,080,982 or 17 per cent of the total membership surveyed. Nevertheless, the branch vote is still the most frequently used method, with 13 unions using a ballot and 4 a show of hands. Of these unions 6 ultimately record a branch block vote. Among the 22 unions choosing their executive at the national conference, 19 hold a ballot and 1 a postal ballot. In this body of unions 6 allow their delegates to cast a block branch vote.

In many ways the conditions associated with executive committee elections resemble those experienced by the president/chairman. The candidates are drawn from within the union and only 5 of the executive committees are, in rule, full-time employees of the union. (In practice, of course, many more spend a considerable amount of paid time on union business.) With one exception, executive committees are required to submit themselves to periodic election (table 2.19). Indeed, almost 50 per cent of unions give their executives only one year's tenure before they face re-election, and 72 per cent hold office for two years or less.

TABLE 2.19   Periodic re-election of executive committees

Length of tenure (years)	No. of unions	% of those with periodic elections
1	46	45
2	28	27
3	19	19
4	3	3
5	5	5
6	1	1

Manual and non-manual unions differ in their electoral methods, although the differences are not as marked as in the case of the elections for general secretary and full-time officials. Hence 71 per cent of manual unions in the survey, compared with only 50 per cent of non-manual unions, elect their executive committees by a membership vote; the proportion of craft unions is as high as 81 per cent. All unions with a full-time executive, i.e. ASB, AUEW(E), AUEW(F), EETPU and UCATT, have craft origins, and 4 have a major presence in the engineering and related industries.

There is no association between size and method of electing executives, except that the smallest unions elect by a membership vote at annual meetings. For example, 13 unions with between 10,001 and 50,000 members elect their executive at conference, and 11 elect their executive by vote of the membership. Postal ballots and branch voting occur in direct membership elections in all but the smallest unions (table 2.20).

TABLE 2.20   Size of union and method of conducting membership election of executive committee (14 not specified)

Union size	Full postal ballot	Half postal ballot	Ballot (branch meeting)	Show of hands (branch meeting)	Discretion as to 1–4	Ballot (AGM)	Show of hands (AGM)	Other ballot
1 – 1000	—	—	—	—	—	—	3	—
1001 – 10,000	3	3	3	—	1	1	1	—
10,001 – 50,000	1	1	3	—	—	—	—	5
50,001 – 100,000	2	1	2	—	—	—	—	4
100,001 – 500,000	2	1	5	3	—	—	—	2
500,001 +	1	1	—	1	1	—	—	—
Total	9	7	13	4	2	1	4	11

Election Survey Conclusions

There are many difficulties in attempting to draw general conclusions about complex systems of union rules governing elections. For instance, in dealing with the election of general secretaries 5 categories are necessary for defining the general method of choosing the secretary, including the catch-all 'Other method'. Further, 9 categories are required to analyse electoral systems, including 'Other ballot' and 'Discretion as to any of above'. Although rules relating to elections are relatively specific, their interpretation is problematic.

There is, however, a set of electoral rules common to a number of unions. With some notable exceptions, certain union posts share common features, and a number of unions with common characteristics employ similar methods for filling these posts. There are broadly two types of post. The first type includes those held by lay members, and subject to regular re-election after relatively short periods in office. Such posts are typically those of president/chairman and executive committee. The second type of post is full time, often appointed and, when elected, is often elected for life: such posts are those of general secretary and full-time officer. In a majority of unions general secretaries are not required to be union members before selection and a large minority of unions also choose their ordinary full-time officials from outside the union.

This classification may be generally thought to reflect views regarding the division of power between executive and legislature. In this model the civil servants or full-time officials, led by the general secretary, are subordinate to the elected executive committee members. But the full-time officers provide the expertise thought to be necessary for the organizational effectiveness and well being of the union. The general secretary is the leading bureaucrat, responsible for managing the internal affairs of the union, and sits at the top of a hierarchy of career officials, each reliant on the general secretary and executive for promotion.

Policy decisions, in this model, are made by the conference and interpreted by the executive committee which also, between conferences, takes other decisions as the circumstances dictate. The executive is kept in touch with membership opinion by frequent election as is the conference which forms the legislature and is the legitimate expression of membership opinion. In the great majority of unions surveyed (table 2.21), the conference is elected by the membership, although only two unions, BALPA and the NUS, both with highly mobile and dispersed memberships use postal ballots.

In practice, however, as Alan Bullock noted when examining the formation of the TGWU and the influence of its first general secretary, 'the position of the trade union official and his relationship to the lay member of his union, have no parallel outside the working class movement'.[16] The union official is normally far more pro-active than the formal position suggests. Full time officials, especially the general secretary,[17] are often

TABLE 2.21   Method of choosing conference delegates

Method	No. of unions	% of total
Election by whole membership	74	72
Election by branch committee	3	3
Election by some other local committee	7	7
Conference consists of entire membership	10	10
No conference	5	5
Not specified	4	4

instrumental in initiating and promoting policies which the executive and/or conference endorse. The tenured general secretary and officers in unions with lay and relatively short-lived executives are thus frequently able to exert considerable influence on both policy formulation and execution.

The executive–legislature model, and the opportunities for full time officer dominance, are more likely to be found in non-manual than manual unions. Among manual unions several elect their general secretaries and full-time officers by a vote of the membership; several manual unions also subject their full-time officials to periodic re-election. Moreover, the 5 unions which have full-time executives have craft origins, and 4 of the 5 are in or closely related to the engineering industry: the ASB, AUEW(E), AUEW(F), EETPU and UCATT. Further, of the 21 unions electing their full-time officials, 12 are craft or have craft origins and these represent 67 per cent of all craft unions in the survey with full-time officers. Unions with extensive electoral systems affecting several of the positions examined tend to be manual unions with craft origins. These configurations are similar to those found in a study conducted in the early 1950s, in which Allen noted that 18 of the 26 '. . . unions which appoint their chief officials' represented non-manual workers.[18] The study also showed that the majority of unions requiring their general secretaries to seek periodic election were either craft or unions with a craft basis, while not one of the non-manual worker unions had such a requirement. Thus in general terms, if not in detail, non-manual, manual and craft unions maintained the same pattern of election methods in 1980 as they showed in the 1950s.

The 1980 Employment Act provisions for reimbursement of certain expenditures incurred in using postal ballots (see chapter 4), and subsequent proposals for mandatory ballots in elections, are likely to have greater effect on some types of unions than others. In the first instance, the subsidies offered would only be open to 8 unions in respect of choice of general secretaries, 10 unions for president, 6 for treasurer, 5 for full-time officers and 15 for executives. Moreover, the dispersal of election methods over widely different sizes of unions means that the 1980 legislation could not hope to reach a majority of members. If all 15 unions electing their executives by postal ballot took up the subsidy, only 17 per cent of union members would be involved. In contrast the Trade Union Bill 1983 could have a much greater impact if activated by dissatisfied members. The unions open to the most radical rule changes are the 44 currently not choosing all members of their executive committees by a direct vote of the membership. These unions could be required to widen their electorate and to adopt new methods of voting. Moreover, only 15 of the 59 unions electing all their executive members by a direct vote of the membership have rules requiring postal ballots and could therefore be confident that they complied with the conditions listed in the 1983 Bill. However, it is possible that a number of the unions whose rules provide for branch ballots actually ballot in workplace based branches. The potential effect of the Trade Union Bill 1983 on the formal electoral process is thus considerably greater than the effect of the Employment Act 1980.

TRADE UNION ELECTORAL PRACTICES

Unions were examined according to their choice of primary balloting method, whether postal, branch or workplace ballot. 'Primary' balloting method is referred to because of the tendency for unions to employ more than one method of choosing officials for different posts. For example, although the AUEW(E) elects its full-time officers, executive and final appeal court by postal ballot, it continues to elect its national committee, the equivalent of a national conference, by indirect branch ballot. Some unions even use different methods for choosing representatives on the same body; for example, the GMWU has on its executive an elected general secretary, appointed regional secretaries and indirectly elected lay members. Thus, some unions are rather arbitrarily allocated to a certain category of balloting method largely because that is the kind of system employed in the particular or main elections studied. The unions included may therefore have balloting methods other than the one examined; where this is important it is noted in the introductory discussion of the union's general features.

The justification for categorizing unions according to their primary balloting method is that Conservative policy is primarily aimed at promoting one method of choice, postal ballots, to the exclusion of other methods, although Conservative policy evolved during the course of the project (see chapter 1). It is hypothesized that the choice of balloting method has an important effect on such issues as turnout, competition, political choice, activity of organized factions and, not least, the election of moderate or militant leaders. For this reason a number of the studies and elections have been included to indicate how similar or different balloting systems affect the outcome of elections where there is a choice between moderate and militant candidates. The following cases do not therefore include all the unions studied, or all elections in the unions.

A further reason for including the unions and elections explored below is that they provide an opportunity to place balloting in a number of different contexts. Unions which differ across several factors which could be thought important for influencing elections, such as size, type of membership, constitution, structure and the degree of factional activity, are included in the study. It should therefore be possible to explore what, if any, configuration of factors allows a certain kind of balloting system to influence the result of elections.

Six unions using *full postal ballots* are examined: the AUEW(E), EETPU, FTAT, Bakers, NUS and Equity. The AUEW(E) provides the main focus as it elects (rather than appoints) all its decision makers, and recently, in 1972, introduced postal balloting for the election of full-time officers. Although the other five unions in this category do not all use postal ballots to the same extent, they provide useful comparisons because of the differences in size, nature of membership and degree of factional activity. Unions using primarily *branch ballots* tend to choose either an individual voting method or a branch block vote. The unions to be examined which operate the individual voting method are the TGWU and the ASTMS and those employing a block vote system, the GMWU, NUR and POEU. Again, these unions span a wide range of size and other factors. Finally, the CPSA and the NUM, which both use *workplace ballots,* are discussed. The NUM is, of course, of interest in its own right because of its history of militancy and importance to the economy, and the CPSA is of interest because it adopted a form of workplace ballots for electing its executive in 1979 and senior full-time officers in 1981.

In each of the cases described, a brief commentary will be provided on the salient features of the unions studied before turning to examine their system of balloting. Attention will be drawn, where appropriate, to those aspects of elections referred to in the Government's proposals. Some general points of interest will be discussed at the end of each series of case studies before turning to consider the next system of balloting. Finally, a summary and conclusion will draw together the main points from each of the balloting sections.

Postal Ballots

The postal ballots to be examined involved the union or an agent of the union posting ballot papers direct to the member's home and the member returning the same by post to the union or its agent for counting. The four craft or craft origin unions using this method, the AUEW(E), EETPU, FTAT and Bakers will be examined before turning to consider the NUS and Equity.

The Amalgamated Union of Engineering Workers (Engineering Section)

The AUEW(E), which adopted postal ballots in 1972 for the election of all its full-time officials, is one section, albeit the dominant one, of the AUEW. The AUEW is a loose amalgamation of four sections organizing engineering, foundry, construction and white collar workers. Each section operates its own system of rules for choosing its officials, and the engineering section thus runs its election system as a virtually autonomous process. The AUEW(E) was, before the amalgamations of 1967 and 1971 which established the AUEW, the Amalgamated Engineering Union (AEU), which was itself formed out of merger in 1920. In 1982 the AUEW(E) had 1,024,240 members, making it by far the largest union using postal ballots for choosing all its full-time officers.[19] It is a highly decentralized union, with a tradition of shop steward involvement. It recruits largely in the engineering industry, but it also has craft members in maintenance jobs in virtually all other industries. However, craftsmen probably accounted for less than half the union's membership in 1982.[20] Nevertheless, as will be seen, the 25 per cent of members in section one, the craft exclusive section, predominate in elections and hold the overwhelming majority of posts within the union's hierarchy. The union is subject to marked internal political divisions variously described as factions[21] or parties.[22] This is not a new development as 'The Manchester district [of the union] formed a Progressive Party to hold regular meetings . . . and above all to organize the voting for members of the executive and district organizer' in 1892.[23] The existing politically opposed groups continue to behave like parties[24] and their role in the more recent past will be further discussed in the following examinations of the AUEW(E)'s electoral method.

The AUEW(E)'s system of government has been described as embodying '. . . the principle of the separation of powers . . .'[25] as expressed in the constitution of the United States. It operates a complex system of checks and balances and power is diffused at the national level over several different positions and bodies. These are the president, general secretary, executive council (7 members), national committee (52 lay members)[26] and the final appeal court (11 lay members).

The lay national committee is chosen by indirect election through branch meetings and district and divisional committees, as it has been since 1919. Before 1972 the full-time posts were filled by direct election using a branch ballot; since 1972 they have been elected by full postal ballot. This system was first introduced in 1972 for all full-time officer posts, including those of president, general secretary and executive. Successful candidates to these posts require either an overall majority on the first ballot or a simple majority in a second ballot which is only contested by the two leading candidates from the first ballot. Once elected they face a further election after three years, and then periodic election every five years until being 60 years of age or over, and having fought at least two elections, they continue in office until retirement at 65 years. The lay members of the final appeal court have also been subject to full postal ballot elections since 1980. They are also chosen under a second ballot system, but face re-election at regular three-yearly intervals.

The rule changes requiring postal ballots were processed through the formal rule-making machinery of the AUEW(E). Amendments of this kind are finally determined by a vote of the lay rules revision meeting, which is the 52 strong national committee under another name. If the rule-making process or the rules themselves are not rigorously adhered to they may be enforced by reference to the High Court. This has happened on a small number of occasions in recent years including action in the High Court by Terry Duffy in 1975 to prevent a boundary change and action by John Weakley in the same year to prevent his disqualification from a key national committee vote on the retention of postal ballots. There is, however, one important exception to the strict application of rule. This concerns the circulation of unofficial election material which is formally proscribed in rule[27] but generally distributed by the two parties fighting for control of the AUEW(E). Both parties make extensive use of such literature as they promote and organize support for their candidates. Use has been made of this material, including the moderates' paper *Engineering News and Views* and *IRIS* and the militants' *Engineering Voice* and *Engineering Gazette*, to monitor the political composition of the union's leadership before and after the introduction of postal ballots.

When postal ballots were used in full-time officer elections in 1972 and adopted for the final appeal court in 1982 (following the rule change of 1980), they were initiated by the moderate right, or, as they are known in the AUEW(E), the Group. This organization has its origins in the general anti-Communist movement which spread throughout British unions in the 1940s. It remains essentially a group opposed to Communist, Trotskyist and left-wing Labour influence and supports the centre/right of the Labour party. It therefore has some similarities with the Bloc in the POEU, the Moderate Group in the CPSA and the present ruling body in the EETPU. Between 1950 and the mid 1960s, the Group had considerable electoral success, and in 1959 only one Communist, C. Berridge, retained his seat on the executive. It was also calculated by *IRIS* in July 1963 that the left held only 42 (26 per cent) of the 160 full-time officer posts in the union.[28] By 1973, however, the left had captured the presidency, won 3 of the 7 executive seats and both assistant general secretary posts. The left had also, according to *IRIS*, increased its hold on full-time officer posts from the 42 held in 1963 to 62 (34 per cent) in 1973.[29]

There are a number of reasons why the left won elections in the period 1967–72. The economic problems encountered in the period and the reaction against the Labour government's restriction on wage increases no doubt helped the left. However, the degree of organized voting in support of left-wing candidates was very significant in producing unusually high and biased votes in a small number of high polling branches.[30] For example, although the overall turnout in the presidential elections of 1967 was 11 per cent, some branches recorded 40 and 50 per cent polls. The left's organization ensured that a clear majority of the high polling branches gave their support overwhelmingly, if not almost solely, to the left's candidate. This was also the case in the executive contest in 1970, when 27 of the 41 branches recording twice the average vote produced large majorities for the left's candidate.

It was against this background that the Group initiated a proposal to introduce postal ballots. This was first discussed in the mid 1960s, and the Group's majority on the rules revision committee forced it through against strong opposition in 1970. It was subsequently challenged by the executive at a recalled rules revision committee in 1971, but the Group's majority on that body again reaffirmed its commitment to postal ballots. At the Group's pre-committee meetings a number of the full-time officials opposed postal ballots on the grounds of the administrative problems associated with operating the scheme and its cost. However, the slogan 'what price democracy' was effectively used to counter those who opposed postal ballots on the grounds of cost. The same argument was subsequently used in the Group some ten years later when the executive unsuccessfully proposed that the union should apply to the certification officer for financial assistance under the 1980 Employment Act.

Proposals to introduce postal ballots for election to the final appeal court were also primarily the outcome of the Group's political considerations. The court was perceived by leading national officials associated with the Group as a 'power body' exercising its judgements according to party political advantage rather than more objective criteria. As the general secretary, Sir John Boyd, saw it the final appeal court had 'lost its judicial character'.[31] The left controlled court was considered prone to give undue weight to rank and file appeals against the decisions of the right-wing executive. In one case this involved overturning the executives' refusal to meet a claim for dispute benefit from members at Rolls-Royce locked out during the 1979 engineering dispute. This act reputedly cost the union £250,000 in retrospective payments. Further, the court also challenged the validity of the overwhelming majority secured by Terry Duffy in the presidential election of 1980 by claiming that, contrary to rule, the AUEW(E)'s *Journal* had been used to publicize Duffy's election campaign.[32] Thus, faced by a 7 to 4 majority for the left on the final appeal court, leaders of the Group promoted postal ballots as a means of reducing the number of left-wingers and hence harmonizing the political views of the court with those of the executive.

A survey of all the 461 elections held under postal ballots in the AUEW(E) between January 1972 and February 1982 reveals that 332 were contested and 129 (30 per cent) uncontested. None of the 43 elections involving a position of national importance went uncontested.[33] The largest number of uncontested elections occurred at the district secretary level. Of the 278 district secretary elections, 105 or 38 per cent were uncontested. However, the great majority of seats that went uncontested (91 per cent), involved a sitting full-time official seeking re-election. Thus, all but 12 (13 per cent) of vacant seats were contested. By comparison, a less comprehensive study of elections held under branch ballots in the AUEW(E) between 1950 and 1960 showed that of 143 district secretary elections surveyed 48 per cent were uncontested, but that only 2 out of 59 national posts were uncontested.[34] It can be reasonably suggested, therefore, that the introduction of postal ballots did not reduce, and indeed may have been associated with an increase in, the number of contested elections affecting all levels of the union's hierarchy.

The average number of candidates seeking election in the 332 contested elections held between 1972 and 1982 was 4. There were, however, quite wide variations between posts. For example, at the top of the scale the average number of candidates in general secretary, assistant general secretary and national organizer elections was 11 in each case. In contrast, the average for district secretary and divisional organizer elections was 3. There are no comparable figures for the earlier period of branch balloting, but fragmentary evidence suggests that there was a similar range of candidates for election to the various positions examined, with again more candidates entering for national than local elections.[35] Postal ballots therefore did not alter significantly the number of candidates entering for contested elections.

A further feature of the union's electoral system is the degree to which candidates in elections come from the union's craft exclusive section. Time-served section one members account for under 25 per cent of the union's total membership.[36] However, they provided 77 per cent of all candidates for full-time officer posts between 1972 and 1982. Successful candidates were even more likely to belong to section one: only 14 per cent of the successful candidates were without section one membership. The full-time officer posts therefore remain firmly under craft control, despite the movement to postal ballots which may have been thought to threaten craft supremacy by taking the votes away from presumably craft-dominated branches and into the homes of the wider and less skilled membership.

Turnout in elections rose quite sharply following the introduction of postal ballots. Over a 20-year period before the introduction of postal ballots branch attendance, as measured by votes in the election of TUC delegates dropped from 8.6 to 6.5 to 5.4 per cent.[37] Voting in a cross section of 40 elections held between 1964 and 1972 produced an average vote of 7 per cent, within a range of 4.5–19.9 per cent of the membership participating.[38] The presidential election of 1967 which attracted an 11 per cent turnout was the highest national poll recorded in the period 1952–72. Many branches did not even participate in the national elections. For example, in the first ballot for selecting a national organizer in 1970, 708 (25 per cent) of the 2,790 branches eligible to participate did not register a vote.

It is possible to make a direct comparison of the turnout under branch and postal ballots by comparing the figures given above for branch ballots with those cast in the same cross-section of 40 elections under postal ballots. Between 1972 and 1980 postal ballots produced an average turnout of 27.4 per cent of those registered as voters on the union's electoral roll. The voting ranged from 19.7 to 42 per cent of the registered electorate. However, because of problems in recording and maintaining members names and addresses, the roll totalled 939,475 members in 1979 whereas the total membership was 1,212,320. Hence only 77 per cent of the members were registered to vote and the turnout as a percentage of total membership in consequence only averaged 21 per cent. Nevertheless, this is still three times the number of votes recorded under branch ballots. Furthermore, the decline in branch attendance continued during the period of postal ballots with branch ballots for the TUC delegates in 1976 falling to 2.2 per cent in two divisions.[39]

Over the period of postal ballots studied, 1972–82, there was a marked reduction in turnout. In the first year (1973) of postal ballots the average turnout over 27 elections was 38 per cent of those on the electoral roll.[40] By 1982 the most important national election of that period, the contest for the vacant general secretary post, only produced a 23.7 per cent vote of those on the electoral roll or 18.6 per cent of total membership. Hence, although the introduction of the postal ballot initially provided a major increase in participation, it tended after ten years to give an average turnout in the area of 19 per cent of total membership.[41]

One of the difficulties associated with the AUEW(E)'s introduction of postal ballots was the collection of information at head office for the electoral roll. Initially a number of branches opposed to postal ballots refused to contribute names and addresses. Even when this temporary difficulty had been overcome, some 270,000 members remained disenfranchised throughout the period 1972–82 because they were not on the roll. This is perhaps not surprising since the union relies on more than 2,500 lay branch secretaries working in ill-attended, geographically based branches for its basic information on who is entitled to vote. With the normal movement of members in and out of the union and changes in address, the union has considerable problems in maintaining an accurate and comprehensive list of members. This is also reflected in the number of ballot papers returned unused. For example, in the 1982 general secretary election 14,295 or 2 per cent of envelopes dispatched were returned unused. However, it would be misleading to conclude that more members were in practice enfranchised under branch than postal ballots. As mentioned above, 25 per cent of branches did not record a vote in a national organizer's election held in 1970, suggesting that they did not organize a ballot. In June 1980 the union calculated that in 41 elections held between 1964 and 1972, a total of 2,018 branches did not participate in the first and 596 in the second ballots. Hence, under branch ballots many members, sometimes 25 per cent, were *de facto* disenfranchised because their branches did not choose to participate in the election, compared to the 23 per cent disenfranchised under postal ballots in 1979. In practice postal ballots therefore marginally increased the size of the potential electorate, even if they did not provide all members with an opportunity to vote.

Political outcomes were directly affected by the move to postal ballots. The unofficial literature which circulates relatively freely within the union shows that the two parties which dominated the electoral process in the late

1960s and early 1970s continued to contest all the major elections after the introduction of postal ballots in 1972. The following discussion of political outcomes may, however, understate the broad left's influence on elections as the copies of the left-wing publications *Engineering Voice* and *Engineering Gazette* available for identifying the political bias of candidates did not cover the whole of the 1972–82 period. It cannot be assumed therefore that where the total or left- and right-wing candidates mentioned in a particular series of elections does not equal 100 per cent that the remaining candidates were independents. Moreover, it is not clear how many of the uncontested seats were held by the Group or the broad left during the period under examination.

In the 332 contested elections held between 1972 and 1982 the Group fielded candidates, in the first ballot, in 277 (83 per cent) elections and the broad left fielded candidates in 216 (65 per cent) elections. The Group placed 261 or 95 per cent of their candidates into the second ballot and the broad left 186 or 86 per cent. In addition, the Group advised its supporters to vote for one of two candidates in the first ballot in 20 elections; this advice is usually given when the Group's pre-nomination selection meetings have failed to reach a decision on their candidates, or the members producing the literature receive conflicting information. The broad left suffered from the same problem in 7 elections. The elections in which these difficulties occurred tended to be at the divisional organizer or district secretary level. In the more important national and executive elections the broad left never fielded more than one candidate and the Group only prevaricated on two occasions, both in 1973.

The Group's original nominee won in 203 or 74 per cent of the 277 elections they contested. In contrast, the broad left won in 72 or 33 per cent of the 217 elections they contested. If vacant seats only are considered, the Group won 56 per cent of all vacancies contested and the broad left 21 per cent. Some major gains were made by the Group in seats involving sitting candidates. The broad left lost 10 such posts to the Group, including two key executive seats (previously held by Les Dixon and Bob Wright). Indeed by 1982, apart from one independent executive member, the Group had complete control of the executive having also retained its own seats in vacant elections and captured a vacant seat traditionally held by the broad left or one of its sympathizers.[42]

It is therefore clear that the Group gained seats and defeated the broad left in several important contests under postal ballots. The result is that the Group held at the start of 1983 the presidency, general secretaryship and all but one of the seven executive council positions.[43] It also continued to hold a majority of local full-time officer posts and it could normally count on majority support from the national committee, even though this body continues to be elected by indirect votes at the branch and the district and divisional committees. However, the Group failed to defeat the broad left in direct branch elections to the final appeal court, and neither the Group nor the broad left revealed the rate of success expected in the elections to what may be termed less salient full-time posts.

In addition to the major national posts of president, general secretary, assistant general secretary and executive councillor, and the more localized regional, division or district officer posts, there are seven national organizers. These seven are the less salient national posts. Although they are elected by a vote of the total membership, in common with the president, general secretary and assistant general secretaries, they are not policy makers and they tend to work under the direction of the executive councillors. They also carry responsibility for certain industry level negotiations. The result is that they are given considerably less publicity both inside and outside the union than the more senior officials. They are not well known in the union and do not attract the attention of the media. Yet the total membership participates in their election. Since the two political machines concentrate upon promoting either known local figures or exploiting press interest in their candidates contesting major national seats, candidates for the post of national organizer are more dependent on the unofficial literature and the two parties national network of supporters, than are candidates for most other posts. Consequently, they are less successful in winning elections when the unofficial parties' machines fail to inform and persuade the wider electorate of their respective candidates' merits. For example, in the 16 national organizer elections held between 1972 and 1982 the broad left's nominee reached the second ballot 10 times (63 per cent) and the Group's 13 (81 per cent). (This compares with a success rate in all elections of 86 per cent for the broad left and 95 per cent for the Group in the first ballot.) Moreover, in the second ballots held between 1972 and 1982 two sitting national organizers were defeated by politically unaligned candidates. Similar political upsets also occurred under the postal ballot system at the intermediate level. For example, a sitting officer holding an assistant divisional officer post and supported by the broad left was defeated in 1979 by an unknown candidate, who on this occasion did not submit an election address and who on winning the election refused to take office.[44] Following this election, the rules were changed and candidates were required to submit election addresses. Thus, the defeat of sitting candidates under postal ballots not only occurred when the Group unseated broad left officers but it also, in the less salient elections, led to unknowns defeating incumbents, something rarely if ever experienced under branch ballots.

In the circumstances surrounding less salient elections held under postal ballots, a number of factors play a more prominent role than they do in other more important elections. The ballot paper, which carries the candidate's name, age, years in the union, branch, section of membership and trade, assumes, in the absence of other information, more import- ance.[45] It would appear from an examination of the results of national organizer elections that candidates with a strong parochial vote – such as is generated in the north east – the almost mandatory section one membership and a name identical with that of a better known member (preferably close to the start of the alphabet) stands a better than average chance of breaking the two parties hold on the first ballot. The introduction of postal ballots in the absence of relevant political information may, therefore, introduce a political randomness which does not exist under branch ballots.

Although significant, such elections are the exceptions in the AUEW(E); over the period 1972–82 elections to the national decision-making bodies, the executive, national committee and the somewhat less influential final appeal court, were dominated by the two parties. Why did the Group manage to win and hold majorities on the first two bodies, but not on the third, between 1972 and 1982? The factors to be considered are the environment, the electoral machines of the two parties and the different systems of balloting used to elect the three bodies under discussion.

Some of the people interviewed argued that the Group won elections to the executive and national committee in the 1970s and early 1980s because of a general political reversion following the brief period when the broad left held the political ascandancy in the late 1960s and early 1970s. According to this view, the membership briefly favoured the left in the election of the president and the executive in the 1960s and early 1970s, but that they subsequently found this a rather costly flirtation because of the disputes arising from the union's opposition to the Industrial Relations Act and the militant pursuit of national wage claims.[46] Thus the membership reverted to type by voting for the Group in the later 1970s and 1980s. There were also suggestions that the later economic recession influenced members' attitudes, and encouraged moderation. The Group therefore regained control of the AUEW(E) because of the unpopularity of the broad left's policies and changes in the external environment. These factors may be important, but they do not explain why, given these general developments affecting all the union's membership, the broad left continued to hold a majority on the final appeal court.

Both parties experienced changes in their electoral machines between 1960 and 1982. The Group overhauled its electoral machine in the mid 1960s. Its organization, based on district, division and national groups, was reviewed and the constitution re-written.[47] In particular, an attempt was made to reduce the frequency of multi-candidatures. This involved requiring the different localized groups to meet and determine their nominations for seats, which cut across group boundaries, before calling a combined group final selection meeting. However, the national Group does not expel members who run against the Group's official candidate, so there is always the chance of multi-candidatures although a member's claim on their support in future is obviously threatened by breaking Group policy. In contrast, the broad left suffered over the same period from internal difficulties which threatened its unity. Difficulties arose over editorial policy in the left's unofficial newspaper and some dissatisfaction was also expressed with Hugh Scanlon's behaviour as president, particularly towards the end of his period in office. A number of leading members also resigned from the Communist party. Moreover, as the Group gathered momentum and gained control of a number of district committees, a small number of ambitious members and full-time officials changed sides and/or were converted to the Group's aims. Thus, the balance of organization moved towards the Group over the period of postal ballots, which may have influenced the elections. This does not on its own, however, explain the variation in results between the executive, national committee and final appeal court.

The changes and variations in the two parties' political fortunes can, however, be explained by reference to the alternative balloting arrangements which combined with the effects of environmental changes and electoral re-organization to produce contrasting electoral results. The final appeal court, which the broad left continued to hold, was elected before 1982 by a direct branch ballot, the same as that previously used in the election of full-time officers. This meant, in effect, that only union activists voted in final appeal court elections. Thus the broad left was able to influence elections by organizing a limited number of geographically concentrated and high polling branches, the kind of organized voting which won the broad left the presidency and executive seats in the late 1960s and early 1970s. In contrast, the election of candidates to the national committee, which was by a different form of branch ballot, was less amenable to this method of organized voting, because the method of indirect election employed (starting from the branch and progressing through the district and divisional committees) limited the extent to which any one branch with a high voting potential could influence the composition of a district committee, composed of representatives of all the branches in the district plus one shop steward for every 3,000 members.[48] The Group was thus able to exploit its wider base of support in the large number of smaller branches not dominated by the broad left to maintain its control of the national committee, even though it could not win a majority on the final appeal court.

The broader based organization enjoyed by the Group was also important when the introduction of postal ballots in 1972 for full-time officer posts dispersed the vote from the branch to the home. This clearly drastically reduced, almost overnight, the importance of the broad left's electoral machine, narrowly based as it was on a small number of high polling branches. By shifting the locus of the vote from branch to home the Group introduced a whole new category of voters into the elections, the non-attender at branch meetings. Further, given the Group's national network of supporters and the popular press' tendency to publicize in a favourable light the Group's rather than the broad left's candidates, postal ballots clearly boosted the Group's candidates' election campaigns.

Thus in the period 1972–82 the interaction between the environment, party organization and balloting systems enabled the Group or moderates to hold and gain majorities on the national committee and executive, respectively, while the broad left lost ground on both these bodies but retained control of the final appeal court. It is clear that the Group benefited from the increased turnout associated with postal ballots. Turnout rose by more than 100 per cent on the introduction of postal ballots despite problems of compiling and maintaining an electoral roll. In 1982 the average turnout was 19 per cent of total membership. Competition for full-time officer posts remained reasonably constant under both branch and postal ballots with more members contesting national than local elections. But sitting left-wing officials previously elected under branch ballots were more prone to defeat by the right after postal ballots were introduced. However, in a large minority of local elections the sitting members of both left and right continued to be returned unopposed. In the less salient elections the increase in participation caused difficulties for both parties' electoral machines as without media interest, particularly the national and local press, the members appeared unaware of the candidates' political allegiances. It can be concluded, therefore, that in the circumstances affecting the AUEW(E) in the period studied, the choice of balloting method had an impact on some aspects of the process of election and a major influence on political outcomes. The Group or moderates regained under postal ballots the control of the presidency and executive which they had lost under the direct branch ballot.

The Electrical, Electronic, Telecommunication and Plumbing Union   Three other craft or craft origin unions also use postal ballots for the election of certain leading officers. These unions are the EETPU, FTAT and the Bakers. The introduction of single transferable voting by postal ballot in the forerunner of the EETPU, the ETU, followed the well documented trial of its leading full-time officials for fraudulent conspiracy in rigging the election of the general secretary in 1959.[49] The trial exposed the manner in which the Communists in the ETU had, under a system of branch ballots, succeeded in preventing the opposition from winning the general secretaryship by interfering with the ballot and with the counting of votes. Communists were subsequently barred from holding office in the union and the moderates or right who instigated the court case gained control of the union.

The ETU became the EETPU in 1968 after a merger with the Plumbers. In 1980 the union had some 420,000 members, broadly divided between those concentrated in the engineering industry and those working on maintenance across a wide range of industries. The original ETU was one of those unions influenced by the Engineers' rule book. It adopted a similar system of election for choosing its full-time officers. However, since its experiences in the late 1950s, the union has undergone a radical restructuring internally, and changed the system of choosing its officials. Except for the general secretary and the full-time executive,[50] all full-time officers are now appointed. The union maintains a panel of potential full-time officers composed of members who apply for and are successful in completing an assessment course at the union's college. An appointments committee of three executive members and three full-time officers determines which applicants are admitted to the course and oversees its organization and content. Members who complete the course successfully are eligible for appointment by the executive to vacant official positions when vacancies occur.

Despite the system of appointing full-time officers, the rule barring Communists from office and the established right-wing leadership's control of all the main centres of power, the broad left still contests union elections. In 1982, the broad left held 2 of the 13 executive (divisional) seats. One is the plumber's seat in Scotland and the other the electrician's seat in South Wales. The broad left also has 2 publications circulating in the union, *The Flashlight* associated with the Communist party, and *Rank and File Contact*, promoted by the Socialist Workers Party.

The broad left does not, however, press the right very closely in national elections, as can be seen from the general secretary election of 1982. In this election the broad left backed a left-wing member of the Labour Party, John Aitken, against the established leadership's candidate, Eric Hammond, and a middle of the road independent candidate, Roy Sanderson. The result on a 32 per cent turnout in a postal ballot supervised by the Electoral Reform Society was that Hammond polled 73,506 (56 per cent), Aitken 32,436 (25 per cent) and Sanderson 26,945 (20 per cent). In an interview for *Socialist Challenge* following his defeat Aitken argued that this result augured well for the broad left as it had promoted only one candidate, found ways of publicizing its campaign despite the rules against electioneering and had established the broad left's nominees 'as credible candidates for national office'.[51] Nevertheless, right-wing control was not seriously challenged, and it maintained its position in the same round of elections by winning the electrician's executive seat in Scotland and the national secretaryship of the plumbers' section.[52]

The EETPU therefore underwent a radical change in its system of government following the High Court case of 1961 and the rise of the right within the union. Among other changes, the union barred Communists from holding office, moved from the election of all officials to a mixed election and appointment system, made its executive full-time and introduced single transferable voting by postal ballot under the auspices of the Electoral Reform Society. The members who brought the case against the Communists inherited the union, and the malpractices of their predecessors served to justify the subsequent rule changes which helped consolidate the right's position.

As in the AUEW(E), the introduction of postal ballots raised the turnout in elections from approximately 10 per cent to over 30 per cent. However, it is unclear how far the change to postal ballots and the increased vote contributed to the right's electoral success. In the short run, the change did not of itself overturn a left-wing majority. For, if the branch ballot held in 1959 to elect a general secretary had not been interfered with the right would not only have won this election but it would also have unseated a sitting general secretary, Frank Haxell. There are therefore good grounds for suggesting that, if elections held under branch ballots had conformed with the union's rules, the right would have overthrown the left without the aid of postal ballots. Postal ballots in the ETU therefore served to eliminate malpractice rather than radically change the balance of voting.

On the other hand, and in the long run, postal ballots no doubt made it more difficult for the left, bereft of its leaders and without access to union official publications and records, to win office. Nevertheless, the left continues to work within the union, under the title of broad left; and, despite the badly tarnished image it inherited from its Communist forbears, it still wins some elections. In view of the court case and media interest in the union's affairs, it is unlikely that the left would have regained control of the union under branch ballots.

The Furniture, Timber and Allied Trades Union   The FTAT and the Bakers union experienced different political outcomes from the AUEW(E) and the EETPU under postal ballots.[53] FTAT had some 69,000 members in 1982, geographically concentrated in the main furniture making centres of London, High Wycombe, Manchester, Birmingham and Glasgow. The Union is organized internally into six trade groups, including a white collar section. It has suffered in recent years from a sharp decline in membership.

All FTAT's 49 full-time officers are elected by postal ballot and are subject to re-election every five years. The lay executive which meets monthly was recently reduced to 19 members, and is also elected by postal ballot for a five-year period. Election addresses are published on the ballot papers and members are required to sign their ballot papers when returning them to be counted by the union's chartered accountants. Like the AUEW(E), the union depends on its branch secretaries for the information necessary to maintain a comprehensive electoral roll. The union replaced branch with postal ballots in 1949 when the general secretary of the period and his supporters instigated a rule change after he appeared under electoral pressure from the 'Furniture Trades Organization Committee' which was supported by the Communist party. The general secretary was himself a former member of the Communist party and had won his election in 1939 with their support.[54]

After the introduction of postal ballots in FTAT, participation in the union's elections immediately rose to average 30 per cent between 1950 and 1960, compared with some 5 per cent under branch ballots. However, turnout subsequently dropped, and by the 1970s was approximately 10 per cent. In the 1970s competition for office also declined, and almost one-third of the executive is reported to be elected unopposed. The union has a governing left-wing majority, against which there is no well-organized opposition. Indeed, the general secretary, Ben Rubner a well-known member of the Communist party, was not opposed when he stood for re-election after the completion of his first term in office. Moreover, when he won his election on the retirement of the previous general secretary, he succeeded the man who had initiated the introduction of postal ballots in 1949 as a means of restricting the rise of the left. In FTAT the postal ballot has not produced a right-wing majority, nor has it stimulated the formation of an opposition faction capable of contesting the leading positions in the union. It did, however, increase the turnout in union elections, at least in the short term.

The Bakers, Food and Allied Workers Union The Bakers union is smaller than FTAT, and has also suffered a recent fall in membership, from 56,000 in 1975 to 42,000 members in 1982. It has the normal union structure of branch, district and regional organization. The general secretary, president and district secretaries are all full-time posts and elected by postal ballots which are returned to the union's accountants for counting. There is no periodic re-election for any of these posts. Nominees for the post of general secretary are required to pass an examination before being allowed to contest the election. The 18 strong executive is a lay body elected by and at the annual conference, and holds office for one year.

The Bakers union has experienced a quite marked change in political direction over the period 1974–83. In 1975, the left-wing Sam Maddox won the vacant general secretaryship by a vote of 7,548, against the moderate John Addison's 5,394 in a 23 per cent poll; Addison subsequently resigned from office as a full-time officer and left the union.[55] Maddox's success was followed by further victories for left-wing candidates. In 1978, Terry O'Neil won the presidency following the enforced resignation of a right-winger, and in 1980 Joe Marino retained the general secretaryship for the left, following Maddox's death. The leading figures on the left in the Bakers, unlike the left in a number of other blue collar unions, are closely aligned with the Militant Tendency. Both O'Neil and Marino are supporters of the Tendency.

Before 1975 the Bakers had been a relatively moderate union, for example registering under the Industrial Relations Act and being consequently expelled from the TUC. It also followed a moderate industrial policy which provoked a series of unofficial strikes in the late 1960s by members protesting at the union's tendency to settle agreements without reference to the wider membership. In 1974 Maddox's predecessor as general secretary, Stan Gretton, and the national officials were subject to intense criticism regarding the national wage claim. The left led and actively organized the protests against the moderate leadership. 'Unofficial literature was widely distributed in support of unofficial strike action . . . Press statements were issued in violation of union rules. . . Flying squads were recruited and appeared at other bakeries calling for stoppages of work . . .'[56] These disputes and opposition to registration under the Industrial Relations Act provided the issues around which the left developed its predominantly localized organization. Thus the union underwent a change of political direction as the left gained the ascendancy under an existing system of postal ballots, with turnouts similar to those experienced in the AUEW(E).

The National Union of Seamen   The two remaining unions which use postal ballots in elections are the NUS and Equity. These are the only two unions identified in the survey of union rule books which elect by postal ballots and do not have a craft origin. However, the two unions do have similar kinds of membership, since both seamen and actors are highly mobile. It is thus difficult for the unions to organize meetings within a branch and district structure. The NUS does not have a district organization and Equity has no branch structure. Postal ballots therefore provide a method of recording votes which is both appropriate to their members' work environments and their internal union structures.

The NUS has suffered a major decline in membership over the past twenty years. In 1960 it had 62,500 members, but by 1981 this had fallen to 34,000. The union appoints its local full-time officials but it elects the three senior national full-time officers, i.e. general secretary, assistant general secretary and national secretary by postal ballot.[57] They are not subject to re-election and are elected by a simple majority. The lay executive is also elected by postal ballot and holds office for three years. The 13 lay members of the executive are joined by the general and assistant general secretary with full voting rights to compose a 15 man executive plus the non-voting national secretary. The biennial general meeting (or conference) is also elected by postal ballot, should there be a contest for places: in 1982 7 ballots were held out of the 20 which would have been required if all branches entitled to nominate had chosen to do so. Full-time officials can seek nomination to the executive but they are limited under rule to no more than one-third of all the places. In order to vote in these and other elections the individual member is responsible for placing himself on the electoral roll.

Balloting in the NUS has undergone important changes since 1967. These changes followed fierce internal factional conflict and a ballot rigging scandal which surfaced in 1964 and led to four officials leaving the union.[58] The scandal appeared to involve a small number of shore-based officials who intercepted voting papers properly intended for members working at sea, and an unfair exploitation of the union's then plural system of voting, under which members with 16 years or more membership had four votes, 11–15 years three votes, 6–10 years two votes and 1–5 years one vote. Thus, in elections where each member had to register in order to vote, an organized registration of long-serving members who could then be persuaded or used to vote for certain candidates produced marked effects on the results. In the general secretary election of 1962, for example, although only 16,640 ballot papers were returned by registered voters the right polled some 31,000 votes and the left 10,000.[59] Rule 17(1) of the *1967 Rule Book* also recognized another problem caused by a highly mobile membership by asserting that '*No member shall vote on any national or local question if he has already voted elsewhere on the same question'* (emphasized in rule). Given these difficulties, the union overhauled its system of government by rule changes in 1967 and 1972 and the executive, responsible under rule for conducting the postal ballot, acted to remove the opportunities for electoral malpractice.

By the mid 1970s, the NUS had ceased to use plural voting, and adopted a system of one man one vote. The Electoral Reform Society was invited to organize and advise on the method of voting and it distributed, received and counted the ballot papers. Members were still required to register but encouraged to record permanent home addresses and not use the name of ships for the receipt of ballot papers. As the members were given three months in which to cast their votes this did not provide a major obstacle to membership participation. Signatures were also required on the envelopes containing the ballot paper.

In 1980 the NUS computerized members' names and addresses by reference to the member's electoral constituency. This produced further opportunities for changes in its electoral system. Most importantly it meant that members did not have to register separately for each election. Once registered for voting, members now receive the appropriate ballot papers if in benefit. Also, the introduction of the check-off system of paying subscriptions enabled the NUS at the head office to identify which members were paid-up and thus entitled to vote. In consequence, the union no longer requires its members to sign the envelopes or ballot papers. Having 'cleaned-up' its method of voting, the union felt confident enough to dispense with the services of the Electoral Reform Society and to require ballot papers to be returned to its bankers before being counted by its own staff under the direction of scrutineers appointed by the executive.

In contrast to the EETPU the left, rather than the right, initiated and subsequently benefited from the changes made in the NUS. The changes were mainly the product of a drive by the left to reduce the power of full-time officials and make the union more responsive to the needs of the rank-and-file membership, regardless of the length of that membership. The left-wing National Seamen's Reform Movement, in which Jim Slater was a leading figure, benefited from the scandal surrounding the ballot rigging cases of 1964.[60] Strikes in 1960 and 1966 also fuelled the left's campaign and Harold Wilson's naming of Slater in 1966 as one of the 'tightly knit group of politically motivated men' promoting the strike gave him further national publicity.[61] Following the sudden death of Bill Hogarth (general secretary) in 1973, the left fielded two candidates in the election and still captured the first two places in the ballot, with Slater polling 1,700, McCluskie 1,204, while the right's candidate came a poor third with 676 votes.

Thus, in the NUS the left pressed for the extension of elections to more full-time offices, promoted greater lay influence on the executive, urged changes in the system of plural voting and pressed for the loopholes in the system of balloting to be closed. It did not, however, seriously question the validity of postal ballots. In the NUS's situation, with its highly mobile and dispersed membership and in the absence of an intermediate channel of communication between branch and head office, postal ballots probably provided the only logical and satisfactory way of giving the membership a chance of participating in elections. But even this method, as shown above, had its problems. It failed to produce a high level of membership participation. In the Slater election of 1974, for example, only 11,000 (25 per cent) of the total membership were registered and received ballot papers, and the 3,580 valid votes cast represented only 8 per cent of the total membership. This position improved following computerization: in the 1982 executive elections 12,340 or 36 per cent of the total membership received ballot papers and 5,091 actually voted; giving a turnout of 15 per cent of total membership.

The NUS's use of postal ballots in all its main elections, an exception among manual non-craft unions, is therefore closely associated with the special nature of its membership. However, in the circumstances surrounding the NUS it was not easy for the executive to maintain an incorruptible system of voting. Postal ballots did not themselves guarantee that the highly mobile and widely dispersed NUS membership received and returned the ballot form. The union encountered extreme difficulties in maintaining a reasonably comprehensive electoral roll composed solely of paid-up members. In such circumstances, turnout was relatively low compared with postal ballots in other unions and, as will be seen, abysmally low compared with that achieved in the NUM's pithead ballots. Also (contrary to what may have been expected from the AUEW(E) case study) as the size of the NUS's turnout increased and the union reduced the opportunity for the organization of biased voting, the left gained influence. This change, as in the Bakers union, was largely due to the membership's growing dissatisfaction with the established right-wing leadership's industrial policies. Moreover, the left in the NUS inadvertently gained from the media's attention to the scandal of 1964 and the right's lack of effective organization.

Equity   The British Actors Equity Association (Equity) had 29,151 members in 1982 and 28 appointed full-time officials, including an appointed general secretary. The union has no branch structure but it does have a number of area councils. The structure of policy-making institutions differs from that normally found in larger and more traditional unions; it has an annual general meeting, which all members may attend, and a biennially elected general council of 65. The general council elects the 17 strong executive and, when necessary, chooses the general secretary. The general council is elected by postal ballot. There is also provision under rule for holding a referendum by a postal ballot of all members. The referendum can be initiated by either the council or the general meeting on any issue it chooses. The ballot paper has to be signed by the voting member, and his union number written in. This allows the union to check whether or not the member is in benefit and entitled to vote. It also, of course, means the vote is not strictly secret, although it is counted by the union's accountants. As will be seen later (see chapter 4), the referendum rule was activated on the question of whether or not to apply for a government subsidy to help cover the cost of the union's postal ballots.

Elections to Equity's council are highly contested by a number of different factions and some well-known individual or independent candidates. For instance, 94 members contested the 29 'general list' places in 1982, and many of these were identified with one of the following four groups: moving from right to left, Act for Equity, Centre Forward, Equity Left Alliance and All Trade Union Alliance (the Workers Revolutionary Party). Act for Equity, although emphasizing its non-political nature, is probably the faction identified in the study closest to the Conservative party. Before the 1982 elections it was the majority group on Equity's council.

The election of Equity's council in 1982 attracted 3,761 votes or 13 per cent of the membership, and some further 90 votes were not counted because the voters' membership had lapsed. The Centre Forward group, representing a wide range of centre-left interests, made some important gains but it did not gain control of the council. Act for Equity, which lost ground to Centre Forward, had previously controlled the council and used its majority to promote a motion seeking a subsidy for the union's postal ballots under the Conservative government's 1980 scheme. Thus the election resulted in a few independent candidates holding the balance of power between the two main factions but, nevertheless, the victories gained by Centre Forward represented a move to the left under a system of postal ballots. Moreover, this was not achieved by leaving the electorate ignorant or misleading them about the nature of the choice of candidates. Equity's electorate is provided with an official booklet containing each candidate's election address. Also, in contrast to the AUEW(E), a majority of Equity's candidates declared their political position in no uncertain terms. For example, in the 1982 election, candidate number 40 stated 'I hope you will vote for me and all other Centre Forward candidates', while candidate 83 declared 'I stand on Equity Left Alliance policies . . .' and 67 'I stand for the All Trade Union Alliance', and finally 59 '. . . vote for the Act for Equity list of candidates.'[62] Thus there can be no doubt that in Equity's case the membership, faced by a known political choice under a system of postal ballots, moved to the left.

Adoption of Postal Ballots The unions which either introduced or modified postal ballots tended to be influenced by a number of considerations. These were often inter-related and included: political advantage, increased participation, consistency of choice, the elimination of malpractice and administrative convenience. The AUEW(E), EETPU and FTAT were all concerned to increase participation and gain political advantage by replacing branch with postal ballots. In each case the right saw postal ballots as a means of combating the left's electoral influence which it considered was disproportionate to the left's support within the union as a whole. Once postal ballots had been adopted and the electoral roll established, the AUEW(E) extended its system of postal ballots to the final appeal court in the hope, as yet unfulfilled, that the membership would be consistent in its choice and elect a moderate court in tune with the executive. In both the EETPU and the NUS postal ballots were, respectively, adopted and modified to combat the malpractice exercised by some of the two unions' existing full-time officials. These officials came from opposite ends of the political spectrum. Finally, administrative convenience made postal ballots the logical way of ensuring membership participation in the decision-making processes of the NUS and Equity. In both unions a widely dispersed and highly mobile membership, and the lack of an intermediate structure of union organization, made any other voting method highly unsuitable. Both unions thus opted for postal ballots primarily because they suited their particular memberships.

Relationship between Postal Ballots and Process of Election   Turnout rose when postal ballots replaced branch ballots in the AUEW(E), EETPU and FTAT. The initial impact led to a three- or fourfold increase in participation. However in the AUEW(E) and FTAT this declined over a period of years, although it still remained considerably higher than that achieved under branch ballots. For instance, the general secretary election in the AUEW(E) in 1982 recorded an 18.6 per cent vote of the total membership compared with 11 per cent in the 1967 presidential election. Nevertheless, postal ballots do not produce majority participation in union elections. In some cases they produced quite low turnouts. For instance, in the highly competitive Equity elections of 1982 only 13 per cent participated and in the NUS an 'improved' turnout in 1982 saw a 15 per cent vote. The range of turnout under postal ballots therefore varies widely. Across unions the 32 per cent vote in the EETPU's general secretary election in 1982 contrasts with Equity's 13 per cent vote. Within unions there is also a wide range of voting, for example, the AUEW(E) in its March 1982 elections recorded a 25.1 per cent turnout in its Blackpool district secretary election and 13.7 per cent in its division nine election to the final appeal court.[63]

In some instances the turnout is unexpectedly low under postal ballots because of the difficulties of maintaining a comprehensive electoral roll. For example, under the NUS's scheme of self-registration, only 36 per cent of the total membership were on the register in 1982. Similarly, despite major efforts to increase the roll, 23 per cent of the potential electorate in the AUEW(E) were still disenfranchised in 1979. With a highly mobile and widely dispersed membership the postal ballot does not always reach the correct address. A high turnover of members may also contribute to a low level of participation in postal ballots. Thus, it is possible under full postal ballots for a large minority, and in extreme cases, a majority of members not to be registered voters. Postal ballots therefore, while raising the level of participation compared with branch ballots, do not always achieve the level of vote hoped for or expected.

Secrecy is sometimes assumed to be greater under postal ballots than under other methods of voting. The voter marking the ballot paper in the privacy of his or her home is less likely to be observed than if the same vote were cast in the branch or the workplace. They are also immune, at the time of voting, from the group pressures which may be exerted when voting in the branch or workplace. However, FTAT, Equity and, until recently, the NUS required voters to record their name and/or union number on either the envelope or the ballot paper. This was considered necessary to prevent non-members, or members who had lapsed through non-payment of subscriptions, from voting in the elections. Hence, even though such papers may be returned to the banker or the accountant for counting, there is still the possibility of the individual voter's preferences being noted. In unions which do not record voters' names, for example, the EETPU and AUEW(E), there is less chance of tracing the individual voter but, of course, a greater chance of non-members inadvertently receiving a ballot paper and completing and returning the same for counting. Both systems therefore have their problems, as secrecy is traded-off against the possibility of malpractice.

Malpractice appears relatively difficult to organize under a system of postal ballots. Of the unions using postal ballots only the NUS, with its unique sea-going membership and the associated difficulty of maintaining a list of permanent home addresses, experienced this problem. It is noticeable, however, that when malpractice became an issue in the NUS and the ETU(EETPU) the introduction of a third party, in the form of the Electoral Reform Society, to administer the distribution, reception and counting of balloting papers, was thought desirable to prevent any further difficulties of this kind.

Outcome of Elections and Political Choice   It is only possible to consider the effect of postal ballots on the right/left or moderate/militant question in elections where the membership concerned is faced with a relevant political choice. This obvious point is worth stressing, as will be shown in later comments on the TGWU, the GMWU and the ASTMS. In all the unions using postal ballots there was a political choice in one or more of the elections studied. Thus each union had a degree of factional organization, often of both left and right, but sometimes of only one identifiable persuasion. The most extreme case of factional organization of both left and right was the AUEW(E), with its two party system.[64] This union therefore stands at one end of a continuum where factionalism is so well developed and established that it is best described as a political party.[65] The EETPU has a somewhat less formalized version of this organization on the right and the left. Equity is more complex in its political divisions while FTAT, the Bakers union and the NUS tend to have leaders at least originally nominated and supported by less well-organized left-wing factions or in some cases local caucuses. What has happened to the right-wing following its defeat in these latter three organizations is unclear; it does not appear to have regrouped to form competing factions.

The membership of the six postal balloting unions therefore faced a political choice between candidates of left and right political persuasions in some if not all the elections examined. In the great majority of second ballots in the AUEW(E) this was the only choice, although in the less important elections independent candidates stood some chance of election. In some unions the membership showed a preference for the right or moderates, as when postal ballots were introduced in the AUEW(E) and the EETPU. However, in both unions this was not entirely due to postal ballots, for in both the AUEW(E) and in the EETPU the moderates had won major elections under branch ballots. Before the late 1960s the Group held a majority position on the main decision making bodies in the AEU [AUEW(E)], and it was only malpractice which prevented the right in the ETU (EETPU) from defeating a sitting general secretary in 1959.

On the other hand, in the elections studied in FTAT, the Bakers union, the NUS and Equity the leadership moved to the left under postal ballots. In each case the established right-wing leadership's hold on the union was either reduced, as in Equity, or overturned as in FTAT, the Bakers and the NUS, under existing systems of postal ballots. Factors, other than the choice of balloting system therefore clearly influence the political outcome of elections. In some cases, evidence of malpractice led to the defeat of the offending faction. In other unions, the union leadership's bargaining effectiveness, and the degree of internal factional organization, interacted to play an important part in changing the union's political orientation.

Branch Ballots

There are two main kinds of votes cast at the branch meeting: the individual membership vote, which results in the actual votes cast being recorded for the respective candidates, and the block branch vote, in which the candidate winning a majority of votes cast is then allocated the vote of the total number of branch members. Branches themselves may also be organized in two different ways. Some unions, such as the GMWU, organize the great majority of their branches on a geographical basis, with members from several different firms or industries attending the same branch which may be close to their work or their home. In contrast, the TGWU has encouraged the formation of factory or workplace branches and these now account for the majority of its branches. In these branches meetings are normally held conveniently close to the main employing unit. The unions studied will therefore be divided into, first, those employing individual voting, and, secondly, block voting, and the type of branch organization will be noted. In the first part the TGWU and ASTMS will be examined and in the second the GMWU, NUR and POEU.

The Transport and General Workers Union   The TGWU is the largest union in the TUC and in 1980 it had 2,004,245 members. It recruits across a very wide range of industries and occupations, but the greater part of its membership is composed of semi- and unskilled manual workers. Internally, the union is vertically divided into a series of trade groups. In 1980 the union had 11 such groups. It is also geographically divided into 11 regions, although the regional influence in the TGWU is much less significant than in the GMWU. The TGWU pursued mergers in the 1970s and it accommodated the major incoming unions' demands for autonomy by giving them the dominant position in established or new trade groups and allocating their leaders places of national importance within the TGWU's hierarchy of appointed officers. This occurred, for example, in the case of the National Union of Vehicle Builders (NUVB). The incoming unions on their part adopted the TGWU's rule book and system of government.

In the TGWU, apart from the elected general secretary, all full-time officials (some 500) are appointed by the general executive council. Candidates for appointment must have two years' membership of the TGWU. The general secretary does not face re-election and holds office 'during the pleasure of the union'.[66] In contrast, the executive is composed of between 50 and 55 lay members and is subject to re-election every two years.[67] This body delegates much of its responsibilities to the 8 strong finance and general purposes committee, which is elected from within the executive. Election to the executive itself is by individual voting normally conducted at the branch or workplace by marking a ballot paper. However, the rule governing elections states that '. . . the methods used may include any or all of the following . . . voting at branch meetings or at works, garages, etc., or by postal ballot'.[68] Over and above the executive is the 1,000 or so strong biennial delegate conference (BDC) composed of regional trade group delegates again elected at the branches.

In 1977 Moss Evans replaced Jack Jones as general secretary of the TGWU by defeating 13 other candidates in a branch ballot. A total of 740,460 votes were cast for the 14 candidates giving a turnout of approximately 39 per cent. As the only elected full-time official, the tenured general secretary has considerable status within the union. He can exercise patronage over the careers of other appointed officials and extensive influence over the lay executive and has often dominated the union's conference. In the 1950s and early 1960s this highly centralized system of government was termed a 'popular bossdom'.[69] In more recent times, the TGWU has decentralized much of its decision making to district committees and shop stewards, and disciplined full-time officials who appeared unwilling to concede more power to lay representatives. This has in turn affected the system of government, and had a marked effect on the national level of decision making within the TGWU. For example, in 1977 the BDC revealed a newfound independence of mind by taking the unprecedented action of overthrowing a major policy recommendation initiated by the general secretary.[70] Also in the late 1970s, more senior shop stewards were successful in gaining election to the executive.[71] This body subsequently started to question, if not challenge, the general secretary's traditional prerogative. It is elections to the executive, the lay body in the TGWU, which will now be examined.

The executive is elected from a number of constituencies. The size and location of these constituencies are determined by the executive, which 'if deemed desirable' is entitled under rule to divide the regions into different constituencies for electoral purposes. This discretion is normally used to prevent any one part of a geographical area, or one particular firm or industry dominating all the elections held in a region. Members in some regions vote mainly at the branch which, in contrast to the AUEW(E) and GMWU, is often factory based. (Estimates made by regional secretaries in interview suggest that 50–80 per cent of branches are based on the workplace.) However, in regions with large concentrations of membership in a small number of employing units there is evidence that many ballots are now held, as the rule allows, in the workplace itself. Two scrutineers oversee the actual voting and mark the union card of each member as they vote. The scrutineers also count the vote and send the details to the regional office where all the branch returns are then totalled. Candidates can, if they wish, attend the count.

An examination of the TGWU's executive elections conducted in the winter of 1979–80 reveals that they attracted a large number of candidates and produced a turnout in the range of 10–40 per cent, thus equalling in some instances that achieved in the 1977 general secretary election. In region 5 (Midlands) 38 candidates stood in three constituencies for three posts, while regions 9 and 4 (Yorks and Wales, respectively) each had 30 candidates contesting two places. The turnout in region 5 was 87,293 or 23 per cent of the region's membership. Some of the contests produced close results; for example, in region 9 the top four candidates received 9,013, 8,920, 5,207 and 4,240 votes. In contrast, the successful candidate for the central constituency in region 5 polled 19,246 votes while his nearest rival recorded 3,772 votes and the other 16 candidates shared a total of 40,461 votes between them. The winner on this occasion was a senior shop steward from the Rover car plant who had completed two terms of office on the executive and was very well known in the region. However, previous experience on the executive did not guarantee success in the 1979–80 election. In Wales, for example, the two sitting members were both comprehensively defeated.

Unlike the AUEW(E), the outcome of the TGWU's executive elections were not determined by internal party political allegiances. Apart from region 1 (London), in which the Communists have a long-standing influence, there was little if any evidence of an organized faction capable of swaying the electorate's decision on the basis of political choice. Despite the removal of the ban on Communists in 1968 and the devolution of bargaining responsibilities to lay activists, which may have been thought to encourage, or at least permit, the development of independent sources of power opposed to the national leadership, the TGWU did not have factional organization on anything approaching a national scale in 1979–80. The members voting in the executive elections were thus not subject to the kind of unofficial election materials which circulates when the AUEW(E) holds executive elections, nor did they receive advice from the popular press on how to cast their votes. Further, the TGWU itself issues no election addresses and disallows canvassing. The ballot form contains only the candidate's name, trade group and the 'numbers' of the branches nominating the candidate. (These numbers tell the initiated the branches location and the nature of its membership.) If a candidate is supported by several branches then, as is the case in the NUR, he can be taken to be a front-runner.

In the absence of political information, the candidate's trade group and geographical location, as in the AUEW(E)'s less salient elections, become of increased importance. Support from the membership in the candidate's own factory or firm can be quite influential in determining the result, particularly if one of the candidates comes from a large and well-organized workplace. This is why representatives from road passenger transport have for many years held a disproportionately large number of places on the executive.[72] Garages which often contain large numbers of members can, as allowed in rule, be used as polling stations and the members persuaded to cast their votes at work for the local candidates or some other busman. It is therefore not surprising that in 1978 the overwhelming majority of executive members came from places such as garages and docks or major multinational companies with large concentrations of membership in a particular region.[73] Further, candidates starting with this advantage who have also been active in multi-trade group district committees and have attended TGWU and TUC educational and other courses and hence become 'known' outside their own workplaces, stand even better chances of being elected.

It may be argued that casting a vote in the giant and vertically divided TGWU according to the non-political factors mentioned above, such as the trade identity of the candidate, is an appropriate choice to make in a union as diverse in its industrial recruitment as the TGWU. Members of the same trade groups and factories may have interests which they hold in common but which are also contrary to those of members in other trade groups or factories. For instance, the dispute over containerization brought the docks and road haulage membership of the TGWU into conflict. In this situation the preservation of jobs could be said to dictate that votes should be cast on a trade and occupational basis. Moreover, if the majority of activists find themselves in accord with the established leadership's political stance and politics there would be no need to organize a counter-faction. It is possible that this was the case in the TGWU during the period studied when the devolutionary policies of Jack Jones (general secretary 1968–77) defused any left-wing opposition that may have been developing around the demands for shop-steward power. Also, there are no signs of an organized right-wing backlash against this policy. It is possible that the activists and the membership see no need to organize in opposition to the established leadership. On the other hand, it may be that, given the size of the TGWU, the continuing authority of the new general secretary Moss Evans and the constitutional divisions into trade group and regions, it is beyond the abilities of the political activists to do any more than organize locally and then, if they are elected to the executive, combine on an *ad hoc* basis according to the issues.[74]

The Association of Scientific, Technical and Managerial Staffs   ASTMS is the largest of the predominantly private sector non-manual unions, with approximately 420,000 members in 1982. It was originally based on the engineering industry, but has more recently expanded into other industries largely through mergers, and its engineering membership now accounts for less than 50 per cent of the total. It has also expanded vertically from its clerical and supervisory beginnings into the professional and management fields. ASTMS has a standard branch, division and head office structure, but has probably given greater autonomy to its branches than any other major union. All its 115 full-time officers, including the general secretary, are appointed by the executive, although for minor positions the responsibility may be delegated to an appointments committee. The last major appointment in 1979 was of a deputy general secretary, which was determined by a secret ballot of the executive after they had limited the candidates to those holding the three assistant general secretary posts.

National elections involving the total membership in ASTMS are reserved for the lay posts of president and vice-president and the other 22 positions on the executive, which are contested every two years. The general secretary is also a non-voting member of the executive. Unlike most unions, the executive of ASTMS is in rule given the right not only to interpret but also to formulate policy in cooperation with the annual delegate conference.[75] In practice, however, this does not give the executive control over the policy-making process. It has on a number of occasions been overturned by the conference, sometimes on quite important issues.[76] There is therefore a system of checks and balances within ASTMS which in respect of policy making leaves the general secretary, executive and conference interdependent. Nevertheless, in the absence of any nationally organized factions of note (the Socialist Workers Party and other fringe groups have only a minor influence), there is no coordinated opposition between meetings of the annual conference to the executive and general secretary.[77] The executive, which tends to promote left of centre policies, while retaining a pragmatic view of what can be achieved in a highly decentralized union which recruits members in traditionally conservative occupations, is therefore the primary decision-making body in the union.

Elections to the executive are conducted at the branch by either a show of hands or marking a ballot paper, although rule 18(4) allows members unable to attend the branch to claim a postal ballot. Many branches are in turn divided into groups which correspond with members' bargaining units. Attendance at the branch may therefore be quite small as activists congregate at the group and not branch meetings. However, the branch still remains the focal point for elections and it returns the vote, including any conducted by postal ballot, to the head office for totalling by strutineers previously elected by conference. Any postal ballots used have to be claimed by the individual member and the paper signed. Each candidate is entitled to produce an election address of up to 150 words and a brief history for publication in the union's *Journal*, which is sent to the home address of each member. Sixteen of the executive seats are contested at the divisional, 4 at regional and 2 at national level, as are the posts of president and vice-president.

In 1975, 11 (85 per cent) of the 13 executive seats up for election were contested with an average of three candidates per contested seat, and in 1983 of the 21 seats due for election 16 (76 per cent) were contested, again with an average of 3 candidates per seat. A number of the contested seats are closely fought. For instance, the first and second candidates for the national level seat contested in 1982 polled 1,737 and 1,706 votes respectively, with the sitting member being defeated. Turnout in this election, which was a by-election held outside the normal electoral period, was approximately 2 per cent. The turnout in executive elections normally varies between 2 per cent and the 7 per cent recorded in a division 10 election also held in 1982.

ASTMS's elections, as in other unions with both a low average turnout and large concentrations of members in a small number of workplaces, or in its case, office-based branches, can clearly be influenced by organized voting. ASTMS has not been immune from such voting, even though it tends to be a union largely devoid of political factions on a national scale. What appears to happen is that some large closed branches (that is, those reserved for membership in one particular office or firm) hold meetings and ballots in their office canteens over an extended period of time, thus allowing more members access to the ballot box. Further, in a few cases the clause allowing postal ballots has been exploited and used to produce high turnouts by encouraging members in large firms with dispersed offices to vote via the company internal post. As the president, L. Wells, commented in 1978 with regard to the postal ballot option, '. . . no one envisaged some branches would have a branch meeting vote of three for one candidate and three for the other candidate and 344 postal votes; nobody imagined that'.[78] Efforts in 1978 to persuade the rules revision meeting to repeal the postal ballot option were unsuccessful. However, the procedure was tightened up to prevent the use of internal office post. Nevertheless, the large concentration of certain groups of members, for example insurance and chemical workers in closed branches, which account for one-third of all ASTMS branches, does enable such groups to win a disproportionate number of seats on the executive.

The absence of nationally organized factions and a relatively low average turnout, despite wide publicity given to the elections in the *Journal* and the opportunity to claim postal ballots, suggest that ASTMS's membership is either less interested or more satisfied than its counterparts in other unions. It may well be that in this left of centre but pragmatic union the dissatisfied members of the left, when they feel moved to protest against the leadership, find it difficult to mobilize support against the established leadership because of the 'standing' many of them have acquired having held office in the union since it was first founded. Further, the highly devolved system of decision making developed in ASTMS, with branches and sometimes groups within branches adopting their own rules and procedures, may cause a large proportion of the membership to involve themselves at the local level in the 'groups' which determine bread-and-butter issues while leaving the 'politicos' the responsibility for deciding the broader national questions.

The General and Municipal Workers Union   The GMWU is the first of the three block branch voting unions to be considered. It is the third largest member of the TUC, with 967,153 members in 1980 and, in common with the TGWU, it recruits across a wide range of occupations and industries. In contrast to the TGWU, however, the GMWU is not internally divided into a series of vertical trade groups. Power within the GMWU is dispersed over its national executive council and its ten regions. Each of the regions enjoys a high degree of autonomy in the way it manages its own affairs. Moreover, the ten regional secretaries all sit by right on the national executive council accompanied by two lay members from each region. The national government of the GMWU is therefore dependent to a great extent on the relationship between the general secretary, the ten regional secretaries and the lay members of the executive, which has quite wide powers to 'perform all such acts . . . as may be necessary . . . whether such powers, duties and obligations are specifically mentioned in these rules or not'.[79]

The GMWU, like the TGWU, elects its general secretary for life or until retirement. Members attend branch meetings and vote mainly by a show of hands, although some branches may hold a ballot. The branch then casts its total vote for the favoured candidate. Apart from the general secretary and confirmatory elections for regional organizers, following a two-year period in office as an appointed officer, all other full-time officials are appointed. The GMWU is one of the few manual unions which appoints from outside the union's membership.

This process of appointment and confirmatory elections was not always used for choosing officials in what is traditionally one of Britain's most moderate unions. In 1926 the union moved away from choosing officials by elections when it repealed rules requiring periodic re-election of certain full-time officials. This change was initiated by the leadership in reaction to the activities of the Minority Movement, a Communist front organization, which ran candidates against the established leadership in major elections.[80]

Further rule changes in 1936 established the present system of choosing officials in the GMWU.[81]

Thus the only full-time officer elections frequently experienced in the GMWU are the block branch votes used to confirm the appointment of regional organizers. Not surprisingly, these confirmatory elections tend to be rubber-stamping operations. The existing official, having had two years to get himself 'known' in the region, is not normally opposed by leading lay officials, not least because such candidates would find themselves out of favour with the regional committee and senior full-time officers for 'rocking the boat' by seeming to question whether or not the officer had satisfactorily completed the probationary period. The Liverpool region provides the exception to this formal confirmatory process. In both 1978 and 1979 the sitting official seeking confirmation in Liverpool was opposed by leading lay members. However, even in these two cases the well-known lay activists failed to threaten the security of the sitting officials who won by approximately 35,000 to 11,700 in 1978 and by 35,000 to 9,000 votes in 1979.

The national executive of the GMWU is composed of 'three representatives from each region, two of whom shall be lay members and one of whom shall be the regional secretary'.[82] The two lay members are elected from the regional council every two years. Voting for the executive is conducted at the regional council by show of hands or secret ballot. The councils vary in size, and according to rule range between 16 and 120 delegates elected from branches on the basis of one councillor per 1,000 members. Although the rules allow a choice of branch voting methods for election to the council, all regions in practice again use the branch block vote.

Competition for places on the regional council, which chooses the lay member of the executive, varies widely. In at least two regions, London and Southern, it is not unusual to have fewer candidates than there are places. For instance, London with 102 seats on its regional council only received 90 nominations in 1979. However, in Scotland and Liverpool elections are fiercely contested. In Scotland in 1979, the 368 branches submitted 330 nominations for 110 places. Each member has 110 votes and the branch secretary records a block vote for each of the favoured candidates. Also, in Liverpool the 1979 elections saw 149 candidates contesting 89 places and approximately 250 of the 350 branches voted. This is a higher level of branch participation than normally occurs in the confirmatory elections for regional organizer. Liverpool region also appears to be the most political in the GMWU. It tends, with London, to support or promote resolutions urging the election and re-election of full-time officers. In a union largely without factions political activity of this kind may help to explain why it is that the Liverpool region of the GMWU experiences a higher number of contested elections.

Elections in the GMWU are therefore unlike those experienced in any other manual union studied. This union combines a highly regionalized system of government with indirect election of lay representatives to the executive and confirmatory elections of regional organizers following successful completion of a two-year probationary period. Given that confirmatory elections very rarely, if ever, lead to the defeat of the sitting official, the only open contests involving the mass membership are those to the regional council. These elections attract some competition, but a significant number of branches do not participate in the election. Turnout in the elections that do occur to regional council is, of course, difficult to calculate under block branch voting. However, it is reasonable to suggest, recognizing that a majority of the GMWU's branches are geographically based, that it is unlikely to be higher than that experienced in the AUEW(E) before the introduction of postal ballots, probably 5–10 per cent. Also, the GMWU's elections are, apart from one or two regions, free of organized political activity associated in other unions with right- and left-wing groups. It is rather that activists are elected because they have proved themselves in particular roles or that it is 'their turn' to be elected to council or the executive. In this process the local full-time officer's influence over which candidates should or should not be supported is extensive. Those who 'rock the boat' are liable to be dropped next time round or opposed by someone more in tune with the values prized in the traditionally moderate GMWU.

The National Union of Railwaymen The NUR is the largest of the railway unions, with 180,000 members in 1981. This represents a major reduction in membership since 1960, when it had 333,844 members. It recruits across a wide range of occupations within railways, and also has some members in other transport industries. Within railways the union competes with ASLEF, which recruits the majority of drivers, and the TSSA, which organizes the majority of white collar workers. Since 1970 the NUR has elected its general secretary, three assistant general secretaries and all its full-time officers, the 26 strong lay executive and its 77 man annual general meeting (conference) by a system of transferable branch block voting (in some 580 branches).[83] All potential candidates for senior office, apart from those seeking the general secretaryship, are required to pass an examination.

Before 1970 the union employed individual branch voting. This method was considered to have fallen into disrepute with collectors circulating ballot papers and persuading members to support the branch's nomination, before sending the completed forms for counting to the Electoral Reform Society. The introduction of branch block votes therefore served to regularize what had tended to happen in practice by allowing the branches to cast all their votes formally for their preferred candidate.

Within the government of the NUR the annual general meeting (AGM) is in theory 'the supreme governing body'.[84] In practice, the relationship between this body and the general secretary is crucial to the running of the union. Although in rule 'the general secretary has to obey the orders and be under the control of the executive committee',[85] in practice the general secretary and the president can normally, with the AGM's acquiescence, direct the union's business and interpret policy without support of the executive. Sid Weighell was the first general secretary elected under the block vote. He won the election easily on the first ballot, recording 85,553 votes to F. Cannon's 34,855, R. Tuck's 29,476 and C. Turnock's 10,190 votes.[86] This victory probably owed much to Weighell's standing within the union and his position since 1969 as senior assistant general secretary. Weighell was a radical and innovative general secretary. This kind of role was facilitated by the continuity of office enjoyed by all full-time officers compared with the regular turnover of members on the AGM and executive who, after holding office for three years, could not then serve again for a further three years. Hence, at least one-third of the AGM and executive were newcomers to office, and open, particularly in the absence of factional organization, to the persuasive powers of the senior elected officials.

Weighell's leadership in the NUR did not depend for its effectiveness on organized factional support. The constitution gave the tenured general secretary, if he had the president's backing, the opportunity to appeal to the AGM over the head of the executive. The AGM was also indirectly influenced by the annual branch secretaries conference, which in turn was addressed by the general secretary, and often persuaded to support his actions and proposals. It was therefore crucial for Weighell's success that he maintained the confidence of the majority of branch secretaries and hence the support of the AGM which was not normally subject to intense competition for places. Indeed the four or five branches usually grouped for the purposes of electing from 77 electoral constituencies the 77-man AGM, often took it in turns to nominate the candidate, who was then elected unopposed. For example, in 1965 36 per cent of AGM places were uncontested.[87]

Weighell, however, resigned in 1982 following a highly publicized miscasting of the union's vote at that year's Labour party conference, when he failed to vote as mandated for Eric Clarke, a left-wing NUM candidate for the party's executive.[88] This resulted in Clarke being defeated. The NUR's left-wing executive took extreme exception to this action and pressed for Weighell's suspension or dismissal. Weighell then pre-empted their threatened action by resigning while appealing to the wider membership and the AGM for support. However, Weighell misjudged the mood of the membership and the effect this would have on his traditional supporters on the AGM. This body at a special meeting in October 1982 rejected a motion for Weighell to remain general secretary by 41 votes to 36.

In the following election Weighell threw his full weight behind Charlie Turnock while the emergent left-wing faction, after considering a number of possible contenders, finally backed Jimmy Knapp, who had already declared his intention of contesting the election. Turnock as the most experienced of the three assistant secretaries should in normal times have been the favoured candidate. He was a well-established senior official while Knapp was a headquarter's officer who had recently failed to pass the qualifying test set for candidates wanting to progress to more senior posts. However, Knapp was the candidate for change, and had a wide range of contacts and support among the NUR's activists. He also represented a less authoritarian approach to the job of general secretary. In the period before the election, Knapp secured 177 branch nominations to Turnock's 96. Two other candidates, Dodd and Entwistle attracted 43 and 37 nominations, respectively. The NUR's branch nominations are a good guide to voting patterns, particularly as the branch subsequently casts a block vote. The election result declared in March 1983, which gave Knapp 90,078 votes and Turnock 35,353, Dodds 11,131 and Entwistle 6,203 therefore ran to form.[89]

It is, of course, not possible under the block vote system to calculate from these figures how many of the union's 160,000 or so members actually participated in the ballot. But there can be no doubt that it was far less than the 90 per cent turnout formally recorded. The union uses the check-off system for collecting subscriptions; many of its members work shifts and they are often dispersed over a wide geographical area and hence unable to attend branch meetings.[90] The actual vote was thus probably much closer to single percentage figures than the 90 per cent recorded. Nevertheless, this was also the system which gave Weighell a convincing victory in 1975 and hence Knapp's success cannot be ascribed solely, if at all, to the low actual turnout. It was rather that the circumstances in which Weighell resigned reduced the ability of the established hierarchy to influence the election. Given that it had relied on individual contacts and in particular the general secretary's ability to manage the union's constitutional machinery and not factional organization for its influence, the emergent left was provided with a completely unexpected and golden opportunity to prevent the most senior official from inheriting the general secretaryship. The left capitalized on this opening by supporting a 'clean' and popular candidate unassociated with the established leadership.

The Post Office Engineering Union   The POEU is the last of the block branch voting unions to be examined. In 1982 it had 132,000 members, the great majority skilled, and – in contrast to some of the traditional craft unions – it enjoyed a marked growth of members over the preceding period from 70,000 in 1960. Approximately half of its membership is employed in the south-east of England, with a large concentration of about one-third in London. Its internal structure is similar to that found in many unions with branch (297 branches), regional (10 regions) and national levels of organization. Each region also contains a number of areas.

All the POEU's 21 full-time officers, including the general secretary, are appointed by the lay executive, which is itself chosen by conference delegates on a system of block branch voting. The lay executive, which spends a considerable amount of time on union business, appoints officials by an exhaustive ballot on the recommendations of a sub-committee which interviews and short-lists the candidates who may come from within or outside the POEU. In practice, about 60 per cent of officers are members and 40 per cent recruited from outside, often for their specific expertise, such as research experience. The chosen officials are presented to conference and ratified by a subsequent conference normally one year after appointment. Objections to ratification may be made at conference, although this is not usual. Although the POEU has only 21 full-time officials, it also has a much larger number of branch secretaries working full-time on union business paid by British Telecommunications under the national facilities agreement. All officials are by rule subject to the policies adopted by the conference and interpreted by the 23 strong executive composed of 12 regional and 11 occupational representatives.[91] There is a tradition in the POEU, however, of strong leadership particularly from the general secretary.

The POEU is a union with a high level of factional organization. The right is represented by the Bloc, which was formed as an anti-Communist group in 1948.[92] Apart from a period in the 1960s when there was a general revulsion against factional infighting, it has had a major and continuing influence on the policies of the normally moderate POEU. The left has traditionally been much less successful than the right at conference and in securing places on the executive. However, a new broad left was formed from the various left-wing groups in 1978 and since that date the left has undergone a revival. This has polarized the union quite sharply; for example, in 1982 there were no independents remaining on the executive, which was divided 15 to 8 in the Bloc's favour. Moreover, in 1979 the broad left initiated a number of rule changes, including the introduction of election addresses and the recording of votes cast at conference. It did not, however, succeed in forcing through the election of full-time officials, which was one of its main policy objectives. Thus, in the POEU which has no election of full-time officials and indirect election of its executive by the block votes of conference delegates, the Bloc or right remained in control in 1982.[93]

Reasons for Modification of Balloting Systems Unions were influenced by a number of factors in their modification of branch balloting systems. The same factors identified as influencing the introduction of postal ballots also affected changes in branch ballots. The level of participation, political advantage and, if not malpractice, the perceived unfair use by certain branches of the discretion given them under rule to organize the ballot, all interacted to produce marginal but significant changes in ASTMS and the NUR.

Process of Election This varied widely under branch ballots. Actual turnout rather than declared votes is, of course, extremely difficult to assess in unions using block branch votes, but it would be surprising, given the extensive use of the check-off, dispersed memberships, mainly geographical branches and relatively low level of competition for national lay office, if the GMWU's and NUR's actual turnout exceeded the 10 per cent or so encountered in the AUEW(E) before the adoption of postal ballots. In the unions recording individual votes cast at the branch, the turnout varied both within and between unions. For example, ASTMS experienced votes of between 2 and 7 per cent in executive elections in 1982. The opportunity, when provided, to vote at the workplace helped to produce significantly higher turnouts in the TGWU than when voting was restricted to those attending meetings at geographically based branches. Indeed, it should be noted that the higher figures recorded in the TGWU were in excess of some of those recorded in the postal ballots previously examined.

Secrecy did not appear to be an issue in the unions examined. In those unions using a show of hands system, the GMWU and ASTMS, the vote is clearly open. In contrast, branch ballot papers can, presumably, be marked in secret if the voter so wishes. It is far more likely, however, that the casual voter will seek or be given advice from branch activists on the candidate most favoured by the branch or the activist himself. On the other hand, none of the branch voters marking a ballot paper appear to be required to record their names or union number on the ballot paper, and thus their vote is secret when counted and pressure to conform with branch policy therefore reduced.

Malpractice is probably easier to perpetrate under branch ballots than any other system of voting. Ill-attended branch meetings can, if the few members attending collude, result in high and biased voting through stuffing the ballot box with bogus voters' ballot papers. Alternatively, one or two bogus votes can be 'planted' and the total votes cast declared null and void after it is 'discovered' that one or two votes were rigged.[94] However, there is little if any evidence from the case studies to suggest that this is a problem, but the rules were interpreted liberally by some ASTMS branches in order to organize high turnouts, and in consequence the union amended the offending rule to meet the objections raised and to bring the practice nearer to the spirit of the rule. In the NUR's case, the method of voting was changed to branch block voting to formalize what, under the previous rule, had been a somewhat questionable practice. Unions are therefore under branch, as under postal, ballots sensitive to the possibility of malpractice and ready to act to remedy the problem.

Outcome of Elections and Political Choice   These cannot always be assessed by reference to political choice. Elections in the TGWU, GMWU and the ASTMS were not consistently contested by supporters of the left- or right-wing factions. The NUR showed some signs of factional organization but not on the scale encountered in the POEU. In the POEU all contests involving major national offices were won by a candidate supported by one of the two factions. In contrast, elections in the TGWU, GMWU and ASTMS were generally determined by criteria other than the political allegiance of the candidates. In these three unions industrial, occupational and geographical affiliations were often of more importance than the candidates' political stance, which would often not be known to the electorate. The prevailing political ethos in the TGWU, GMWU and ASTMS was therefore not systematically challenged by an opposition group, and hence the outcome of elections in these unions cannot be said, under branch ballots of the individual or block kind, to favour either left or right. In the POEU, with a high level of factional activity the Bloc successfully defended its position against the broad left throughout the 1970s. Branch ballots do not therefore necessarily facilitate victories of either left or right, and in three cases they were not normally associated with a political choice of any kind.

Workplace Ballots

The Civil and Public Services Association The two unions to be considered under this heading are the CPSA and the NUM. The CPSA's balloting method is not easily classified. It is called a branch ballot in the rules but the members normally vote at their place of work. This is because the branch is required to call meetings in the workplace for the purpose of conducting ballots for the election of the executive and the senior full-time officials. The members are entitled to time off during working hours to vote in these elections under the union's facilities agreements with the employer. However, if the members are employed in small employing units they may have to travel to a larger office to vote or if dispersed over a wide area in very small units they may be entitled to a postal ballot. Thus, the balloting method is a hybrid but the main location of the vote is the workplace.

The CPSA is the largest civil service union. It had 216,415 members in 1982, compared with a peak of 231,000 in 1976. It recruits primarily clerical, typing and office machine grades in the Civil Service, and is divided internally into 18 departmental sections and public sector groups. Its membership is dispersed over more than 1,000 branches, although there are a small number of very large branches; for example, the Newcastle DHSS office branch has approximately 7,000 members. The CPSA therefore has both a large number of small branches with widely spread membership and a small number of very large branches with a concentrated membership. The membership is largely female, and young: in 1978 65 per cent of members were women, and in 1977 60 per cent of the 30,000 DHSS security grade 2 officers, a major recruitment field, were under 30.[95] This membership is, not surprisingly, subject to a very high level of turnover as people enter and leave the Civil Service, and the ambitious and able members are promoted up and out of grades recruited by the CPSA to the grades recruited by the Society of Civil and Public Servants (SCPS).

The CPSA is highly volatile politically:

Since the Second World War, internal struggle has been almost continuous, with great emphasis on political differences between the moderates and the left. It has led to several law suits and one inquiry by a Commons Committee on Privileges . . . In the 1970s, rival factions each started their own publications, printing their own list of candidates for elections to the National Executive Committee and other offices, chosen at factional meetings or conferences. Control of the executive changed four times in four years.[96]

This internal division was given a degree of formal recognition in 1976 when rule 9(4) which barred such factions was repealed (largely because it had been ignored). The CPSA is therefore unusual, having a predominantly young and female membership, high turnover of members and yet also a long history of left–right struggles for power which, as will be shown later, affected the decision to move to the election of full-time officers in 1981.

The CPSA's lay executive is composed of 26 members plus the two vice-presidents and the president. Before rule changes made in 1981, the executive appointed all the full-time officials, the more senior appointments being subject to confirmation by the annual delegate conference. This confirmation was not a formality. For example, John Raywood, backed by the moderates, successfully appealed against the left-wing executive's decision to appoint Peter Thomason to the post of assistant general secretary in 1977.[97] In this period the executive was elected by block branch vote recorded at conference by delegates previously mandated by majority voting at special branch meetings.

In 1979 the executive, then dominated by the right or Moderate Group, promoted a motion to change the method of choosing the executive from block branch voting to individual member voting as described above. This motion followed a major row at the 1978 conference when it was discovered that some branches in the vice-president election had voted, contrary to rule, for candidates other than the ones they had actually nominated.[98] As the broad left had been the main beneficiaries of this dubious practice, the subsequent decision to declare all elections null and void and order new elections gave the Moderate Group the opportunity to exploit the publicity given to the broad left's practices. The Moderate Group won the next round of executive elections by a convincing majority. Fortunately for the Moderate Group the broad left, which if united would have dominated the 1979 conference, was in some disarray over the preferred method of election. The Socialist Workers Party faction, unlike the Militant Tendency, favoured election by individual membership ballots held at the workplace during branch meetings, but it would not support the executive's proposal. The executive therefore dispensed with its own abortive proposals and instead supported the Socialist Worker-dominated British Library branch's motion in favour of individual voting. A combination of the Moderate Group and the Socialist Workers Party thus initiated a motion which attracted other unaligned but predominantly left-wing support, and opened elections to the wider membership.

The left then pressed in 1980 and 1981 for the extension of periodic elections to the appointed full-time officers and in 1982 to all full-time officers. This was not universally popular and was criticized in 1980 as designed to allow the '. . . politically blind of the extreme Left activists to infiltrate the top positions of the union'.[99] Nevertheless, the principle of elections was accepted in 1980 by 105,203 votes for and 104,936 against. In 1981 an attempt to limit elections to a single test of popularity was comprehensively defeated at conference by 143,144 votes to 57,873, and a subsequent motion calling for periodic elections passed by the wide margin of 147,936 to 49,149. These votes were cast under the block vote system. The motion for periodic elections was sponsored, moved and seconded by leading figures on the left. It was passed despite the vigorous opposition of the general secretary who protested to no avail that 'you will be throwing the CPSA into turmoil every 5 years when the officers will be running around trying to get elected instead of running the affairs of the union'.[100]

It is extremely difficult to judge the effect of the change from block branch voting to individual membership voting at the workplace on the political composition of the CPSA. In 1980 and 1981 the Moderate Group won majorities of 27 to 2 and 18 to 11 respectively over the broad left on the executive. However, true to form, the broad left had a majority of 25 to 4 on the same body in 1982. The Moderate Group also won the first of the full-time officer elections held under the new system in 1981, when their candidates took the general secretaryship by 44,447 votes to 28,009 and the general treasuryship by 32,374 to 29,233. In both full-time officer elections the turnout was almost 40 per cent. These elections were given extensive press coverage in the week of the election. For example, the *News of the World*, under the headline 'Bully boys hit union vote', attacked the broad left's activities in the CPSA, and the *Newcastle Journal* carried a similar story under a headline proclaiming 'Row over voting for top union job'.[101] There can be little doubt that these stories were promoted by the Moderate Group to draw the membership's attention to the broad left's campaign and candidates and hence solicit a higher vote for the Moderate Group's candidates. Or as the leading left-wing candidate John McCready, a supporter of the Militant Tendency, stated in the *Socialist Worker*: 'It is an attempt to help the media interfere with the election process. They think they can persuade voters not to back us.'[102] The result suggests the Moderate Group was successful.

The broad left regained control of the executive in the less well-publicized 1982 elections when the turnout dropped to around 30 per cent. Following this election, two defeated Moderate Group candidates started a High Court action to have the result set aside because they claimed a significant number of branches and hence members had not been given an opportunity to vote in the election. The general secretary was later reported as stating that 149 of the 1,000 or so branches had not participated.[103]

Concern over the level of the 1982 turnout and also the court action provoked proposals to change the CPSA's regulations governing elections so as to give those members finding it difficult to attend branch meetings held in distant workplaces an opportunity to receive ballot papers through the post. These papers would be posted by and returned to the branch. Hence, the CPSA, in common with other unions, showed its sensitivity to criticism and suggestions of possible malpractice by adjusting its balloting system.

This adjustment may not be sufficient for the Moderate Group. It considers that the left deliberately encouraged a low overall turnout in the 1982 elections, while organizing a high vote in the larger branches which the left appears to control. Further, the Moderate Group in its unofficial paper *Daylight* issued in December 1982 carried a statement by the two members who pursued the court action entreating '. . . the national government to legislate for the use of secret postal ballots for trade union elections . . .'. As the union polled almost 40 per cent in its full-time officer elections under the present system of voting it is unlikely that postal ballots would add much, if anything, to participation rates, although it would, of course, move the location of the vote from the workplace to the home. Such a move could assist the moderate Group in the CPSA, as it did in the AUEW(E), if by limiting the impact of a small number of high polling branches such as Newcastle, it disproportionately and adversely affected the broad left. However, this is by no means a certainty, as the Moderate Group probably suffered as much from the after effects of the somewhat less than successful strikes pursued by the CPSA in 1981 as it did from the change in turnout. In a union as volatile as the CPSA, with a tradition of rejecting the sitting majority of whatever colour under whatever balloting system, it is unlikely that any one balloting system will on its own create stable government.

The CPSA study therefore shows that both left and right factions can come to similar conclusions regarding the kind of changes needed to increase membership participation in elections. However, it was the left in the CPSA which pressed for election and re-election of previously appointed officials. This is a common theme of the left opposition in unions which are both under moderate control and appoint their officials. But the change did not in the first round of full-time officer elections augur well for the broad left. Indeed, those on the right who eventually expressed a preference for workplace ballots, as against elections at the increasingly left-dominated conference, were vindicated by the results of the 1981 elections. But given the political volatility of the CPSA this may be only a passing phase. Finally, the CPSA shows as did the POEU study, that it is possible to have well-organized factions of left and right in relatively centralized unions which appoint all their full-time officers.

The National Union of Mineworkers   The NUM had 253,142 members in 1981. In common with other industrial unions studied (the NUR and NUS), the NUM has suffered a marked decline in members since 1960, when it had 638,988 members. The government of the NUM is based on a federation of 14 areas, each with a high degree of autonomy. There are therefore some minor variations in the way in which the areas organize their elections. However, full-time officers of the NUM are generally elected by pithead ballot (the pithead being the miners' equivalent of the workplace). Full-time officials do not face periodic re-election and attempts to introduce such changes, initiated by the left-wing Kent area in 1979 and 1981, were defeated at annual conference.[104] Members cast a single transferable vote by marking a ballot paper and these are collected by the union and transported to the Electoral Reform Society in London for counting.

The two major posts in the NUM are those of general secretary and president. Although the two posts are of almost equal constitutional importance, in practice the relative influence of the posts differs according to the abilities and energies of the respective incumbents. Both president and general secretary are members of the executive, the first with a casting vote only and the second with no vote at all. In contrast the vice-president, elected biennially at the annual conference, is a full voting member. Apart from these three officers, the executive, in 1979, was composed of 18 representatives from the 14 areas and 1 from each of the 6 associated groups, including COSA (the white collar section). The great majority of the executives' membership is composed of full-time officials elected to represent their own areas or groups. Although they hold their area posts until retirement age, they are required to seek re-election to the executive at two-yearly intervals. There are several different methods used for electing the executive, including indirect election by the area council in Yorkshire and branch votes in Nottinghamshire. The executive, given the autonomy enjoyed by the areas, is not easily dominated by either the president or general secretary. However, because the union is politically divided into left and right groupings, the president and general secretary can normally rely on support from whichever faction claims their allegiance. Until 1981 the tendency has been for the president to be on the right and the general secretary on the left.

It is possible to gain an appreciation of electoral practices in the NUM by examining the presidential election of 1981. In this election Arthur Scargill, the broad left's candidate, contested a position previously held by Joe Gormley for the right. Of the 248,980 ballot papers distributed, 200,247 were returned, giving a poll of 80 per cent. In the count 197,299 valid votes were accepted and Scargill received 138,803 or 70 per cent of these votes. The other candidates received votes as follows: Trevor Bell, 34,075, Ray Chadburn 17,979 and Bernard Donaghy 6,442. The NUM case therefore gives an insight into how a declared, if not notorious, left-wing candidate can win an election which both attracts the media's closest and mainly hostile attention, and a very high turnout. It provides the opportunity to consider which variables mediated between the turnout and political outcome to produce a comprehensive win for the left. As the following comments will show, the environment, factional organizaton and the candidate's relative standing all contributed to the outcome.

In order to assess the impact of the environment on the 1981 election, it should be recognized that the broad left had been gaining ground in the NUM before 1981. External circumstances had over a period helped the broad left establish itself in a number of key areas, including Yorkshire which, with its 65,000 members, has nearly twice the voting potential of the next largest area, Nottinghamshire, with 34,000 members.[105] A sign of this growing influence was that the broad left more than doubled its representation on the executive from an 'uncertain bloc of five' in 1967 to 10 or 11 in 1982.[106] It is generally agreed that the broad left benefited from the 1972 strike in which Scargill played a leading role. Further, the broad left's successful campaign against the national incentive schemes put to the members in ballots in 1974 and 1977 again raised their profile in the union. Scargill's appearance on behalf of the NUM at the Lofthouse and Houghton main disaster inquiries suggested that he had the ability to defend miners' interests, and in January and February of 1981 Scargill again 'hit the headlines' with an attack on pit closures.[107] As Gormley later acknowledged, the Coal Board's reluctant statement that between 20 and 50 pits were to be closed over the next five years 'gave the "militants" the perfect platform they needed . . .'.[108] The executive, under pressure from the broad left, then moved towards a national strike ballot; several areas took unofficial action before the Government agreed to ease the situation by relaxing its financial constraints on the Coal Board. Thus, Scargill's and the left's militancy was justified by the Government's own action.

Both the left and right had histories of political organization earlier than the 1970s. Caucus meetings of both interests sometimes took place before meetings of the executive. However, there were no factions meeting regularly on a national scale and coordinating local activists in the 1960s. The union's federal structure and the locally determined payment system militated against such national organizations. According to Allen, the first abortive attempt to establish a national broad left faction occurred in 1964 at the instigation of activists in Derbyshire and South Wales.[109] Changes in the environment, particularly the rise of national negotiations following the National Power Loading Agreement of 1966, provided a major incentive for the factions to organize themselves more effectively at the national level. The executive now became the forum for making decisions on matters of real import, i.e. earnings. By the general secretary election of 1968 and the presidential election of 1971, both factions had sufficient coordination to select and nominate only one candidate to each election.

The broad left unanimously endorsed Scargill at a gathering in Birmingham in March 1979 and subsequently organized meetings at which Scargill addressed the members.[110] Hence, by the time Joe Gormley announced his decision at the conference held in July 1981 to retire in March 1982, Scargill had been a declared candidate for over two years and he launched his manifesto 'Miners in the Eighties' on 1 September 1981.

One of the major aims of the broad left's campaign was to secure area nominations. As noted by Edelstein and Warner, successful candidates in NUM elections tend to have a number of such nominations.[111] Scargill, confident that the broad left could deliver nominations in South Wales, Derbyshire, Kent and, of course, Yorkshire, concentrated much of his campaigning in other areas, including the right's normally reliable Nottinghamshire coalfield. He addressed meetings in Durham in late September, the Midlands area on 24 October, Northumberland on 25 October and Nottingham 28–30 October;[112] all just before the close of nominations on 2 November 1981. He succeeded in securing 12 of the 16 nominations actually made, including Yorkshire, Scotland, South Wales, Kent, Derbyshire, Nottinghamshire, Northumberland, Durham, Leicestershire, North Wales, Midlands and the Scottish Craftsmen. The election was held over 2, 3 and 4 of December, and between the 18 October and the ballot he attended 37 election meetings plus television and radio appearances, culminating in a rally in Sheffield on 28 November, with Tony Benn as the main guest speaker. It is therefore little wonder that Sid Vincent (general secretary of the Lancashire area and a leading member of the right) should comment 'He's always on the ruddy telly . . . people don't know any other bugger.'[113]

In contrast to the broad left's success in promoting its one candidate and getting him 'known', the right suffered from a multiplicity of 'unknown' candidates. Contrary to popular belief, the single transferable vote does not in practice, at least in the NUM, prevent polarization or help a faction which offers the electorate more than one candidate. The left had been made painfully aware of this fact by the election of Sid Ford (COSA and right-wing) to the presidency in 1960. In this election the left fielded 4 candidates out of 7, and although a left-winger (Moffat) received more first preferences and the 4 left-wingers between them carried over 50 per cent of first preferences, Ford who ran third on the initial count eventually won on transfer.[114]

The right had no natural successor to Gormley. The right's initial candidate appears to have been selected by a series of caucus-type meetings called by Gormley in 1979 and 1980.[115] From these meetings Trevor Bell of COSA emerged as the right's choice. But Ray Chadburn the leading moderate in Nottingham, the area with the second largest vote and hence with some claim to the nomination, did not attend some of these meetings, possibly because he was out of favour with the caucus at that time. Chadburn was reported in the press on several occasions to be seeking or not seeking the right's nomination.[116] Moreover, the right's reliance on caucus-type meetings, rather than carrying the question of candidate selection, or at least endorsement, to relatively open meetings of the political faithful, placed it at a disadvantage when faced by the broad left's electoral machine which deliberately chose to involve and mobilize its rank-and-file supporters through well-publicized meetings. It may well have been that the right's reliance on individuals and not factional organization had reduced its ability to generate support for its cause amongst the wider membership.

Given the above conditions, it is therefore not surprising that in the run up to the election Bell's campaign did not appear to be gaining momentum. In the end, he only received the nominations of his own section, COSA, and of the Midlands Craftsmen. Faced by the possibility that Scargill would be successful in gaining the traditionally moderate areas' nominations, Chadburn was reluctantly persuaded to reconsider his position and offer himself for election. In the event his entry into the contest in mid-October 1981 was too late to prevent his own area, Nottinghamshire, nominating Scargill on 26 October by 15 branches to 9, with 8 abstaining. Ultimately he was only nominated by one pit area, Cumberland. The right's problems were further exposed when Bernard Donaghy of the Lancashire area entered the contest, also on an anti-Scargill ticket. Donaghy had no national reputation and had never sat on the executive, but he did, as intended, prevent Scargill gaining the Lancashire nomination.

Of the four candidates, Scargill was therefore the only one to have widespread area support, as shown by his nominations, and to be backed unanimously by a well-organized faction. Moreover, the nature of this factional support and its strong left-wing bias was not hidden from the electorate. Both the unofficial election material published by both sides and the national media made it abundantly clear that Scargill was committed to left-wing policies. Indeed, in his own election address he proclaimed that he was 'proud to be a militant'. Thus it cannot be argued that he won the presidency because the electorate were unaware of, or misled about, the nature of his policies. Nevertheless, it is possible that the electorate believed that the costs associated with a more militant stance could, if they so wished, be limited by the rule which required a ballot before they took national strike action. On the other hand, individual miners voting for Scargill could not know in advance of future ballots that their colleagues, if and when asked to support strike action, would vote collectively against pursuing a more militant industrial policy. The interaction between strike and election ballots may therefore have influenced the outcome of the election. However, superior organization and a favourable economic environment were the main factors which gave the left a comprehensive victory in an election which attracted the highest turnout recorded in any of the unions studied.

Process of Election　It can be concluded, therefore, that workplace ballots had a pronounced effect on both the NUM's and the CPSA's electoral processes. The move to workplace ballots in the CPSA, as a replacement for block branch voting, at conference, attracted both right- and left-wing support. As a result, the participation of members in elections to the executive rose to approximately 40 per cent. This is higher than that achieved in many of the unions using postal ballots. Nevertheless, it is only half that recorded in the NUM's presidential election of 1981, and given that CPSA members are entitled to paid time-off to participate in elections it is not as high as could have been expected. Secrecy in the casting of the vote in the NUM is probably less than in branch and postal ballots, although it does vary across the areas.[117] However, this does not prevent miners voting against the advice of their leaders as will be seen in the later discussion of reference back and strike ballots (see p. 135). Secrecy in the counting of the NUM's vote is secured by the involvement of the Electoral Reform Society. Finally, political outcomes in both the CPSA and the NUM show clearly that the broad left can win major elections which attract high turnouts. In the NUM's case the outcome of the 1981 presidential election was never seriously in doubt. The environment in which it was held, the relative cohesion and organizational ability of the two factions and the standing of their respective candidates gave Scargill victory on a platform of militancy and despite the vigorous criticism of the national press. In the CPSA the position was far more fluid. The union has a history of political volatility and the move to workplace ballots does not appear to have changed the balance of power significantly between the two well-organized factions.

CONCLUSION

Methods Used to Choose Officials and Committees

As the survey showed, there are many different methods and combinations of methods used to choose officials and committees. These vary between unions and across levels of offices within individual unions. Despite these variations, there is a broad distinction between manual and non-manual unions in their methods of choosing general secretaries: manual unions are more likely to elect and non-manual unions to appoint; 76 per cent of manual unions and 8 per cent of non-manual unions elect their general secretaries by a vote of the membership. Only 8 unions opt for a postal ballot. Moreover, amongst manual unions, craft or originally craft unions are more likely than their blue-collared colleagues to elect their ordinary full-time officials. All 21 unions electing their officials by a vote of the membership are manual unions.[118] Five of these unions use a postal ballot. Apart from the smallest unions electing their leaders by a vote of the total membership at an annual general meeting, the size of the union does not appear to influence the electoral method used. This contrast between manual and non-manual unions is long-standing, research in the 1950s revealing a similar pattern.[119]

The choice of union executive committees, in contrast to the general secretary and full-time officers, is more generally determined by a vote of the membership in both manual and non-manual unions. Sixty-five of the unions surveyed use this method, accounting for 61 per cent of the TUC's membership. However, as in other elections, few unions use a system of postal balloting. Only 15 unions use postal ballots for executive elections, accounting for 17 per cent of the total membership surveyed. Nevertheless, unions are more likely to use postal ballots in election to executive committee membership than to any other office.

Postal ballots are therefore only a minority interest and it may be that the Conservatives recognized this in 1983 when they acknowledged that workplace ballots, with certain safeguards, were also acceptable means of holding elections.[120] Legislation which enforced either postal or workplace ballots would, however, still require extensive changes in union rules. The extent of the changes would, of course, be affected by the choice of posts to be elected or periodically re-elected in this manner. If, however, the Conservatives opted to enforce the periodic and direct election of executives, the changes required would be considerably less than if full-time officials were made so accountable. But some major unions, including the GMWU, NUR and NUM would still find it necessary to make changes to their present methods of choosing their executives.

Amendment of Rules Governing Elections

The case studies show that, despite the fact that unions remain generally in the electoral moulds of the 1950s, there were some marked changes in the methods of choosing leaders. For example, the CPSA moved from appointment to election of full-time officers and the AUEW(E), NUS and NUR made a number of significant changes in the detail of elections. The changes noted in the case studies were undertaken for a number of often interrelated reasons. Rule changes are, by their very nature, deliberate acts which occur within the formal machinery of union government, even though they may in some unions be initiated in the unofficial meetings of rival factions. The reasons for their promotion can therefore normally be answered by reference to the motives of the members or factions sponsoring the relevant motions.

In unions with parties or well-organized factions [such as the AUEW(E) and CPSA] questions of political advantage, and the related question of the extent and nature of membership participation, were at the centre of discussions regarding changes in the methods of choosing leaders. In the AUEW(E) and CPSA the alterations to rule increased participation and changed the location of the vote. In the AUEW(E) this was achieved by moving full-time officer elections from branch to postal ballots, and in the CPSA by switching executive elections previously held at conference to election by the membership in the workplace. In both cases the right supported the rule changes, although in the CPSA one of the left-wing factions promoted the resolution which was finally accepted. A move to postal ballots in FTAT, in an earlier period, was also intended to produce an advantage for the right.

However, it was not always the case that the right wished to extend participation in the choice of leader or the left to restrict it. The GMWU's decisions to reduce the frequency of elections in the 1920s and 1930s were instigated by the right in reaction to the Communist party's attempts to mount an electoral offensive against the union's established right-wing leadership. Similarly, in the NUM it was the left which unsuccessfully sought in the 1970s to introduce periodic re-election of full-time officials. In the CPSA the left, following the decision to elect the executive by workplace ballot, successfully sponsored a motion to extend this electoral method to the choice of senior full-time officials who had previously been appointed. Hence, although considerations of political advantage were influential in leading to changes in the methods of choosing leaders in unions with factional organization, the right- and left-wing factions did not always follow the same policies. Regardless of political persuasion, those under threat, or those on the outside, respectively promoted motions to restrict the threat or weaken the hold of the established leadership.

Concern to eliminate malpractice was important in stimulating the electoral changes in the ETU(EETPU) and the NUS. Malpractice was associated with political advantage in both unions. The trial which exposed the illegal activities of the Communists in the ETU(EETPU) had direct bearing on the union's subsequent adoption of postal ballots. In contrast, it was the left in the NUS which gained from the scandal which, in turn, led to the abolition of the plural voting system and improvements in the distribution of the existing postal ballot papers.

Minor amendments to rule in the CPSA, ASTMS and the NUR were concerned to reduce the incidence of practices which did not comply with the spirit of the rules. In the CPSA this involved ensuring, after adopting workplace ballots, that the more geographically dispersed union members had less difficulty in obtaining ballot papers. A court case in which right-wing members in the CPSA protested about what they claimed was an unexpectedly low turnout in a previous election contributed to these changes. In contrast, ASTMS's leadership restricted the use of procedures allowing access to postal ballots. These procedures were being exploited to generate high and selective voting in an otherwise relatively low branch turnout, and hence playing what was seen as a disproportionately important role in determining elections. A somewhat different approach to the problem of local interpretation of rule was adopted by the NUR. In this union the rule rather than the doubtful practice was changed; in effect, the unofficial practice of maximizing the actual branch turnout by canvassing outside branch meetings for support and votes was regularized by the introduction of block branch voting.

Changes to rules governing the methods of choosing leaders were therefore generally stimulated by consideration of (either one or a combination of): political advantage, the degree and nature of participation, malpractice and rule bending. However, it was not the prerogative of the right or left to promote rules which increased or reduced participation, although it was only the right who initiated the introduction of postal ballots. Neither the right nor left had a monopoly of malpractice or rule bending. In all unions where such practices were noted the unions, albeit in one or two cases after court action, attempted to eliminate the problem.

Therefore, apart from the rather limited cases of the NUS and Equity, where the highly mobile membership and lack of intermediate union structure made postal ballots the logical and probably the only effective way of involving the membership in the choice of leader, there was no one 'model method' of choosing the leader. Amendments to rule were therefore taken in the light of immediate rather than long-term considerations and were commonly reactions to some recent event.

Effect of Ballots on Electoral Process

Turnout   This was highest under workplace, or in this case, pithead ballots. In the Scargill election of 1981 turnout was 80 per cent of the NUM's membership. The second highest level of voting noted in the 1980s also involved a high degree of workplace balloting, in the CPSA elections. In its first election for full-time officers in 1981, this union recorded almost 40 per cent turnout, although it dropped to 30 per cent in the 1982 executive elections. The CPSA's combination of workplace balloting and limited postal ballot voting thus produced higher turnouts than those achieved in the majority of elections held under postal ballots or in geographically located branches.

Two other unions with a mixture of workplace and geographically based branches are the TGWU and ASTMS. Of these, the TGWU experienced a wide range of votes. In its executive elections of 1979–80 turnouts were claimed of up to 40 per cent. Region 5 recorded a vote of 23 per cent. A study of this union published in 1952 revealed that in 1947 the average turnout in TGWU executive elections was 37 per cent.[121] Given the introduction of check-off, changing social habits, etc., it is unlikely that this level is maintained in the 1980s, although workplace ballots have helped maintain a relatively high level of participation in some regions. ASTMS's turnout in executive elections also varied widely in 1982 from 2 to 7 per cent.

Unions using postal ballots tend to have levels of participation approaching that achieved in the CPSA's 1981 elections. The EETPU produced the highest turnout among the postal balloting unions in the 1980s with a 32 per cent vote in its 1982 general secretary election. In the same year an election for the identical post in the AUEW(E) attracted a lower turnout of 18.6 per cent. But in the 1982 elections the AUEW(E) also experienced a 25.1 per cent turnout in a district secretary election. Participation in the postal ballots organized by the NUS, FTAT and Equity did not approach these figures. Equity, for example, had a turnout of 13 per cent in its 1982 council elections, and the NUS recorded what was for it a high turnout of 15 per cent in its 1982 executive elections.

Unions employing postal ballots encounter particular problems with maintaining complete and accurate electoral rolls. Even a union as committed to postal ballots as the AUEW(E) confesses to leaving some 20 per cent of its membership off its electoral roll, despite considerable efforts to register all its membership. In the NUS the position is even more serious, with only 36 per cent of its members on the electoral roll in 1982 (an increase from 25 per cent in 1974). If the vote cast in these unions is taken as a percentage of the registered electorate, the turnout rises. For example, the 18.6 per cent cast in the 1982 AUEW(E)'s election becomes 23.7 per cent, and the NUS's 15 per cent in the same year rises to 41 per cent. However, these figures cannot be used to support arguments that postal ballots, when compared with branch ballots, necessarily disenfranchise significantly higher numbers of members. Evidence on branch ballots in the AUEW(E) shows that a number of branches did not participate in elections under the previous branch method of election. Thus, the actual opportunity to vote in the AUEW(E)'s elections has increased through the use of postal ballots, and in other unions at the least the opportunity to participate is probably no more restricted than it was and is under branch ballots. Further, the AUEW(E)'s turnout also rose by over 100 per cent under postal compared with branch ballots. Nevertheless, postal ballots do not normally achieve the level of participation experienced under workplace ballots as used in the NUM or in the CPSA.

The lowest level of turnout is encountered in unions with geographically dispersed branches electing representatives by individual or block branch ballots. If these unions also collect subscriptions by check-off and have membership allocated to branches some distance from both workplace and home, branch attendance is likely to be below 10 per cent. There is no evidence to suggest that it is any higher than this in the GMWU or the NUR.

Secrecy This can be discussed by reference to the casting and the counting of the vote. Clearly, the least secret method of voting on both these counts is the show of hands as practised in elections in many branches of the GMWU and ASTMS: in these circumstances the voter's preference is obviously known. Ballot voting in the branch and workplace is potentially more secret in the casting of the vote, should the person voting choose to hide his or her mark from other members by retreating with the ballot paper to some corner of the room. The voter is also assured of secrecy in the counting of the ballot papers in as much as his or her name is not recorded on the ballot paper. Postal ballots give yet greater opportunity for secrecy in the casting of the vote by encouraging the member to mark the paper in the privacy of his or her home. This assumes, however, that the member does not take his ballot paper to work for advice from his shop steward or other activist on how to vote. Secrecy in the counting of postal ballots is not so certain. Equity and FTAT require the voter to sign either ballot paper or envelope. Voters' names are checked against membership lists to ensure that only paid-up members vote in the elections. Thus, it would be theoretically possible in these unions to check individual voter's preferences. In the AUEW(E) the voter does not record his or her name on the paper.

Malpractice This can also occur in the casting and counting of votes. A show of hands election at the branch by members whose cards have been checked is probably the surest way of avoiding malpractice in the casting of the vote. If this is then translated into a block branch vote there is also little opportunity for interfering with the counting of the vote. Branch ballots in ill-attended branches can be interfered with should a small group of members collude to 'stuff the ballot-box'. Unions are well aware of this potential problem and seek to prevent it by, for example, requiring lists of members recorded as attending and voting to be either sent to the regional or head office and/or published within the branch. As the ETU (EETPU) trial showed, unscrupulous officials can also interfere with the counting of branch ballots by a variety of means, such as declaring certain branch votes invalid because of late delivery. Postal ballots prevent individual members stuffing the ballot-box. On the other hand, they provide the possibility for non-membership participation in the casting of votes. The problems of compiling an electoral roll from branch records, and the time-lag between compiling the roll and holding the election, are bound to give non-members the opportunity to vote in elections in which they have no right to participate, especially in unions with a turnover of membership, changes in members' addresses, members moving out of benefit and resigning, etc. This is, of course, why FTAT and Equity require members to sign the envelope and/or ballot paper when voting, but, as mentioned above, this in turn reduces secrecy in the counting of votes. However, the degree of secrecy may be increased by giving the job of counting to the union's accountants or bankers. The EETPU, amongst others, uses the Electoral Reform Society for the administration and counting of its ballots.

In short, no single system of voting maximizes turnout and secrecy and minimizes the opportunity for malpractice. If the concern is for the highest degree of participation, the workplace ballot should be encouraged. On the other hand, if the quest is for secrecy then postal ballots which do not require the voter's signature are probably the most effective, particularly when administered by a third party. However, this kind of postal ballot runs the risk that votes cast by non-members will be included in the count. Choice of voting method therefore affects the process of election in several different ways and arguments can be developed in support of any of the three main methods, depending on the criteria chosen for judging the success of the process. In academic discussion of union democracy the emphasis is normally on the prevention of oligarchy and the nature and degree of membership participation (see chapter 5) rather than, as stressed by the 1980 legislation and regulations, secrecy. However, the question most often raised within unions and in the Conservative government is the relationship between process and political outcome.

Effect of Balloting Method on Political Outcome of Elections

There are a number of variables mediating between the method of voting and the political outcome of elections which need to be considered. Although these often interact, for the sake of clarifying the discussion the relevant variables will be considered in the following order: competition and choice, degree of factional organization, the standing of the individual candidate and the environment in which the elections are conducted.

Competition and Choice These vary not only between, but also within, unions. As shown in the survey, many unions choose their officials and some their executives by a vote of either the executive or conference. Self-evidently members in these unions exercise no direct control over the choice. Further, they only actually exercise a choice in those unions choosing by election if more than one candidate is successful in receiving the necessary nominations and, in certain unions, in passing the examination. Thus, even in the AUEW(E), where virtually all national elections were contested under both branch and postal balloting systems, 30 per cent of the total elections for full-time office held between 1972 and 1982 went uncontested. This is probably a smaller proportion of elections uncontested than occurred under branch ballots in the preceding ten years, but the difference is not significant. Under both systems it was the district secretary posts which attracted the lowest number of candidates, particularly when the sitting officer was seeking re-election: 91 per cent of uncontested elections involved a sitting candidate.

A number of other unions studied offered less choice in elections than those available in the AUEW(E); this restricted choice affected elections of major national importance. For example, the general secretary of FTAT, a postal balloting union, was re-elected unopposed, and almost one-third of FTAT executive seats went uncontested in the 1980s. The NUS's elections to its biennial delegate conference, also subject to postal ballots, only attracted competition for 7 of the 20 places in 1982. Branch ballots similarly failed to provide the membership with a choice in many important elections. For example, in 1983 5 of the 21 executive seats due for election in ASTMS were uncontested. In the GMWU the confirmatory elections for full-time officers are often uncontested, and the process of electing the lay executive members, which starts in elections to regional councils, fails to attract more candidates than places in some regions. Finally, the NUR in electing its policy-making annual general meeting does not provide a choice in some constituencies, particularly as the branches grouped for electoral purposes may in practice 'take it in turns' and hence secure unopposed nominations for their chosen delegate. In 1965, 36 per cent of the NUR's AGM seats were uncontested.

Union elections are not therefore always subject to the same degree of competition. Elections to the highest offices in unions, both full-time and lay, normally attract more competition, both in the proportion of contested seats and in the number of candidates, than elections for less important posts. Nevertheless, not all such national posts are contested. Moreover, there is no necessary or causal relationship between the method of voting and the number of contested seats. The AUEW(E), FTAT, NUS and Equity all use postal ballots, and the ASTMS and GMWU variations on branch ballots. The members of these two sets of unions grouped by reference to balloting method did not have the same frequency of choice in elections. Executive seats were, for example, consistently contested in the AUEW(E) but not in the NUS, FTAT and ASTMS. Postal ballots cannot be claimed therefore necessarily to provide, or where initiated increase, the choice of candidates offered in elections. Thus postal ballots would have no effect on the outcome of certain elections, including some to national office, because candidates would in some unions still continue to be elected unopposed.

Given that there is a choice in elections, the impact of postal ballots on the outcome depends on the nature of that choice and the other mediating factors mentioned above. Choice in some unions is largely limited to voting for candidates of the left- or right-wing faction or party, and in others rests more on the industrial, occupational or regional identity of the candidates. The degree of factional organization varies both across different unions and between the political groupings within individual unions.[122] Factional activity of a political kind is not necessarily associated with unions which are either relatively decentralized [TGWU and AUEW(E)] or centralized (CPSA and GMWU) in their bargaining functions.[123] Neither is it always found in unions with traditions of local autonomy in the region (GMWU) or branch (ASTMS). It does, however, appear to be most marked in the more homogeneous unions, and it is notable for its absence in the more heterogeneous unions. Thus, if postal ballots depend on existing factions for their subsequent political effect they are likely, other things being equal, to have a greater impact on certain kinds of unions, that is, the more homogeneous unions, than others. The unions identified as tending to offer political choices in national elections and therefore to be more susceptible to political change include the AUEW(E), EETPU, NUS, Equity, NUR, CPSA, POEU and NUM. FTAT and the Bakers at some point also offered such a choice. In contrast the TGWU, GMWU and ASTMS, which accounted for some 30 per cent of the TUC's membership in 1983, normally had candidates distinguished more by reference to industrial, occupational and regional factors.

Even if the introduction of postal ballots in the heterogeneous TGWU, GMWU and ASTMS increased turnout, secrecy and removed any opportunity for malpractice, it would not lead to an immediate change in political outcomes, unless there was also a rapid development of factional political organization. It is possible that the introduction of postal ballots would stimulate the development of such factions by encouraging ambitious members, out of tune with the established leadership, to band together for electoral purposes. This might happen because moving the ballot away from the branch and increasing turnout weakened the influence of the established leaders over elections and hence they could be more easily challenged. On the other hand, the existing norms, structures and political cultures of the three heterogeneous unions militate against further internal divisions based on political factions. Thus, the introduction of postal ballots for the election of senior officials and executives in the TGWU, GMWU and ASTMS would not lead to different political outcomes, at least in the short run.

However, the influence of certain industrial groups on the executives of the TGWU (busmen) and ASTMS (insurance workers) which are dependent on generating relatively large turnouts in workplace-based ballots would be undermined by postal ballots which equalized the opportunity to vote between all the unions' members. It is possible, therefore, that the introduction of postal ballots in the TGWU and ASTMS could lead to an executive more representative of the balance of industrial interests within the two unions. It is not clear what, if any, this industrial change would mean for each union's political orientation.

On the other hand, the more homogeneous unions with a more political character, the AUEW(E), EETPU, FTAT, Bakers, NUS, Equity, NUR, CPSA, POEU and NUM, appear to promise more substantial and predictable political changes should they adopt postal ballots. Indeed the two largest, the AUEW(E) and EETPU, have both postal ballots and right-wing leaderships. But, in direct contrast, the Bakers, FTAT, NUS and Equity all moved to the left under postal ballots. Moreover, the NUM and the CPSA, both with higher turnouts than were achieved in the postal balloting unions, moved to the left in some elections in the 1980s. The political effect of postal ballots, even where there is a right and left choice, is therefore problematic.

Degree of Factional Organization Factions within unions do not always have equal or near equal electoral organizations. The Group in the AUEW(E), which was founded in the late 1940s, has many of the features associated with a political party. For instance, it has a history of continuous organization originating in anti-Communist activities in the late 1940s, and is composed largely of democratic socialists associated with the centre/right of the Labour party. It has a written constitution, funds, national and local meetings, an established procedure for selecting candidates and processing motions and a national secretary and chairman who do not necessarily also hold the two comparable jobs in the official government of the union. It therefore appears at the 'party' end of a continuum of factionalism (see p. 193). It is probable that the Moderate Group in the CPSA, the Bloc in the POEU and the established right-wing leadership in the EETPU have many organizational features in common with the Group in the AUEW(E). The broad left in the same unions, the AUEW(E), CPSA, EETPU and POEU, also has many similar arrangements for selecting candidates, promoting resolutions and mobilizing its supporters. These groupings are very rarely, if ever, recognized in rule, although the CPSA's decision to rescind a rule proscribing such organizations in 1976 could be said to represent a *de facto* recognition of their existence, as could the AUEW(E)'s failure to activate the rule which bars unofficial election material. Factionalism in the NUR, NUS and FTAT appears far less well developed and in Equity it takes the form of a multiplicity of groups not found in the other unions.

Thus, if postal ballots are introduced into a union with factional organization, their political effect will be partly, and in certain unions primarily, dependent on the state of the two or more factions contesting for office and the previous system of voting. For instance, if, as in the AUEW(E) and in the EETPU, the opposition group is confident of the breadth of its popular support, then a change to a balloting system which allows it to mobilize that support may change the balance of political power. In the AUEW(E) the evidence for the wider support was reflected in the Group's ability to carry, under the previous system of branch ballots, a majority of branches recording average votes in full-time officer elections and its control of the indirectly elected national committee.[124] In the ETU(EETPU) the right was only denied victory in branch ballots by the Communists' malpractice. Postal ballots in the AUEW(E) reduced the importance of the few but important high polling branches recording almost unanimous support for the left, and in the ETU(EETPU) they prevented the malpractice which had been used to keep the left illegally in control. A change in balloting system in these circumstances which moved voting away from the branch meeting and more than doubled the normal turnout thus gave the organized right important political advantages.

It cannot be assumed, however, that the right in all other unions with factional organization would similarly benefit from a change in balloting method. Not all unions experience the low turnout of the AUEW(E) pre-postal ballots. The organized right and its candidates may not always be the popular choice or, if they are, have the organizational ability to signal the nature of that choice to the membership, and hence to mobilize its supporters. Poor organization, as in the high polling NUM 1981 presidential election, may even lead the right to confuse its supporters by offering a multiplicity of candidates. The right does not have a monopoly of effective factional organization. Thus, the introduction of postal ballots is likely to reduce the effectiveness of any factions based on a small number of geographically concentrated groups of activists, as exist in some unions using branch ballots. But postal ballots would not differentiate in their effect between left and right, neither would they compensate for the lack of effective factional organization and allow the membership to identify the right- or left-wing candidates. In the absence of such organization, and assuming several candidates emerged to contest elections, postal ballots would probably turn elections into a political lottery and give more prominence to non-political factors, as they do under branch ballots in the TGWU, GMWU and ASTMS, and the less salient elections in the postal balloting AUEW(E). Therefore, postal ballots could produce, at least initially, a less predictable form of union government detached from any one political grouping, in which outsiders could more easily defeat sitting officers.

Individual Candidates   The standing of the individual candidates also influences the outcome of elections. Sitting full-time officers, as shown in the AUEW(E) study, have considerable security of tenure under a system of periodic re-election, particularly when supported by an effective electoral organization. Also, assistant general secretaries, and other heirs apparent, often stand to inherit, through elections, the vacant general secretary's position.[125] However, when they are opposed by other prominent candidates, lay or full-time, in an unfavourable climate, as in the Bakers and the NUS, or senior officers backed by the opposing faction, as happened in the last AUEW(E) general secretary election of 1982 (G. Laird, EC *versus* K. Brett, AGS), the heirs apparent may be faced with defeat.

The position with union executive committee members may be somewhat different. Ninety-eight of the 103 unions surveyed had lay executives, and 93 of these were required to face re-election after a period in office not exceeding three years. Lay executives are often subject to quite high rates of turnover. For example, in 1978, 20 of the TGWU's 35 strong executive had less than five years' membership of the EC.[126] Thus, the opportunity for replacing executive members is relatively frequent and the average sitting member is unlikely to enter an election with the standing which goes with length of service. If postal ballots radically increased the voting electorate, they could make it even more difficult for the relatively unknown lay member to retain his seat on the executive. This could seriously weaken the contribution of the executive to union government. The general secretary and other full-time officials would find themselves facing after the periodic elections a new lay executive composed of an even greater number of inexperienced members dependent for their decisions upon the information, advice and guidance offered by the senior officials.

Electoral Environment The environment can also affect the membership's perception of the popularity of certain candidates. Unofficial election material, and the national press in the more important elections, play their part in informing the membership of the candidate's political affiliations and bargaining effectiveness. But the membership's evaluations are coloured by recent developments in the union and the general environment. In common with their Socialist or politically apathetic colleagues, Conservative trade unionists appear as willing as any other member to vote for the leaders that conform to expected standards of behaviour and 'deliver the goods' at least possible cost. Thus, any faction or official who is perceived as having bent the rules or been involved in malpractice normally suffers in the next series of elections, as in the NUS, EETPU, NUR and the CPSA. Also, candidates appearing to offer more satisfactory solutions to outstanding major issues than their opponents normally appeal to voters, as Scargill did in the NUM and Slater in the NUS. A reaction against costly industrial action or costly inaction, for example, in the AUEW(E) in the early 1970s, and the NUS in the mid 1970s, respectively, also influences the outcome. Even with the high turnouts achieved in the NUM, it is possible for the electorate to be both very well informed of the candidate's left-wing credentials and still opt for the broad left's nominee as president.

Postal ballots and high turnouts do not therefore necessarily result in right or moderate candidates winning elections. A necessary but not sufficient condition for any such outcome is that the electorate be presented with a political choice. In a number of large and important unions, the TGWU, GMWU and ASTMS, the electorate is not normally offered such choice. Also, in many elections the candidate is unopposed or so well entrenched in the post as to make opposition of little consequence. Further, in less important elections, the wider electorate may be unaware of the political choice because of the lack of official information and media interest, even where factions exist and contest the election. The unions and elections which fall into these categories are not insignificant. The TGWU, GMWU and ASTMS without factional organization accounted for some 30 per cent of the TUC's membership in 1983, and 30 per cent of the highly competitive AUEW(E)'s elections went uncontested between 1972 and 1982. Thus, postal ballots would not, other things being equal, cause the political stance of three large and influential unions to be recast in any particular mould, nor would postal ballots affect the outcome of many less important posts in a cross-section of unions.

Unions with factional organization are potentially more open to political change from the introduction of postal ballots. In the rather special circumstances of the AUEW(E) and EETPU postal ballots gave the organized right the opportunity to capitalize on its widespread support and win elections denied it under branch ballots. But the right also won elections under other systems of voting, for example, in the POEU and CPSA, and the left similarly made gains under postal and branch ballots, including major elections in the Bakers, NUS, FTAT, Equity and NUM. The kind of ballot does not therefore predetermine the political outcome of elections.

3 The Role of Ballots in Collective Bargaining

Both Labour and Conservative governments have been concerned to encourage the use of ballots in collective bargaining, especially where industrial action is contemplated. The Labour government's White Paper *In Place of Strife*, published in 1969, recommended that the Secretary of State for Employment should be empowered to require unions to ballot their members before calling strikes which the Secretary of State believed threatened the national interest. The Conservative government's Industrial Relations Act 1971 followed this lead, empowering the Secretary of State to apply to the National Industrial Relations Court for an order requiring unions to ballot their members when strikes threatened the national interest (whether economic, defence or public order) and 'there are reasons for doubting whether the workers . . . taking part . . . are or would be taking part in it in accordance with their wishes, and whether they have had an adequate opportunity of indicating their wishes in this respect'.[1] The Industrial Relations Act 1971 was repealed by the Trade Union and Labour Relations Act in 1974, the Labour government not subsequently following up its earlier interest in strike ballots. Conservative governments, however, remained committed to ballots (see chapter 1).

Although politicians have favoured extending the use of ballots in collective bargaining, industrial relations scholars have been less enthusiastic. The still influential Donovan Royal Commission on Trade Unions and Employers' Associations (1968) argued that strike ballots would do little to improve industrial relations, and might cause harm; ballots would not necessarily reduce the number of strikes, but would reduce negotiating flexibility. The Commission therefore did not favour legislation to increase their use.[2] From a different perspective, Lewis and Simpson criticized legislation to increase the use of strike ballots, since it involved an undesirable external intervention in internal union affairs.[3]

Despite the extensive public discussion of strike ballots, little detailed evidence has been available on the use of ballots, and their consequences: forceful opinions have been expressed based on *a priori* judgements, both favourable and unfavourable. This chapter will therefore examine evidence of the constitutional position of ballots in union rule books, and the extent to which ballots are in practice used in the process of collective bargaining. Ballots are treated as one form of decision making and consultation with union members in the process of collective bargaining, not as a universal panacea, nor as the *sine qua non* for union democracy.

The structure of this chapter is as follows. First we outline the formal provisions in union rule books relating to the consultation of union members on collective agreements, and on strike action at both national and local level. Then we discuss the extent of the use of balloting. The third section is concerned with the *de facto* practices of four major unions – the NUM, GMWU, TGWU, and AUEW(E) – making very different uses of ballots in the reference back of agreements and in strike decisions. In the fourth section we discuss the factors which influence the propensity of unions to use ballots, drawing upon the four case study unions and upon interviews with national officials in other unions, and assess the consequences of the use of ballots for collective bargaining.

In general, union rule books regulate collective bargaining procedures less precisely than they regulate electoral procedures. This is as to be expected since collective bargaining is less subject to control by the union itself: collective bargaining responds to varied and changing circumstances, especially employers' strategies and product and labour markets. As will be seen, unions consult extensively before accepting agreements or deciding upon strike action, although the form of consultation and decision making varies widely: among manual workers voting by show of hands at meetings remains the most frequent method, whilst among non-manual workers workplace ballots are most common, although few unions confine themselves to only one method. The form of consultation depends upon bargaining tactics (especially which procedure will put most pressure upon employers or which procedure will be most effective in persuading the membership to accept an agreement which cannot be improved upon) and upon practicalities (what is the most effective way of consulting a dispersed membership) as well as upon beliefs about the need to consult the members affected. The most common form of ballot is the workplace ballot. Where postal ballots are used, they increase the formal nature of the consultation process, and, in certain circumstances, may reduce union militancy.

COLLECTIVE BARGAINING PROCEDURES IN UNION RULE BOOKS

Union officials are representatives of their members, not delegates: they are therefore expected to act on behalf of their members' interests, using their professional judgement of the best method of improving their members' terms and conditions of employment, taking into account the circumstances of negotiations. Democratic theory – and industrial relations commonsense – require representatives to carry their members with them; failure to do so is both undemocratic and likely to cause industrial relations difficulties. Carrying the membership can be done either through relying on the authority of the representative's position or by consulting directly or indirectly with the members concerned. The extent to which negotiators rely upon their own authority or upon consultation depends upon the provisions of the union rules, the custom and practice of the unions concerned, the standing (and preferences) of the negotiators involved and the circumstances surrounding the particular negotiations; the interaction between such factors is indicated in the case studies presented below.

Reference Back of Agreements

Union rule books exercise very little influence on the practice of referring collective agreements back to the membership before signature. Only 9 of the 103 TUC unions whose rule books were examined *require* the reference back of agreements to the members concerned (and, of course, no union has rules prohibiting it). In view of the small number of unions with rules requiring reference back, few generalizations are possible. The minority of unions requiring reference back are highly concentrated, three being printing unions (NGA, NATSOPA, SLADE) two being from the communications industry (NATTKE and UCW), together with NUT, NUFLAT (one trade section only), Power Loom Carpet Weavers and Tailors and Garment Workers (NUTGW).[4] No union with fewer than 1,000 members requires reference back: in small unions negotiators are likely to be in sufficiently close and regular contact with their members for mandatory reference back to be unnecessary. Similarly, no union with over 500,000 members requires reference back by rule: mandatory reference back would clearly constrain officials unduly within a single framework, which would be especially damaging in a very large and diverse union. The degree of concentration is not surprising; unions in frequent contact with other unions already making provision for mandatory reference back are likely to contain members pressing for similar provisions, especially during periods of conflict.

The methods followed in referring back to members vary widely. In the three printing unions and NUFLAT ballots are held of the members concerned. In the Power Loom Carpet Weavers, reference back is to branch general meetings. In the NUTGW the membership is consulted via branches, where decisions are made on a show of hands. In the UCW, reference back is either to branch meetings or to ballot, and in NATTKE reference back is to the branch, without the method being specified. Finally, in the NUT the rules require reference back to a special conference if the Burnham Committee proposals differ from the demands formulated at the NUT annual conference.

Although few unions require reference back by rule, large numbers of unions, including the four case study unions, frequently refer back to the membership before concluding agreements. Such practices occur either under specific rules providing for reference back at the discretion of specific bodies or under general executive discretionary powers. Hence 42 unions specifically provide for reference back by ballot at the discretion of either the executive (27 unions), conference (13) or executive and conference (2); 52 unions do not mention the issue. There is little distinction between unions which provide explicitly for discretionary use of ballots in reference back by rule and unions which fail to mention the issue specifically: union representatives are able to consult their members whenever, and however, they choose in both sets of circumstances. Hence the TGWU and GMWU both use ballots to refer back to their members before signing agreements in certain circumstances, although there is no specific mention of reference back in the union rules. Agreements may be referred back to the members concerned under residual discretionary powers, whether or not specific reference is made to the practice. Hence union executives are characteristically given powers to act in ways not prohibited by the rules between annual or biennial conferences, as in BIFU (rule H.2): 'The National Executive Committee shall be vested with and shall exercise complete executive powers, provided that in the exercise of these powers it shall do nothing inconsistent with these Rules or the general policy of the Union as laid down from time to time by Annual Delegate Conference or a Special Delegate Conference.'[5] Similarly, POEU rules provide the executive committee with authority to act as it thinks appropriate between annual conferences, provided action is not inconsistent with the rules.

The extent to which unions refer back to their members before signing agreements, and the method adopted in referring back, is thus less a matter of rule than of tradition, policy and practice. This is as would be expected: provision for mandatory reference back would only be expected in unions with a highly developed formal system of membership participation, required by a dispersed membership or by profound distrust of officials.

Strikes

In the majority of unions the authority for calling industrial action rests with the executive committee, which may or may not consult the union membership before undertaking strike action. As table 3.1 shows, 53 unions grant authority to the national executive to call national industrial action, and 56 to call local industrial action. There is thus little difference in the allocation of authority for calling national and local strikes: the national executive is the most likely authority in both cases. There is therefore little devolution of authority to lower level institutions in deciding upon industrial action, with only 5 unions granting authority to local committees, although of course unofficial strikes occur on local initiative. The category of 'Not specified' refers to those unions whose rule books make no mention of industrial action.

TABLE 3.1   Authority to call national and local industrial action

Location of authority	National	Local
Executive	53	56
Conference	4	3
Union officers	1	1
Special delegate conference	—	—
Conference and/or executive	4	3
Local committee	—	5
Not specified	15	17
Total	77	85

Union rule books are more explicit about the procedure for consultation when calling strikes than they are for consultation over collective agreements, although even on industrial action the majority of union rule books do not specify a mandatory procedure. Hence, as table 3.2 indicates, only 25 of the 103 union rule books examined explicitly include the procedure to be followed before undertaking national industrial action, in the majority of cases requiring some form of ballot.

TABLE 3.2   Rule book provision for national industrial action: requirement for ballot[a]

Method	No.
No specific provision	78
Provisions specifying	
Postal ballot	2
Half postal ballot	1
Ballot voting (branch meeting)	3
Special delegate conference	1
Ballot (method unspecified)	7
Other ballot	3
Unspecified method	8

Note:
[a] Some unions, e.g. the NUM, distinguish between national and local disputes, with provisions for the former but not the latter. The table relates to 'national' disputes where unions treat the two types of disputes differently.

Although only 25 of the unions surveyed specify the procedures for consulting the membership, a further 40 unions have rules which specifically permit the discretionary use of ballots before undertaking strike action.

The number of unions requiring ballots before calling industrial action is thus small. However, the requirement is more important than the number of unions suggests, since larger unions were more likely to be required to ballot their members than smaller unions: only 7 out of the 33 unions with 10,000 or fewer members were required to ballot their members, compared with 7 out of 25 unions with over 100,000 members. Moreover, the massive TGWU, with almost 2 million members, is required to ballot members in national disputes involving more than one trade group, whilst NALGO, with over 500,000 members does so, although not required to do so by rule. The requirement to ballot members is found amongst unions operating in a limited range of industries: clothing and textiles (NUTGW, Felt Hatters, Power Loom Carpet Weavers and Card Setting Machine Tenters), all of the coal mining unions (NUM, NACODS, BACM), four transport unions (TGWU, NUS, URTU and Radio, Electronic and Officers Union), seven engineering and metal working unions [Boilermakers, AUEW(F), AUEW(TASS), Associated Metalworkers Union, National Union of Scalemakers, Engineers and Managers Association and National Union of Gold and Silver and Allied Trades]. In addition, a small number of unions in other sectors require ballots before national industrial action – BIFU, NATFHE, FDA, ACTT and NATTKE in the communications industry.

Only two unions have rule books providing for a full postal ballot before undertaking strike action, BIFU and the NUS. The provisions of BIFU are unusually explicit and comprehensive. According to rule H6 (a):

> The National Executive Committee only shall have power to direct members of the Union or a particular group of them to withdraw or limit their services and to fix the date of such withdrawals or limitation. The National Executive Committee shall only exercise this power after a secret ballot shall have been taken of the members concerned for the express purpose of determining whether the withdrawal or limitation of services should be ordered and then only in accordance with the wishes of a simple majority of those voting.[6]

Under rule T4 (a) the executive is empowered to determine the form of the question printed on the ballot paper and to prescribe the timetable: no requirement is specified for additional information. Rule T4 also specifies that an external organization, like the Electoral Reform Society, should be appointed as returning officer, except where the number of members to be balloted was under 1,000. The general secretary is responsible for providing the returning officer with a list of members entitled to vote and their addresses.

> The Returning Officer shall send a ballot paper to each member and shall inform the members of the closing date of the ballot. Each member may complete the ballot form and return it to the Returning Officer by the prescribed closing date. On the day following the closing date the Returning Officer shall supervise the counting of votes . . . The Returning Officer shall inform the General Secretary of the result of the ballot within five days of the closing date. The General Secretary shall report to the National Executive Committee accordingly.[7]

Although ballots are required before strike action may begin, 'members who have not been balloted may take part in any withdrawal or limitation of services in support of other members if they are authorized to do so by the general secretary. Any such members shall for all purposes be treated as though they had taken part in a ballot'.[8] BIFU rules thus cover the constituency to be balloted, the responsibility for the formulation of the question, as well as the mechanics of the ballot.

In the NUS, since 1976 the head office has dispatched ballot papers to the home addresses of shore-based members, and telexed offers to branch officers of members at sea. Shore-based members have returned their ballots through the post to head office, whilst shipboard members have taken part in ballots organized by their branch secretary. Counting was previously done by the Electoral Reform Society, but is now carried out by the union itself, the union now being confident that the corruption which had led to the need to use the Electoral Reform Society has been rooted out.

Only one union provides for a half postal ballot, i.e. a ballot in which the ballot papers are distributed at the workplace or branch, and returned through the post (SLADE); SLADE merged with the NGA to form NGA'82.

Of the 41 unions which specifically grant discretion for holding ballots on industrial action, only 5 specify that the method to be followed should be a postal ballot [BALPA, AUEW(E), EETPU, Health Visitors and Equity] and 6 specify that it should be a half postal (table 3.3). The unions providing for half postal ballots are the AUT, Bakers, National Association of Cooperative Officials, National Association of Licensed House Managers, NALGO and the Rossendale Union of Boot, Shoe and Slipper Operatives. In view of the widely divergent methods of consulting the membership, and the large numbers of unions classified as 'other' or not specifying the method to be followed, no conclusion can be drawn from the variations in system provided for.

TABLE 3.3   Method specified for holding discretionary ballots on national industrial action

Method	No.
Postal ballot	5
Half postal ballot	6
Ballot (branch meeting)	3
Show of hands (branch meeting)	3
Delegate conference	1
Other balloting method	9
Unspecified	14
Total	41

Predictably, an even smaller number of unions require the membership to be consulted before taking local industrial action than require consultation before taking national industrial action, 17 compared with 25. A further 43 make specific provision for discretionary consultation of the membership affected. Amongst the unions requiring consultation are the

GMWU, which requires voting in any dispute involving 300 or more members, the AUEW(E) which requires a ballot where a dispute involves a whole district, and BIFU which requires a postal ballot. The majority of unions who require consultation of the membership, or specifically refer to discretionary consultation, do not specify the method to be followed (table 3.4).

TABLE 3.4   Method of conducting consultation on local industrial action

Method	Mandatory	Discretionary
Postal ballot	1	5
Half postal ballot	—	7
Ballot (branch meeting)	3	3
Show of hands (branch meeting)	—	3
Ballot at workplace meeting	1	3
Other ballot	—	8
Delegate conference	—	1
General meeting	—	1
Not specified	12	15
Total	17	43

In view of the lack of specific requirements, few conclusions can be drawn. However, it is significant that fewer unions which require ballots specify postal or half postal than unions which make provision for discretionary ballots. This suggests that unions are conscious of the need for flexibility and for limiting costs: requiring postal ballots reduces flexibility and increases costs. In unions which provide for discretionary consultations, flexibility is retained and the costs, both in time and money, can be taken into account in the first place in deciding whether to hold the ballot or not, and the method of balloting to be adopted.

It had initially been thought that unions which pay strike benefits would be more likely to require ballots of the membership before undertaking industrial action, since industrial action would involve financial costs for the union. However, there is no link between the payment of benefits and the requirement by rule to ballot the membership: unions which pay benefit are no more likely than unions which do not to require ballots before undertaking industrial action, although some unions (for example ASTMS) in practice justify asking officers involved for conclusive evidence of membership support in industrial action, preferably by ballot, on the grounds of financial implications.

Analysis of the union rule books thus shows that the formal role of ballots in collective bargaining is limited. Only a small minority of unions ($n = 9$) explicitly require by rule that officials should consult with the members concerned before signing agreements with employers: none lays down a postal ballot procedure. There is more extensive provision for mandatory consultation with union members before calling official industrial action, 25 unions requiring ballots before national industrial action is called. Such ballots are especially likely in large unions, only 24.5 per cent of unions require ballots, but the membership covered comprises 35.2 per cent of members of TUC-affiliated unions in 1980. The methods provided for in the rules of the 25 unions differ widely, but only 2 unions provide for full postal ballots, with the ballot papers distributed and returned through the post, and only union provided for a half postal ballot, SLADE, a union which has now disappeared through amalgamation. In the majority of unions responsibility for calling industrial action rests with the national executive committee, which might or might not consult the membership affected: 41 unions provide explicitly for discretionary ballots on national industrial action, and 43 for discretionary ballots on local industrial action.

Reliance upon union rule books alone would, however, lead to a very serious exaggeration of the independent authority of national executives, and underestimate the importance of consultation with union members, including the use of ballots. Union officials must carry their members with them if they hope to organize effective industrial action. This can be most effectively achieved when the membership concerned has been able to express its views on the issues involved: ballots provide a mechanism for assessing such views. However, enshrining the requirement to consult the membership, by ballot or by other specified procedures, in union rules inevitably restricts the room for manoeuvre of union officials, even where they may believe that balloting the membership is in general desirable: restricting the room for manoeuvre may limit the effectiveness of the union concerned in collective bargaining. As one union official commented, 'we have secret ballots in principle but we do not want them all the time'. It is therefore not surprising that only a limited number of unions explicitly require ballots of the membership on collective agreements or on industrial action. Nor is it surprising that much more extensive consultation, and much wider use of ballots, occurs than is required under rule.

METHODS OF CONSULTATION AND DECISION MAKING

Trade union action is governed but not wholly determined by the rule book: union officials are required to act according to rule, but large areas of union activity are not specifically covered, or covered only in very general terms, by rule. In such areas officials naturally rely upon their judgement of the best method of achieving their objectives. Union rule books are especially opaque about collective bargaining procedures, including methods of consulting membership opinion, whether on pro-posed settlements or on industrial action. The extent and methods of consultation are therefore not often reflected in union rules, and surveys of union practices reveal considerably more consultation than indicated by the rule books. Although only a minority of unions require voting by the members affected before signing a collective agreement or undertaking industrial action, some form of consultation with the members involved is the norm. A comprehensive quantitative survey of the extent of reference back of collective agreements, or voting on industrial action, was beyond the scope of the present project; national and even regional officials are not fully aware of the precise extent of methods of consultation used, and quantitative analysis would require the collection of data from individual bargaining units. However, data from other sources provide some relevant evidence. Most importantly, the Department of Employment survey of workplace industrial relations indicates that consultations were held before the acceptance of agreements in 72 per cent of bargaining units covering manual workers, and 64 per cent of bargaining units covering non-manual workers.[9] Similarly, evidence from the CBI data bank indicates a wide range of consultation: 87.69 per cent of bargaining units reporting some form of consultation.[10] Unfortunately, no similar figures are available for industrial action; however, in practice decisions on industrial action are an integral part of consultations on agreements. It is unlikely that consultations over industrial action would be less extensive than those carried out before ratifying agreements.

The proportion of bargaining units reporting being consulted over the ratification of their last wage settlement ranged from 90 per cent in the AUEW(E) to 24 per cent in the NUR.[11] However, only in 4 unions was the proportion of bargaining units reporting no consultations over 50 per cent (NUR, POEU, UCATT/STAMP, and NUTGW). Moreover, the extent of non-consultation reported in the four unions concerned needs to be placed in context: the number of bargaining units surveyed was small (10 in the NUR, 4 in the POEU, 7 in UCATT/STAMP and 6 in the NUTGW), and the agreements covering the industries primarily national. The level of consultation reported was, not surprisingly, higher in industries in which local bargaining was of major importance, notably in the engineering industry.

Although there were differences reported in the extent of consultation between unions, in general these reflected differences in the industries in which the unions recruited rather than in the policies of the unions concerned. Hence the extent of consultation was linked to the size of establishment: for both manual and non-manual workers consultation was more likely in large establishments. As table 3.5 shows, no consultations were reported in 55 per cent of establishments employing under 10 manual employees, and 37 per cent of establishments employing under 10 non-manual employees: all establishments recognized trade unions. The comparable figure for establishments employing over 1,000 employees was 3 per cent for manual employees and 11 per cent (but only 1 bargaining unit) for non-manual. In view of the importance of the size of the establishment, it is hardly surprising that the bargaining units reporting no consultation were primarily in professional/scientific services, utilities and transport, miscellaneous manufacturing, distribution and miscellaneous services (for manual workers); professional/scientific services, utilities and

TABLE 3.5 Extent of consultation of members affected (by establishment size): % reporting no consultations

No. of employees	Manual (%)	Non-manual (%)
1–9	55	37
10–24	39	43
25–49	27	37
50–99	34	35
100–199	24	34
200–499	12	24
500–999	8	16
1000+	3	11
Total	27	34

TABLE 3.6 Industrial distribution of membership consultation: % of bargaining units reporting no consultations in each industry

Industrial distribution	Manual (%) (n = 188)	Non-manual (%) (n = 219)
Prof./scientific services	19.7	34.7
Utilities/transport	19.1	16.4
Misc. manufacturing	12.2	2.7
Distribution	11.7	6.8
Misc. services	11.7	7.3
Public administration	3.2	24.7
Others	22.3	7.3

transportation and public administration (for non-manual workers). The evidence is summarized in table 3.6.

Precise statistics on the extent of membership consultation are unreliable, based upon the views of work place representatives who may be discussing practices relating to agreements with which they were unfamiliar. However, the limited quantitative evidence confirms the view that consultation with members [and in a small minority of cases (8 per cent) stewards but not members] is the norm. Not surprisingly, this norm is less likely to be achieved in small establishments, or in the service sector; however, it is also less likely to be achieved by unions organizing non-manual workers in the public sector.

Characteristics of industrial structure (and probably to a lesser extent bargaining structure) appear to exercise the major influence over the likelihood of union members being consulted over proposed collective agreements. The same factors influence, but to a lesser degree, the method of consultation used: many other factors, discussed in detail below, influence the method used to consult members. As table 3.7 shows, the most common method of voting upon collective agreements by manual workers is a show of hands, whilst the most common method for non-manual workers is by non-postal ballot. For all manual unions except the EETPU, whether craft, general or industrial, show of hands is the most frequently used method of deciding upon collective agreements for manual groups. (The NUM was not included in the survey.) However, show of hands is rarely used for non-manual workers, even in the non-manual sections of predominantly manual unions: in the TGWU/ACTTS, for example, 56 per cent of manual representatives, compared with only 6 per cent of non-manual representatives, reported deciding upon the last wage agreement by show of hands. A wide variety of methods is used to consult non-manual union members, of which the most common is non-postal ballot, even in unions making little use of balloting for manual workers. Hence, 71 per cent of non-manual TGWU/ACTTS representatives reported using non-postal ballots for the last wage agreement, compared with 10 per cent of manual representatives; for GMWU/MATSA the same figures were 58 per cent and 8 per cent, respectively.

Relatively little use is made of postal ballots: 5 per cent of manual representatives and 7 per cent of non-manual representatives reported use of postal ballots. Amongst unions recruiting manual workers only the EETPU make extensive use of postal ballots, 24 per cent of their representatives reporting the use of postal ballots to discover membership views of the last pay settlement. The other unions making most use of postal ballots to assess opinion are GMWU/MATSA (16 per cent of representatives) and NUPE (21 per cent of representatives): data on BIFU, which requires ratification by ballot, were not available separately, but 7 per cent of 'other' representatives reported the use of postal ballots.

As the foregoing analysis indicates, unions consult extensively before concluding wage agreements, in the majority of cases with the stewards and members affected, although in a minority of cases (8 per cent) with the stewards only. Three major methods of consultation are used: show of hands at a general meeting, non-postal ballot and postal ballot, of which the traditional mass meeting remains the most common for manual workers and the non-postal ballot for non-manual workers. However, few unions use one method exclusively: for manual workers only the NUR uses show of hands exclusively, whilst for non-manual workers only AUEW(TASS) (non-postal ballot), EETPU/EESA ('other method'), BFAWU (non-postal ballot) and the NUTGW (non-postal ballot) use one method exclusively. The precise method followed therefore differs for different groups within the same union. The use of postal ballots is rare: only in the EETPU was it the most frequently mentioned method of consultation, and even in the EETPU it was reported in only a minority of instances (24 per cent).

It is unfortunately impossible to provide quantitative evidence on consultative practices with regard to industrial action: surveys concerned with decisions on collective agreements have not discussed the issue of strikes separately. However, this omission is less serious than it first appears, since strike action is only one of a number of alternative strategies

TABLE 3.7 Methods used to consult members on last collective agreement (%)

	TGWU/ ACTTS		AUEW/ TASS		GMWU/ MATSA		NGA		NUPE		EETPU/ EESA		UCATT/ STAMP		NUR		POEU		BAKERS		FTAT		CPSA		NUTGW		NSMM		Other unions		Total	
	m	nm	m	nm	m	nm	m	nm	m	nm	m	nm	m	nm	m	nm	m	nm	m	nm	m	nm	m	nm	m	nm	m	nm	m	nm	m	nm
Members (incl. stewards)																																	
Show of hands	56	6	67	–	53	9	54	–	46	2	21	–	9	–	24	–	31	–	18	–	34	–	10	–	18	–	65	–	31	5	46	5
Postal ballot	5	–	2	–	4	16	–	–	1	21	24	–	–	–	–	–	–	–	13	–	6	–	5	–	19	–	–	–	8	7	5	7
Non-postal ballot	10	71	5	20	8	58	–	–	13	21	17	–	–	–	–	–	–	–	18	100	3	–	23	–	6	19	–	–	13	34	10	33
Other method	3	–	3	–	2	–	–	–	5	–	–	15	2	–	–	–	–	–	13	–	–	–	3	–	–	–	–	–	3	5	3	5
Stewards only consulted																																	
Show of hands	6	–	9	–	4	–	2	–	–	–	–	7	–	23	–	–	–	–	–	–	30	16	9	14	–	–	–	–	5	–	6	1
Postal ballot	–	–	–	–	–	–	–	–	–	–	–	–	–	–	–	–	–	–	–	–	–	84	–	–	–	–	–	–	–	–	–	2
Non-postal ballot	2	4	4	2	–	–	–	–	–	–	1	5	5	–	–	–	–	–	–	–	–	–	–	9	11	–	–	–	3	1	3	4
Other method	–	–	–	–	3	–	–	–	4	–	4	3	3	–	–	–	–	–	–	–	–	–	–	–	–	–	–	–	2	3	3	3
Don't know	–	–	2	–	3	–	–	–	3	4	–	–	–	–	3	–	3	–	–	–	–	–	10	–	–	–	–	–	3	4	4	4
No consultation	18	20	10	80	23	16	34	–	31	48	27	80	67	–	76	–	60	–	37	–	27	–	40	–	54	81	19	–	35	34	27	34

M, Manual, MN, non-manual.

Source: Unpublished data made available by the Department of Employment, Policy Studies Institute and the Social Science Research Council.

considered in relation to proposed agreements: the figures relating to strike action are therefore likely to be similar to those for reference back of agreements. Moreover, as indicated above, union rules are more likely to require membership support for strike action than for the acceptance of agreements. It is therefore likely that consultation on strikes is at least as extensive as consultation on collective agreements. It is also likely that the methods used would in general be similar, namely predominantly show of hands at mass meetings for manual workers and non-postal ballots for non-manual workers. However, the greater emphasis in rule upon balloting on strike action than on reference back suggests that ballots may be more extensively used.

In view of the complex structure of British trade unions, it is not surprising that there should be only indistinct patterns in the methods used to assess union members' opinions, with unions using different methods for different groups of workers, and different methods for the same group of workers at different times. Assessment of membership opinion is only one element in collective bargaining, involving processes of formulating claims, conducting negotiations and securing acceptance of agreements. The role of ballots in collective bargaining can therefore only be understood in the context of the overall process of collective bargaining. As an indication of the role of ballots in collective bargaining, recent developments in four major unions, the NUM, TGWU, GMWU and AUEW(E), will be examined to indicate the complex inter-relations between union rules, union action, union structure and environment.

BALLOTING IN PRACTICE

The practices of referring agreements back to the membership and deciding upon strike action are intimately linked to each other; ballot papers sometimes explicitly refer to strike action and on other occasions do not, although the effect of rejecting an agreement may be to decide upon strike action. The close link between balloting on wage offers and balloting upon industrial action was explicitly recognized by the Government with the extension of the 1980 scheme to cover ballots on wage offers in 1982. Ballots on reference back and ballots on strike action are therefore discussed together.

Ballots can be organized for any unit of union membership depending upon the coverage of the agreement or of the strike action envisaged, but this study will concentrate upon national agreements and national industrial action. Such agreements are not always the most important for union members, especially in the private sector. Moreover, national industrial action is not, of course, the most frequent type of industrial action. The coverage of the study has been limited mainly for practical reasons: as indicated above, the resources required to carry out a survey at bargaining unit level were not available. However, where evidence is available [for example, for sections of the GMWU and the AUEW(E)], the factors relevant to ballots on local agreements are indicated. On local agreements, as on national agreements, union use of ballots is primarily moulded by the overall requirements of bargaining effectiveness and responsiveness to membership opinion.

The four unions examined in detail use ballots to differing extents: the NUM makes extensive use of balloting, the other three unions do not. The NUM uses ballots on national agreements, by custom, and on strikes, by rule; it also uses them for other decisions when the NEC regard the issue as important. The use of ballots for the ratification of agreements is a recent development, prompted primarily by political conflicts within the union, although facilitated by the structure of collective bargaining in the coal mining industry. Both the GMWU and the TGWU use ballots in exceptional circumstances, most importantly in the water industry (GMWU) and electricity supply (where ballots are organized by the National Joint Industrial Council, though prompted by the TGWU): in both cases the industries involved are politically sensitive, with extensive membership discontent, and highly centralized bargaining structures; ballots are thus desirable and practicable. Relatively little use is made of ballots in collective bargaining by the AUEW(E), in contrast to the extensive use made of ballots in elections: a premium is placed on following procedures and maintaining the authority of representative institutions, which it is thought would be undermined by increasing use of ballots.

The National Union of Mineworkers

The rules of the NUM require a national ballot before calling national strike action, but they do not require ballots on national wage agreements. Nevertheless, between 1969 and 1977 the union held 19 national ballots, covering wage agreements, national strikes and other major issues. As Joe Gormley, the NUM president from 1971 to 1982, explained: 'There is nothing in our rules which says that we have to have a ballot on every wage agreement. But . . . the union runs itself by custom and practice, and it is clearly more democratic to hold a ballot when the NEC is so narrowly split, and holds such strongly differing views.'[12] There were few national ballots in the NUM before 1969, although individual areas held ballots on specific issues; the use of ballots at national level was a product of the increased internal conflict of the late 1960s.

The NUM rules refer to negotiation only in the initial statement of union objectives, rule 3 including the objective of negotiating a national wage agreement covering the whole of the British coalfield; the rules are silent on how the negotiations should be conducted, and on who should be consulted before agreements are accepted. Colliery and district negotiations are the responsibility of area officials, although no agreement is valid without the previous approval of the NEC, or authority specifically delegated by the NEC. The rules are, however, explicit on strike action.

According to rule 43 a 'national strike' may be called only 'in pursuance of a resolution of conference' and after 55 per cent of the membership have endorsed such action on a ballot vote. Local disputes are covered by rule 41: 'Local disputes likely to lead to strikes or other industrial action are to be reported immediately to the NEC, and no industrial action is to be taken without the previous sanction of the NEC, or a committee to which it has delegated its powers.' Strike pay or other dispute benefits are payable at the discretion of the NEC; the NEC also has the power to determine the level of benefits paid: there is no strike fund. Ballots are thus required for national industrial action, but discretionary for local industrial action.[13] In practice, ballots on local disputes are required by a number of areas: Northumberland, for example, requires a two-thirds majority for branch strikes and a 55 per cent majority in county disputes.

Since 1969 there has been a presumption that the annual wage round would only be settled in the coal mining industry after a ballot. However, this presumption did not follow automatically from the rules, nor from direct historical precedent. The rules required national ballots only where industrial action was in prospect, not automatically. Moreover, since the last national strike before 1972 was in 1926 (long before the foundation of the NUM), there was no direct precedent indicating the scope of issues to be subject to ballot under rule 43. The major pressures leading to the use of ballots were both external and internal – collective bargaining structures and procedures, economic difficulties, uncertainties concerning membership opinion on the issues facing the union and union political conflict.

The development of national ballots in the NUM in the 1970s was influenced by the collective bargaining system within which the union operated. The NUM negotiated a single national agreement with the NCB. (The area incentive schemes operated since 1978 are based on a national framework, although of course operating differently at local level.) Its only other negotiations were relatively small ones involving colliery clerks and managers. On the union side the process involved the formulation of union policy at the annual conference in July, detailed preparations in the early autumn, negotiations in the winter, with a settlement date the following January. The process was thus a relatively extended but simple one: the union officials involved had time to focus upon a single major exercise, instead of being preoccupied with a large number of different sequences of negotiations, as officials in, for example, the TGWU were. Moreover, with the development of a national day wage structure, from 1966 for faceworkers and from 1971 for other underground workers, there was the possibility of encapsulating the basic terms of the operative agreement simply and comprehensively in a single document. The high level of concentration in the industry made it practicable for officials to explain the terms and the NEC recommendation to union members. However, such factors in themselves did not explain the developing practice: rather, they permitted it. For many public sector unions, with similar bargaining structures, including the NUR, POEU, CPSA, rarely or never hold national ballots.

The second factor influencing the growth of ballots was NEC uncertainty about the views of union members in the face of declining earnings, especially among the 'pace-setting' faceworkers who formed an elite group within the union. Discontent with their declining earnings relative to manual workers in manufacturing industry generally, exacerbated by long-term job losses, led to unofficial strike action in 1969 and 1970, centred upon but not confined to Yorkshire. In view of the danger of the NEC losing control of the membership, the NEC itself recommended strike action in 1972. Relative earnings decline in itself does not lead to the increased use of ballots: but ballots provided a way for the NEC of the NUM to reassure itself about the strength of membership feeling in an uncertain situation.

The internal political situation, the third factor involved, was the most important pressure leading to ballots, as Gormley stressed. By 1971 the broad left in the NUM was able to muster a majority at the annual conference, but not a two-thirds majority: it was only a minority on the NEC.[14] The tactics of the broad left were thus to formulate high wage demands in such a way that if the claim were not achieved, a ballot of the membership on strike action would be required. To counter this tactic, the NEC majority itself took the initiative in holding ballots on the annual settlement, with recommendations from the NEC, including from 1974 onwards for acceptance of the Labour government's wage guidelines.

Voting in the national ballots takes place at the pithead. Voting papers are received at the pithead from head office via the area, together with accompanying literature, including special issues of *The Miner*. Members vote on coming on or leaving the shift, the marked papers being placed into conveniently placed ballot boxes. Two scrutineers oversee the voting, often officers from nearby branches, and a register of voters is maintained. The level of secrecy at the polling booth varies: precise rules are not laid down. In Yorkshire voting is relatively open, on long tables, whilst in Nottingham and Derby voting booths are widely available, although not always used since voters are in a hurry to get home or into work and do not wish to queue for booths. Once voting is complete, the ballot papers are parcelled up at the branch, addressed and delivered by hand to the area offices. Area officials deliver the area votes to the Electoral Reform Society. The branch issues a certificate to the Electoral Reform Society showing the number of ballot papers received, the total used and the total unused. The Electoral Reform Society acknowledges by post receipt of the ballot papers from the branches.

The procedures followed by the NUM are thus not those envisaged by the certification officer. In particular, the ballot is not postal: papers are distributed or collected by hand. Secondly, the voting is carried out at the workplace, not in the home; thirdly, although the ballot is in principle (and potentially) secret, it is not always so in practice. Hence the possibility of influence, especially in the long-table system, remains. However, the procedure does permit the union member to vote as an individual, and the ballot is counted by an outside body, with access to detailed registers of eligible voters as well as votes: it is thus possible to vouchsafe the accuracy of the results of the balloting process, although not to assess the independence of the voters.

Ballots were held on the NCB offer every year between 1969 and 1981 except when the union policy was constrained by the Labour government's incomes policy already endorsed by the union. Table 3.8 summarizes the negotiations between the NCB and the NUM, together with the relevant NEC recommendation and the ballot result. In addition to the ballots on national agreements, additional ballots were held on the following specific issues: productivity incentive scheme (November 1974); Social Contract (August 1975); overtime ban (March 1976); TUC/Labour government wage guidelines (June 1976); early retirement (December 1976); early retirement (January 1977); concessionary coal (July 1977); and national incentive scheme (November 1977). The NEC recommendation was

TABLE   3.8   NUM ballots on wage offers, 1969–82

Year	Issue	NEC recommendation	Ballot result	Agree with NEC
1969	NCB offer and surface hours	Acceptance	Yes 82.4% No 17.6%	Yes
1970	Strike ballot[a]	Pro-strike	Yes 55.5% No 44.5%	Yes
1971	Strike ballot	Pro-strike	Yes 58.8% No 41.2%	Yes
1972 (Feb)	Strike ballot	Pro-strike	Yes 210,039 (96.5%) No 7,581	Yes
1973 (April)	Strike ballot	Pro-strike	Yes 82,631 (32.6%) No 143,006	No
1974 (Feb)	Strike ballot	Pro-strike	Yes 188,393 (81%) No 44,222	Yes
1975 (Feb)	NCB agreement	Acceptance Turnout 88%	Yes 171,755 (88%) No 23,686	Yes
1976–9	No ballots on annual round: incomes policy			
1979 (March)	NCB agreement	Acceptance	Yes 131,316 (84.7%) No 23,686	Yes
1979 (Dec)	Strike	Pro-strike Turnout 87%	Yes 107,656 (48.75%) No 113,160	No
1980 (Dec)	NCB agreement	Acceptance Turnout 80%	Yes 117,196 (56.2%) No 91,498	Yes
1982 (Jan)	Strike	Pro-strike Turnout 82%	Yes 91,477 (44.7%) No 113,144	No

Note:
[a] Ballot held under requirement for two-thirds majority: no strike called. Rule changed to 55 per cent 1971 conference.

endorsed in all such specific ballots on which the NEC's recommendation is known, except the national incentive scheme ballot, 1977.[15]

Assessment of the full significance of the ballot results for industrial relations in the coal mining industry would require a full chapter in itself; our concern is with the narrower question of the workings of the political system. In general, the expectation that ballots are likely to endorse the decisions of the NEC is confirmed: even in a politically divided union like the NUM in the 1970s, with the NEC and the annual conference having different political complexions, the NEC recommendations on wage agreements and strike action were normally accepted. However, on three occasions in the period studied (and again subsequently) NEC recommendations for strike action were rejected: in April 1973, December 1979 and January 1982.

As indicated earlier, the NEC of the NUM contained a moderate (or in Gormley's terms 'progressive') majority throughout the 1970s, involved in a sharp conflict with the broad left. The three occasions on which NEC recommendations for strike action were rejected were all influenced by the union's political situation: the recommendations did not mean what they appeared to mean on all three occasions. Hence on all three occasions the moderate majority recommended a vote for strike action for tactical reasons, being anxious to avoid being outflanked by the broad left: the NEC was thus not unhappy when its recommendations were rejected. In 1973 the NEC was influenced by the growing broad left support at the annual conference and on the NEC following the success of the 1972 strike, and the increased time period covered by the agreement, 16 instead of 12 months. In 1979 Gormley recommended acceptance of the NCB offer (20 per cent plus consolidation of £6 from the Social Contract) but was over-ruled by the NEC, who decided to call the broad left's bluff and recommend strike action, correctly anticipating that it would be rejected. Finally, the moderate majority was especially fearful in the 1981–2 wage round following Scargill's overwhelming victory in the presidential election: in the event the strike call was (almost equally) overwhelmingly rejected, only Yorkshire (66 per cent) and Scotland (63 per cent) returning over 55 per cent in favour. (The ballot was the occasion of controversy, Joe Gormley recommending rejection in the *Daily Express* the day before voting began: 'Think – before you destroy what we have built up'.)

Throughout the 1970s the turnout for NUM ballots on wage offers or on industrial action was 80 per cent or more for the ballots for which precise figures on participation are known, levels similar to those achieved in elections to national office in the union. Such levels of participation are the maximum that can be realistically expected, of course exceeding the levels achieved in Parliamentary elections. Workplace ballots are thus an effective means of achieving high levels of participation, and an accurate recording of opinion, at least for unions with large numbers of members employed in large establishments.

The NUM has thus made extensive use of national ballots since 1969. The frequency of balloting has not been because of union rules; union rules require ballots on national strike action but not in other circumstances. Ballots have played a major role in resolving issues in a politically divided union: ballots have provided a means of making 'final' decisions, at least until the next wages round. Neither moderates nor broad left have queried the outcome of the balloting process, even when the ballot has had the status only of advising the NEC. It is difficult to see how the political divisions in the NUM could have avoided fragmenting the union without recourse to national ballots.

In the NUM balloting provides a means of resolving internal conflict. This is facilitated by the essentially simple structure of the collective bargaining machinery in the industry: an industrial union negotiating with a monopoly employer for a very large group of workers. The only other agreements of concern to the NUM cover industrial staff and clerks and are only of limited importance. The national agreement determined earnings (until the general adoption of pit-based incentive schemes in 1978). Although the union covers four major occupational groupings, the overwhelming majority of members belong to one occupational group. Balloting is thus a convenient method of resolving divisive issues. In more complex collective bargaining systems balloting is a less appropriate method, as indicated in the use made of ballots in the three remaining case studies.

The Transport and General Workers Union

In the TGWU the authority for conducting negotiations, authorizing strike action, paying strike benefits and concluding agreements rests with the general executive committee (GEC). According to rule 6(15), the GEC 'shall have power at any time to negotiate on matters concerning the interests of labour generally, and to conclude agreements'.[16] The GEC also has power to formulate negotiating policy and to organize industrial action, except that national strike action, or action involving more than one trade group, requires the endorsement of a recalled biennial delegate conference and a ballot of the membership: such strikes are unknown. The GEC has power to delegate its responsibilities under rule 6(16): '[the GEC] may delegate to any national or regional or district committee such of their powers as are necessary or expedient and consistent with the powers and duties of such committee . . . and may modify or revoke such powers from time to time'. In practice, the GEC delegates its powers to negotiate to the national trade groups, although retaining the power to authorize disputes and the payment of dispute pay in all cases. Within the TGWU the conduct of collective bargaining, including the procedures for consultation with the membership, varies between trade groups; national ballots are used only rarely.

The variety in structure between trade groups has a direct influence on TGWU policy towards reference back in general, and ballots in particular: the continued survival of the union requires organizational flexibility.

Indeed, obligatory reference back was opposed at the 1974 and 1980 rules revision conferences precisely because *obligatory* reference back would reduce flexibility. At the 1974 rules conference it was proposed that trade group secretaries should be required to convene 'lay delegate conferences or hold individual membership ballots before signing any agreement on wages and conditions', but was opposed by the GEC and the branch received no support. At the 1980 rules conference reference back in general, and ballots in particular, were both discussed. A major change appeared to have occurred when the conference passed a resolution requiring national trade group secretaries to convene their trade group or section committees before signing any agreement on wages and conditions: the conference supported the proposal against the recommendation of the GEC, which opposed the resolution. The general secretary thereupon 'clarified' the resolution in a speech to conference:

> Clarification was essential because of the vast implications in the proposal carried by conference for National Secretaries to be required to convene National Trade Group Committees in order to sign agreements. Clearly this was impracticable and conference attention was drawn to the multifarious negotiated arrangements existing in industries such as automative, road haulage and general trades. In addition there were constitutional arrangements with many individual plants and the need for District Officers with shop stewards to sign agreements on behalf of members. The intent of the amendment was understood to be related to the construction industry only, and this was how the Executive would interpret it. Conference concurred with this view – the Sponsor of the motion having indicated acceptance of the executive qualifying statement.[17]

Mandatory recourse to the national trade group committee was practicable, and sensible, in the construction industry, since the committee dealt primarily with two important agreements only, and alternative means of consultation were impracticable with the largely casual and geographically mobile membership; more numerous agreements, and a different membership, made this procedure less practicable and less necessary elsewhere. At the same conference, resolutions on ballot voting, including resolutions on balloting before acceptance of wage agreements, were defeated.

Although the procedures for reference back were not laid down, the general policy of the TGWU was that agreements should be referred back. As indicated above (table 3.7), this policy was followed in practice, 82 per cent of manual TGWU representatives stating that they had been consulted over the last wage agreement. This was one aspect of the comprehensive policy of decentralization in collective bargaining and increased involvement of lay members promoted by Jack Jones and Harry Urwin. The TGWU's policy, as explained at the 1974 rules conference, involved 'the fullest possible participation and consultation with representatives and members . . . there was now a greater degree of accountability in terms of negotiating agreements than in the past in consequence of the determined policy which had been pursued by this Union in recent years'.[18] How this consultation was carried out varied between trade groups, and was heavily influenced by the views of union officials within each group, especially the trade group national secretary. At the beginning of the fieldwork there were 11 trade groups: this was increased to 12 during the fieldwork, with the creation of a separate civil air transport group out of part of the public services group, and to 14 subsequently with the creation of trade groups for agricultural workers and for dyers and bleachers following mergers with the National Union of Agricultural and Allied Workers (1982) and the National Union of Dyers, Bleachers and Textile Workers (1982). There were long-standing procedures for reference back in the docks, passenger transport and vehicle building trade groups. The national secretary of the oil, chemicals and rubber trade group established procedures following his appointment in 1969, as did the newly appointed national secretaries of the public services group and the commercial road haulage group following their appointments in 1976; the national secretaries of the general workers and the food, drink and tobacco groups were considering adopting the public services group's practices at the time of the fieldwork, in 1981. None of these procedures involved the use of ballots.

Ballots were used for national agreements in three trade groups: power and engineering, road haulage, and building and construction, although not all workers covered by the groups have been balloted. Balloting has been most elaborately developed in the electricity supply section of the power and engineering trade group: it is now used regularly in specific circumstances in the oil tanker driver section of the road transport (commercial) trade group, and it has been used only once nationally in the building and construction trade group.

The development of the use of ballots on the National Joint Industrial Council (NJIC) national agreement in electricity supply was due to specific features of the industry, and of the union membership. Four unions represent manual workers: the TGWU, EETPU, GMWU, and AUEW, the largest being the EETPU; the decision to ballot the members concerned was a joint decision, although the pressure for wider consultation came from the TGWU representatives, responding to pressure from their own members: the ballots were organized by the NJIC. Collective bargaining in the industry is highly centralized: a joint trade union committee composed of full-time officials negotiating with a single employer. The centralized bargaining system is paralleled by an hierarchical consultative structure; the Electricity Council does not recognize shop stewards. The national agreement has wide coverage, with little room for local negotiations: earnings are primarily determined nationally. Both the Electricity Council and the unions agreed that the appropriate collective bargaining structure for the industry was a centralized one. The workers covered by the agreement are either widely dispersed, when employed by area boards, or on shift work, when employed at generating stations by the CEGB. Hence collective bargaining structure, membership distribution and shift working favoured the use of ballots. At the same time, there was pressure from workers in the industry for increased consultation. Two unofficial combine committees were active in the industry from the 1960s favouring the reference back of agreements, if necessary by ballot rather than lay conference. The combine committee based in South Yorkshire was especially influential, and was heavily influenced by NUM practices: power station workers had very close links with miners, especially where coal-fired generating stations were supplied directly from the pithead. This pressure was reflected in comments by the Wilberforce Court of Inquiry, which settled the 1970 work-to-rule: 'the NJIC would need . . . to set out procedures for acceptance in principle by appropriate groups of workers. We would suggest that a clear majority in each group must in a vote express themselves in favour of such acceptance already accepted by the unions at national level'.[19] From the NJIC perspective postal ballots were the most practical method of reference back.

By 1983 four ballots had been held in the industry: 1978 (April), 1979 (May), 1979 (July) and 1982 (May). On each occasion ballots were distributed by the Electricity Council with pay packets, and returned in prepaid envelopes to the Electoral Reform Society. In the first two ballots the Electricity Council's proposals were outlined, with the question 'Are you in favour of the Electricity Council's proposals'; there was no recommendation from the union side. On the third ballot, on a revised offer, the trade unions recommended acceptance, stating that the offer was the Council's final one, and made explicit that any rejection would be interpreted as indicating willingness to undertake strike action: the only way of voting 'no' was to vote 'I am against acceptance of the revised offer and am prepared to take Industrial Action which could include a stoppage of work'. The ballots were thus half postal. Union representatives and shop stewards were allowed to be present when the ballots were distributed, although of course voting did not necessarily take place at the workplace. The cost of the 1979 ballots was shared equally between the Electricity Council and the unions involved, although the Council bore the larger share of the 'unallocated' cost since it was responsible for distributing the ballots. The results of the ballots were scarcely encouraging to the Electricity Council's view that strike ballots would foster industrial peace (table 3.9).

All four ballots were highly contentious. In the winter of 1977–8 an unofficial strike in South Yorkshire led to the closure of six major power stations. As the result of fears that failure to refer the Council's offer to the membership would result in further discontent, the NJIC balloted the membership, although with some reluctance on the part of EETPU and GMWU representatives. The ballot was very narrowly in favour of acceptance, the balance being tipped, according to some interviewees, by the foremen, who had received an especially generous rise under the agreement due to the Electricity Council's desire to restructure its management payment system.

The rejection of the first proposal in 1979 was expected by both the

TABLE 3.9   Results of postal ballots in electricity supply (all workers covered by agreement, not TGWU only)

1978 April		
No NJIC recommendation		
For acceptance	41,626	(50.33%)
Against	41,076	(49.67%)
Majority in favour of acceptance	550	
Invalid returns	51	
Turnout	82,753	
1979 June		
No NJIC recommendation		
For acceptance	19,254	
Against	66,162	
Majority against acceptance	46,908	
Invalid returns	20	
Turnout	85,436	(96,000 ballots issued)
1979 July		
NJIC recommended acceptance		
For acceptance	34,097	
Against	46,151	
Majority against acceptance	15,054	
Invalid returns	68	
Turnout	83,316	(96,000 ballots issued)
1982 May		
No NJIC recommendation (stress that rejection would lead to strike action)		
For acceptance	31,801	
Against	41,249	
Majority against acceptance	9,448	
Turnout	73,050	

Electricity Council and the unions: the offer was in line with the Labour government's 5 per cent limit, and no attempt was made to sell the agreement to the membership. The revised offer was made possible by the new government's policy of cash limits, in place of incomes restraint, and the availability of new money through increased revenue. The unions campaigned for acceptance of the revised offer, including conferences of branch secretaries and chairmen, and the ballot questions were worded to secure acceptance. The offer was rejected by a substantial majority, to the surprise of the Electricity Council and union NJIC members. Following the rejection, the Electricity Council increased its offer slightly, on condition of immediate acceptance; the union side agreed to accept any improvement without reference back. The haste was partly due to embarrassment, and partly to the need to reach a settlement before the end of the current financial year (nationalized industries cannot carry financial surpluses forward). The fourth ballot, in 1982, also resulted in a rejection of the

Electricity Council's offer, and strike action was authorized. However, before industrial action began the dispute was settled by ACAS: the NJIC accepted the ACAS formula without ballot.

There have therefore been four major national ballots amongst manual workers in electricity supply: three have resulted in a rejection of the offer submitted, and the fourth resulted in acceptance by a majority of under 1 per cent. There are three major reasons why ballots have resulted in the rejection or narrow acceptance of offers, despite the tacit endorsement of the offers by the union side of the NJIC on two occasions and explicit endorsement on a third.

The first reason is simply that the members had grievances which they did not believe that the offer submitted settled. There were particular grievances associated with the implementation of productivity schemes; the lead-in payments recommended by the Wilberforce Court in 1971 were tightly constrained and much criticized. The sense of grievance was increased by close awareness of the miners' successes, especially in South Yorkshire, where the miners militancy rubbed off on the electricity workers. Elsewhere engineers working for the CEGB believed that engineers working for other organizations were receiving more where local labour market conditions required it: they themselves were bound by a tight national agreement. Such grievances were articulated by an active combine committee, based upon but not restricted to Yorkshire. At the same time the experience of 1978 indicated that rejection of offers led to improvements: power workers were aware of their considerable bargaining strength.

The second reason involves the rigidity imposed on negotiating procedures by the use of ballots. On the one hand, the centralization and relative simplicity of the industry's bargaining structure was appropriate to the structure of the industry, with a single employer concerned to control labour costs and with a trade union side sharply aware of the danger to the national economy posed by their members (and to the members themselves if industrial action led to violence, as it had in 1970). On the other hand, ballots did not allow great flexibility: where particular items caused difficulty they could not be renegotiated. Moreover, the reasons for rejection were not clear, and little guidance was given to negotiators. Consultation through delegate conferences, preferably before the offer was put to members, would increase flexibility; on the other hand, it might lead to a questioning of the industry's centralized structure. Despite their obvious procedural limitations, ballots were therefore seen as the most appropriate method of consultation.

Finally, managers were thought to have been influential in the second ballot in 1979. The managers were themselves in negotiation with the Electricity Council, and had a strong claim to receive an award comparable with that achieved by NJIC manual workers; managers were responsible for distributing ballot papers locally and it is thought that they canvassed for a 'no' vote, anticipating that an enhanced offer would be passed on to them.

The overall TGWU policy of increasing consultation with the membership thus resulted in the use of postal ballots in the very specific circumstances of the electricity supply industry: such circumstances were not repeated elsewhere. The second area in the TGWU in which ballots were used was in the road transport (commercial) trade group. Amongst the national freight corporation membership reference back is to national and regional conferences, and then to depots. However, amongst oil tanker drivers balloting is used as a matter of policy, following a decision of the senior stewards conference in oil in 1979. There were three major reasons for the stewards' decision. Throughout the 1970s stewards from large depots were increasingly concerned that they were being outvoted at conferences by small depots in formulating wages policies; there was therefore pressure for some sort of proportionality. This could have been achieved by a system of block voting at conferences. However, two other factors combined to make balloting at depots a preferred solution. Most importantly, stewards complained that managers were interfering in depot meetings, particularly by announcing the results of meetings in other depots (when they favoured settlement); this led to pressure for secret ballots, and for a common timetable. Finally, there was some feeling that conference delegates were not always reflecting the views of their depots in the way they voted. Although the senior stewards conference recommended that depots should vote by secret ballot, the final decision was left to individual branches; not all branches followed the recommendation.

In addition to ballots in electricity supply and amongst oil tanker drivers, occasional ballots have been organized at regional and local level in other sectors. However, the practice is rare, and usually adopted in two types of situation: first, when ballots are the most convenient method of consulting a mobile (or widely dispersed) membership, as amongst airline cabin crew in the public services and civil air transport trade group; secondly, as means of resolving local difficulties as a last resort. Hence, for example, in the chemical industry a full-time officer initiated a plant-level ballot because the lay convenor was advocating at mass meetings the rejection of offers he had endorsed as a member of a national negotiating committee. Secret ballots are especially likely to be used to resolve such conflicts where the organization of work precludes decisions at a single meeting, for example among shift workers. The frequency of such ballots as a way of resolving conflict between full-time officers and convenors, or between different groups within a branch or plant, is unknown, but likely to be rare.[20] Similarly, some branches organize their own ballots before endorsing a wage agreement, for example in the Courtaulds and glass container branches: again, the prevalence of shift working is significant.

The detailed examination of the use of ballots in electricity supply indicates the circumstances under which ballots are used, and the difficulties encountered. Although there was universal commitment within the union to the 'Jones philosophy' of reference back, there was little pressure from elsewhere in the union to adopt the methods followed in electricity supply, even in the power and engineering trade group. The union's policy was one of flexibility; ballots, especially postal ballots, might be useful in some circumstances, but there were major disadvantages in using them, and in any event there were better alternative methods of consultation. Officials' reservations about balloting were based on principle, practice and interest. In principle, lay representatives should be fully involved in the negotiating process through the union's representative system; this could be obtained most easily by organizing lay delegate conferences to formulate policies and to discuss proposals in detail with full-time officers, rather than by relying upon a system of full-time officers dealing directly with the membership. Moreover, negotiators feared that management would, in effect, be negotiating directly with the membership if offers were required to be put to members. In practice, ballots would reduce negotiating flexibility and draw out the process of negotiation. It would also make the process of communication, explanation and persuasion more difficult, necessarily involving elaborate documentation of agreements and arguments. The process of consultation makes it possible to air differences and to give negotiators advance warning of potential difficulties. Such flexibility was advantageous to management as well as to full-time officials. Finally, full-time officers would simply become post-boxes if postal ballots were made routine, substantially diminishing the significance of their role: they could hardly be expected to support procedures which reduced their own significance.

In place of postal ballots, in the mid 1970s the public services trade group (London region) developed a dual system, subsequently considered by the general workers and the food, drink, and tobacco trade groups. Nationally, if the offer is complex, the trade group organizes a lay delegate conference (which may or may not be followed by a systematic canvass of membership opinion, depending on the mood of conference, timing of negotiations, etc.). If the offer is straightforward, forms are sent to the branch secretary for completion following relevant meetings. However, in the London region a more complex procedure is followed, involving the steward completing a form. The form requires: branch; workplace name; number of members at meeting; voting figures; signature of steward; steward's home address. The system was designed to foster the stewards system (in a sector where stewards were not long established), to enable members to participate in small groups, to provide detailed information on variations in membership opinion and to gauge membership opinion accurately. Individual branches, especially large branches or branches with a scattered membership, can decide whether to hold individual ballots; Great Yarmouth Hospitals branch is known to use individual ballots, the ballots being collected by stewards at members meetings. The system has been encouraged because it provides detailed information, and individual and collective involvement. The ballots of course are neither secret nor postal, and the considerable expenses involved could not be reclaimed from the certification officer under the 1980 Employment Act even if the union wished to do so.

The role of ballots is thus considerably more limited in the TGWU than in the NUM. Although there is no prohibition in the *Rules* on the use of ballots (indeed the rules require them in national disputes involving more than one trade group), and although the union has pursued an explicit policy of consulting widely with the membership since the late 1960s, ballots have been used only rarely on national agreements, and postal ballots even more rarely. The major exception has been in electricity supply, where the TGWU, as a member of the NJIC, has used postal ballots on four occasions. As outlined, there were specific reasons for the use of ballots in electricity supply: bargaining structure, employers' attitudes, coverage of agreements, inter-union convenience and internal political pressures. Elsewhere in the union ballots, although not postal ballots, were used in the commercial road transport trade group, and on one occasion in the construction trade group. However, the union full-time officers preferred to consult via lay committees, shop stewards meetings or, as in cars, mass meetings rather than to use formal ballots, arguing that the method was more flexible, and less open to employers' influences. There is an increasing tendency to adopt the public services group methods. The overall intention is to maintain the authority of representative institutions (especially the shop steward system) whilst obtaining detailed information about membership opinion.

The General and Municipal Workers Union

Under rule, authority within the GMWU remains concentrated in the hands of the executive council. No strike may be called without the express sanction of the executive council, strike benefit is only payable if strikes are sanctioned by the council and the EC is given explicit authority to refer disputes to arbitration. According to rule 27 (3):

> No cessation of work shall take place unless two-thirds of the members belonging to the Branch or body immediately concerned shall have voted in favour of the adoption of such course, and then only with the express sanction of the Executive Council and after legal notice to terminate contracts of service has been given. Every member affected shall have an opportunity of recording his vote at a special meeting, for and against handing in notice to cease work.

Voting at the meeting may be by show of hands or by ballot. Strikes involving no more than 300 members could be approved by the regional committee where all specified procedures have been followed. The role of the executive council in negotiations is less clearly defined, although all claims must be reported to the executive council. According to rule 27.(2):

> Should any Branch or body of members of the Union desire steps to be taken for an advance of wages or improved conditions of employment, the Branch Secretary shall report the claim to the Regional Secretary . . . who shall forward the same to the Executive Council. With respect to those on whose behalf the claim is being preferred, there shall be stated, on the form

provided, the number of members entitled and not entitled to benefit, the number of non-members, if any, and also the number of votes recorded by the Branch or body for and against the claim.[21]

In practice the regional secretary's comments on the claim are central.

As in the TGWU, the practice of referring agreements back to the membership directly affected increased during the 1970s: as one official commented, the days when full-time officers could make unpopular decisions behind closed doors have gone. According to the Department of Employment Workplace Industrial Relations Survey, 67 per cent of GMWU manual worker stewards reported that the last wage settlement had been referred to the membership for ratification (see p. 129). Reference back became more common partly because of the enhanced role of shop stewards and partly because of a general liberalization of institutions. However, reference back was not obligatory: negotiators were expected to use their judgement. The methods used in referring back varied, depending largely upon the circumstances and the views of the relevant national industrial officer, or in particularly important circumstances (as in water) the general secretary and the EC. There was less flexibility over strikes, primarily because of the importance attached to following prcedures to secure payment of strike benefit. The use of ballots before strikes was determined by regional organizers in the light of their relationships with shop stewards. However, members had to be consulted, and either regional committee or executive council sanction had to be obtained if dispute benefit was to be claimed.

Ballots have been used only rarely in the GMWU on national agreements. In addition to electricity supply, discussed earlier, ballots on national agreements have been held in the fibreboard packing case industry, glass containers, Pilkingtons, water and gas. In some sectors ballots have come to be used on a regular basis, e.g. fibreboard and Pilkingtons; in water they have been used repeatedly to resolve major industrial relations problems; in gas only one ballot has been held, to call off a strike in 1973.

Ballots have been held on the fibreboard packing case industry agreement since 1977. Before 1977 consultation was informal, the national officer involved consulting branches by letter; where the opinions of the branches were unclear national conferences were held. However, active members of the union believed that the national officer was ignoring their opinions, and campaigned for holding a ballot on the same lines as the ballot held by SOGAT. A new national officer was appointed in 1976, who believed that ballots would reduce membership discontent. Accordingly, ballots have been held on the agreement annually since 1977, the offer put to the membership being rejected once: since the union is only a minority alongside SOGAT, the results have paralleled those in the other union.

GMWU ballots in the fibreboard packing sector were neither secret nor postal. The ballots were carried out by the branch secretary, under the supervision of the national industrial officer: the ballot papers were issued by the NIO to the branch secretary, who carried out the ballot as he thought best and forwarded the results to the NIO. There were no procedures laid down, and practices varied from branch to branch. No outside agency was involved. Ballots thus provided a means for rank-and-file members to express their views on the employers' offers; but they did not do so under precisely regulated conditions, and the procedures followed would not have qualified for the reimbursement of the expenses involved under the scheme drawn up by the certification officer.

The union officials involved have become increasingly sceptical of the procedures, owing to the length of time involved, the lack of flexibility and the view that members are not voting on comparable bases since the agreement affects different groups of workers differently. Such general reservations were underscored by experience in the 1979 wage round. The employers' association convinced the union side at an early stage that the offer made was a final one. However, the offer was rejected on a ballot. When negotiations reopened, the employers forthwith increased their offer, thereby implying that more money might have been available earlier. The second offer was balloted upon and accepted by a very substantial majority of GMWU members (2,283 for, 615 against) and a substantial majority of SOGAT members (5,880 for, 2,356 against). The lesson the officials drew from the 1979 round was that regular balloting encouraged employers to make initial 'final' offers, without serious negotiations, on the basis that if the offer was accepted the employers had made a good deal, and if not accepted the process of negotiations could begin without serious loss: ballots were a 'no-loss' gamble when employers knew an offer must be put to ballot. Union negotiators had difficulty in resisting employer requests to put offers to their members. It was also likely that the time involved in the balloting process would lead to the settlement date being missed, leading to pressure upon the members involved to accept the offer because of the backpay involved. Moreover, the negotiators were in difficulties over whether to submit the offer to the membership with or without a recommendation; in 1979 the GMWU made no recommendation in either ballot, whilst SOGAT recommended acceptance.

Structural conditions favoured the use of ballots in the water industry, as in electricity supply. Collective bargaining was centralized, between the National Water Council (since 1974) and a joint union committee (GMWU, TGWU, NUPE and until 1982, NUAAW). Moreover, the annual agreement was a comprehensive one, leaving limited scope for local variations. All members voting were likely to be similarly affected by the terms proposed. Moreover, the multi-union negotiating structure made it desirable that all unions adopt comparable consultation processes, with clear-cut outcomes: ballots provided a mechanism for visible comparison although, in water supply, unions did not always consult their members by the same methods. Finally, the membership was dispersed, working in small groups, and consultation through branch meetings was difficult. However, although structural conditions facilitated balloting, the major reasons for holding ballots in water supply derived from problems of union management: ballots were used when negotiations with employers were at the end of the road, and the union was faced with the alternatives of acceptance or strike action. Ballots were held in March 1978 (on the 1977–8 wage application) and in March 1980 (on the 1979–80 wages application); they were not held in 1979 (on the 1978–9 wages application), nor in 1981 (on the 1980–81 wages application). Since fieldwork was completed, a further ballot has been held, in December 1982. The union officials concerned recommended, or rejected, the use of ballots on their perceptions of how ballots would help in securing orderly settlements in an industry with major industrial relations tensions, not on the basis of their views on the desirability of ballots *per se.*

Before 1974 water industry workers were incorporated in negotiations with other local authority manual workers; they were not a separately identifiable group. Following local government reorganization in 1974, and the creation of separate water authorities, with industrial relations handled by a separate NJIC, water workers became increasingly aware of their potential bargaining power. Their 'natural' comparisons were with electricity supply and gas workers, a comparison acknowledged by the Conservative government in 1979 when it recognized water workers as key workers whose power had to be respected. However, water workers' earnings were below those of the other two groups, and 'catching up' was difficult because of the operation of incomes policies during the Labour government and financial constraints under the Conservatives. At the same time, the water workers' bargaining strength was not always an advantage: members were conscious that strike action might endanger health and result in 'sewage on the streets', which was both morally offensive and likely to incur public hostility (as strikes in electricity supply do). Water workers were thus aware that the weapons available were powerful, but blunt. This dislocation was increased by inter-union rivalry, the NUPE assistant general secretary, Ron Keating, raising expectations amongst water workers as a means, according to the other unions involved, of winning support for NUPE. It was therefore likely that industrial relations would be turbulent in the industry, that union negotiators would face major difficulties in obtaining agreements satisfactory to their members and that unofficial action would develop: this expectation was realized.

The use of ballots was thus one element in union officials' 'managerial' strategy. The standard procedure for formulating wages policies was for the regional organizers to hold regional conferences to formulate demands; these were incorporated into a programme by a national industrial conference, organized by the national industrial officer. Agreements were reported back for approval to the same national industrial conference. The national industrial officer played the leading role in negotiations with the employers, all union side members of the NJIC being full-time officers. In 1977–8 it was anticipated that the settlement reached would not be acceptable to the national and regional conferences, since it was within the

Labour government's guidelines, to which the union was committed. Accordingly, the agreement was referred directly to the membership, with a recommendation for acceptance: on a turnout of 14,320 or 68.2 per cent (out of 21,000), 9,429 voted for acceptance, 4,842 for rejection, with 49 spoilt, giving a majority for acceptance of 4,891. Only one region out of 10 voted to reject the settlement, Yorkshire and North Derbyshire. In 1980 the national industrial conference rejected the recommendation by the union side of the NJIC, the executive council and the national industrial officer concerned to accept the offer, calling instead for industrial action. The NIO asked the EC for a ballot, and received permission. A detailed statement of the offer, together with a recommendation for acceptance, was circulated in February, and accepted by a substantial majority (10,052 for, 4,927 against, 34 invalid). Both ballots were half postal, i.e. distributed through the union but returned by the individual member through the post to the Electoral Reform Society.

Ballots were used in 1978 and in 1980 to resolve intra-union problems. There were fewer internal problems in the 1980–81 wages round, the major difficulties arising in the negotiations with the employers. The major method of consultation was through regional conferences, which were recalled on three occasions. Following the initial rejection of the union claim, which included a £20 per week increase, the regional industrial conferences were asked to endorse industrial action: they agreed to do so. Following an increase in the employers offer from 7.9 per cent to 10 per cent the union agreed to place the offer before the conference, but with a recommendation to reject: the offer was rejected. Following this rejection the employers offered to pay for a ballot on the offer organized by the union, or to organize one themselves: the union refused the first suggestion, and expressed strong resentment at the second. When industrial action appeared inevitable, the employers increased their offer by 2.5 per cent. The union side of the NJIC thereupon recommended acceptance, subject to membership agreement. Since the offer did not meet the initial claim, and the extensive and highly visible process of negotiation had heightened expectations, it was not inevitable that the recommendation would be accepted. However, it was known that a recourse to ballot would be highly unpopular with union activists, the regional conference procedure had not lead to difficulties earlier in the round, and the NIO concerned referred the recommendation to the regions, leaving them to consult as they thought best. The regions reconvened regional industrial conferences. Five regions rejected the agreement, three accepted and one tied. However, since the regions accepting the agreement represented more members than those rejecting, the EC decided that there was no support for industrial action, and that the agreement was accepted.

In the 1982–3 wages round, the balloting process itself was a source of contention. Under pressure from the Government, the National Water Council offered 4 per cent in response to a claim for 15 per cent. The offer was put to the membership (regional conferences) largely as a formality, and rejected overwhelmingly. Following an overtime ban, a mediator was appointed, who recommended 7.3 per cent over 16 months. The offer was put to the membership, with the explicit interpretation that rejection would lead to a national strike. The offer was rejected and the industry's first national strike began on 23 January 1983. Public controversy surrounded the balloting process, indicating the difficulties involved in using ballots even when apparently clearly specified in rules. Under rule, a two-thirds majority of members affected is required for strike action; on a turnout of 82 per cent the union claimed a majority of 3 to 1 for strike action (61.5 per cent of all relevant members). Conservative spokesmen claimed that this did not justify strike action under rule, since two-thirds of members affected had not supported strike action. In reply, GMWU officials claimed that the executive council had full authority under rule to decide upon strike action, the rule providing for executive authority over-riding specific provisions. Whatever the interpretation likely in a court of law, the executive was correct in industrial relations terms: voting turnout was almost the maximum that could be realistically expected, the vote was overwhelmingly for strike action, the executive would have lost control of the situation if it had not called a strike, and the interpretation of rule was at least plausible. A five-week strike was ended with the unions accepting the recommendations of the Johnston Committee, which recommended a settlement the unions could interpret as 11–12 per cent, without a ballot.

In the glass container industry, the GMWU (and the TGWU) organized plant by plant secret ballots on the national agreement in 1980–81. There were both long-term historical reasons for this, and particular circumstances. As a continuous process industry, with shift working, balloting was a convenient method of consulting members: branch or workplace meetings were difficult to organize. Moreover, balloting provided a means of consulting members without raising tension between two groups with antagonistic interests, the glass makers and the bottle sorters, in effect responsible for quality control. Specific plants within the sector, especially in Yorkshire and Merseyside, had thus used ballots on agreements irregularly since the 1950s, although the major pressures at local level came from TGWU rather than GMWU members. In 1980–81 there was uncertainty about membership views on the agreement, which was regarded as poor but the best likely to be obtained, and it was therefore decided to ask for secret ballots in all plants to ensure thorough and consistent consultation. The offer was put to the membership without any recommendation from the NJIC, although the Yorkshire Glass Committee (TGWU) recommended acceptance. It was accepted. Secret ballots have also been held regularly on the Pilkington's agreement since 1978, primarily on the insistence of representatives of the larger plants, who felt that the 1978 agreement had been accepted without adequate consultation.

Below national level, the use of ballots for reference back within the GMWU depends on the attitudes of the regional officials and, at plant level, shop stewards. The key to the method used in referring agreements back is the relationship between the regional organizer and the branch officers and shop stewards: ballots are most likely to be used as a method of consultation where the stewards' organization is weak, where the stewards themselves think it would be convenient or where practical obstacles inhibit the use of alternative methods. More rarely, full-time officers may insist on secret ballots because they do not believe that the stewards are representing the views of their members effectively. Examples of all circumstances were mentioned in interviews with regional officers, and will be examined in turn.

Below national level, secret ballots on agreements are normally initiated by full-time officials or agreed with shop stewards for tactical reasons, usually (if not quite invariably) to secure acceptance of an offer. No regional organizer said that he would use a ballot if looking for rejection. Ballots would be especially appropriate if the agreement being presented was not a good one, but where there was little prospect of further improvement, since it would allow the stewards to absolve themselves of responsibility. Very few instances were reported of ballots being forced on union members against the wishes of stewards, as it was only likely in extreme situations, involving either the ending, or calling of a strike. However, the tactical use of secret ballots is not widespread, being used only very rarely in Lancashire or the Northern region: secret ballots are only one of a repertoire of tactical options. Ballots are used elsewhere for practical reasons, where the membership is dispersed and direct contact is impossible, for example in the managers in hotels and catering sector in Scotland, or where shift working makes workplace or branch meetings difficult, as in glass containers or the Scottish whisky industry. At plant level, stewards occasionally use ballots on plant negotiations, either tactically or on a regular basis, but the extent is unknown: the full-time officers interviewed would only be involved where difficulties arose, and few were reported.

As explained above, GMWU rules laid down that strike action could only be official if approved by the EC, or the regional committee if involving 300 or fewer workers, and by at least two-thirds of the members affected at a special meeting. In particular, strike benefit could only be paid if both conditions were met. If regional organizers wish to hold a local strike on a local agreement detailed procedures are laid down: detailed forms are filled in; approval is sought from the regional secretary who makes a recommendation on the bottom of the form; the national industrial officer for the industry is consulted; sanction is required from the general secretary (if straightforward), finance sub-committee (if awkward), or whole EC if very serious (water). The effect of the procedure is to introduce a gap between the issue arising and the strike occurring, providing a period for putting pressure on the employer. If the procedure is followed, a strike vote is invariably sanctioned. The method by which the vote is carried out varies between regions, ballots being very frequent in the Northern region

(33 between 1970 and 1980) and rare in Birmingham; where ballots are held they are workplace not postal. There was no difference in the outcome of the consultation process according to the method of consultation followed. Authorizing strike action did not invariably result in strikes occurring: in the Northern region in 1980 there were 8 strike ballots requested, of which 1 was refused, 4 requests were granted without strikes taking place, and 3 strikes occurred (one in industrial catering, one in contract cleaning and one in the rubber industry). In the Southern region there were 33 requests to the regional committee for strike votes between July 1970 and July 1980, including 7 specifically indicating the intention to organize ballots; of the 5 for which the ballot results could be traced, 2 resulted in acceptance of the management offer and 3 in a majority in favour of strike action, but in all cases the disputes were resolved without the strikes taking place. The hope throughout was that insistence upon an elaborate formal procedure would result in frequent delays, increasing pressure upon employers, but without reaching the point at which strike action would be required.

As in considering alternative methods of reference back, the tactical advantages of different methods of consultation on strikes were important. Ballots are most likely to be used when mass meetings reject a recommended offer, but the official suspects there is inadequate support for strike action: the officer goes for secret ballot on industrial action, expecting rejection. Similarly, following rejection of an offer mass meetings may be asked whether they wish to hold a secret ballot or a show of hands: secret ballots are likely to be preferred by the meeting when there is little support for strike. Secret ballots are also likely to be preferred where members are unwilling to repudiate union principles publicly, but also unwilling to support them in practice, as over discrimination issues: secret ballots provide a means of voting against virtue. Secret ballots are thus likely to produce less militant responses than alternative methods of consultation, in part because secret ballots are likely to be used in circumstances in which it is known or suspected that the membership holds non-militant views: the circumstances in which the method is likely to be used, rather than the method itself, is the crucial factor.

The role of ballots in collective bargaining in the GMWU has thus been limited. As in the TGWU, there has been increased reference back of agreements to the groups affected, but the normal method used has been to national and regional industrial conferences, even in sections in which ballots have occasionally been used. Ballots have been used in limited circumstances in some areas: gas (in 1973 only), water and electricity supply at national level, primarily for tactical reasons. The officials concerned were fearful of the consequences of the industrial action demanded by groups in the industry. In addition, in all three cases the bargaining structure of the industry, the operations of the bargaining system and multi-unionism provided favourable circumstances for the use of ballots. Elsewhere ballots have been used in specific circumstances, either for practical reasons (dispersed membership, continuous shift working) or for tactical reasons (enabling stewards to avoid responsibility for unpopular settlements). Where ballots have been held they have usually been either half postal, papers being distributed by the union and returned to the Electoral Reform Society (as in water) or, more frequently, workplace, returns being made to the union regional office (as in the regional strike ballots). However, GMWU officials, like TGWU officials, preferred to avoid committing themselves inflexibly to using ballots either on agreements or on strikes: the flexibility to use whatever method of consultation appeared appropriate, including ballots, was highly prized.

The Amalgamated Union of Engineering Workers (Engineering Section)

The AUEW(E) makes extensive use of postal ballots in union elections (see chapter 2). However, the union makes very little use of ballots in considering collective agreements or in deciding upon strike action: primary reliance is placed upon decision making by the relevant authoritative body, normally either the national committee or the district committee. The union rules empower the EC to organize postal ballots of the whole union, or part thereof, 'in matters which in their opinion affect the interests of the union', but the provision is rarely used. Provision is also made for balloting at district level, where a strike involving the whole district may be called only if endorsed by a 3 to 2 vote of members by ballot, but the provision is also infrequently used since disputes rarely involve the whole district membership. Nor is there any intention to extend the use of ballots either in reference back or in disputes: extending the use of ballots in such circumstances is seen more as a media preoccupation than as a real concern of union politics. The major exception to this negative conclusion is the organization of a ballot on the ICI agreement, where the members involved and the EC had different views: the circumstances are explained below (see pp. 153–4).

Under rule, and practice, policy-making responsibilities in the AUEW(E) are shared between the national committee, the executive council and the district committees. According to rule 13:

> The National Committee shall review agreements with the Engineering Employers Federation, or other employers, and suggest any alteration or amendments deemed necessary. They shall discuss past and future policy of the Union, with a view to giving the Executive Council instructions for the ensuing year, and may initiate any policy which they think would be beneficial to the Union. The function of the National Committee shall be to review working conditions and rates of wages or any other matters affecting members' interests.[22]

The National Committee is explicitly empowered under the same rule to call or to terminate a general strike when in their opinion time would not allow the members to be balloted. The national committee is thus the major policy-making body. At the same time the executive council is responsible for day-to-day administration, and is explicitly empowered to hold ballots of members whenever it believes it appropriate. Finally, district committees are empowered 'to deal with and regulate rates of wages, hours of labour, terms of overtime, piece-work, and general conditions affecting the interests of the trades in their respective districts', subject to the approval of the executive council and the exclusion of issues specifically referred to branches.[23] Where disputes affecting the whole district arise, the committee is required to organize a ballot, and a majority of 3 to 2 is required; where disputes affect only a single shop, the district committee can give approval forthwith. Responsibility for the conduct of negotiations, and therefore for the conduct of disputes, is thus split between the national committee, the executive council, and the district committees, according to the level of discussion and the urgency of the issue. Except in the case of district disputes, the appropriate body is able to follow any method of consultation (or none) with its members.

Although rules permit, even encourage, the use of ballots in negotiations, in practice little use is made of them: ballots are regarded as outside the 'normal tried process' of consultation. More importance is attached to bodies following proper procedures and confining themselves to decisions falling appropriately within their sphere of responsibility than to wide membership consultation. According to one interviewee, 'the custodian of the legal action is the district committee, which is subject to EC approval'; strikes are therefore capable of being carefully controlled. Full-time officers would not be able to negotiate effectively if all decisions were taken by postal ballot, thus undermining their authority. The district committees are in close touch with convenors, and convenors with stewards; stewards in turn consult their members either through mass meetings or through departmental meetings. An even higher proportion of AUEW(E) manual representatives reported consultations over the last wage agreement than TGWU or GMWU representatives, 90 per cent compared with 82 per cent and 77 per cent, respectively (see p. 129). There was thus an effective two-way channel of communication between decision-making bodies and the rank and file. Shop stewards were also subject to annual recall and re-election. The effectiveness of the reporting back process was reinforced by ensuring that full-time officials had direct experience of working at the trade; full-time officials were representative of the membership. It was therefore unnecessary to use ballots in collective bargaining because of the union's effective means of ensuring responsiveness through the electoral system. It was unlikely that the union would adopt the use of ballots in reference back or in disputes in the immediate future. There was no feeling that the increased use of ballots by other unions with whom the AUEW(E) conducted negotiations, for example the TGWU, would exert pressure on the AUEW to act similarly.

Although the AUEW(E) made little use of ballots in general, the union did ballot its ICI membership over the issue of withdrawal from the ICI weekly staff agreement, which covered eight manual unions. The experience illustrates the AUEW(E) view that ballots are only to be used in exceptional circumstances in collective bargaining rather than as a regular part of the process of consultation. There was long-standing discontent in ICI with the operation of the negotiating procedure, the skilled AUEW(E) members believing that participation in the joint committee reduced their stature and bargaining power. Resolutions seeking withdrawal had been submitted to the national committee for several years. The resolutions had been heavily defeated in the past, but in 1979 the committee was evenly split. The issue reappeared in 1980 and the national committee decided that a ballot would be the most appropriate way of resolving the issue. The initiative for the ballot arose from the members concerned. To maintain constitutional propriety the ballot was in the form of a request to the national committee: if unsuccessful, the national committee would be asked to withdraw from the joint negotiations. Since the EC was opposed to withdrawal and the EC was responsible for approving the wording of the ballot, the ballot paper contained several statements arguing against withdrawal – from the EC itself, from the other unions involved and from management. The majority of stewards were in favour of withdrawal. By a narrow majority (1,676 to 1,540) the members concerned voted for the status quo. Even the workers directly concerned who favoured withdrawal accepted that the ballot was decisive. There were significant practical difficulties involved in organizing the ballot, since the union had difficulty in obtaining the addresses of the relevant members. Moreover, major constitutional problems were seen in attempting to extend the practice, most notably the undermining of the responsibility of the national committee.

The only major example of the use of balloting nationally is the ICI manual staff agreement. However, there has been a small increase in the use of ballots at district level. As indicated earlier, districts can consult their members by whatever method they deem appropriate: 84 per cent of district secretaries stated that they and the stewards reported back to their members 'always' in general engineering, and 64 per cent reported similarly in companies with national or corporate agreements. The practice of referring back has increased slightly over the past three years, 16 per cent of district secretaries reporting an increase in reference back in general engineering and 17 per cent an increase in companies with national or corporate agreements. The major method of recording members' views on agreements remained a show of hands, very little change having taken place over the past three years. As table 3.10 shows, 77 per cent of officials indicated that agreements in general engineering were very frequently or always voted on by a show of hands, and 49 per cent in companies with national or corporate agreements.[24] Agreements were more likely to be voted on by non-postal ballot when they were corporate agreements than when they were in general engineering.

The pattern of responses on strike action was very similar: members

TABLE 3.10 Frequency of use of alternative methods of recording votes in AUEW(E)

Method of voting	General engineering (%) (n = 67)	Corporate agreements (%) (n = 60)
Show of hands	77	49
Ballot paper (non-postal)	5	7
Postal ballot	—	—

were normally consulted on both the calling and ending of strikes and the method most commonly used for recording decisions was a show of hands. Hence 99 per cent of district secretaries reported that members were very frequently or always asked to vote on strike action in general engineering, and 80 per cent in companies covered by national or corporate agreements. Similarly, 94 per cent reported that members were asked to vote on calling off strikes in general engineering and 78 per cent in companies covered by national or corporate agreements 'very frequently' or 'always'. More officials thought that the number of strike proposals being put to members had decreased than had increased, although this may have reflected the view that the number of strike proposals was decreasing not that the proportion of strike proposals being referred to members was declining. The methods used in recording strike votes are as would be expected from the methods used in reference back: the overwhelming majority of proposals are voted on by a show of hands, but some use of non-postal ballots is reported, especially in companies covered by national or corporate agreements. The opinions are summarized in table 3.11: only 2 per cent reported that postal ballots were frequently used in companies covered by national or corporate agreements, and 2 per cent always. Few

TABLE 3.11 Use of different methods of recording strike votes in the AUEW(E)

	Never	Very infrequently	Infrequently	Half/ half	Frequently	Very frequently	Always
General engineering							
Show of hands	—	—	—	9	9	43	38
Non-postal ballot paper	25	33	17	10	10	5	—
Postal ballot	87	8	5	—	—	—	—
National or corporate agreements							
Show of hands	3	8	6	10	11	32	29
Non-postal ballot	31	24	17	10	10	8	—
Postal ballot	79	12	5	—	2	—	2

officials believed that there had been any significant change within the last three years.

The amount of change reported by the district secretaries was thus small: the large majority believed that agreements were very frequently or always referred back, that strike proposals were very frequently or always voted upon and that the method of voting in all circumstances was most likely to be by show of hands. However, there were some changes, most significantly a substantial minority reporting an increase in the number of offers being referred back to the membership. The increase is attributed partly to members' increased expectation of consultation and partly to the recession: officers are unwilling to take responsibility for accepting or rejecting offers they know to be unsatisfactory. As one Midlands district secretary reported: 'We could not now be sure of automatic support from the membership as we may have done in the past. A low offer may have been rejected out of hand a few years ago – now it has to be referred back and in many cases is accepted.' Moreover, offers are increasingly having strings attached, adding to official uncertainty about their acceptability: reference back is the safest procedure in an uncertain situation. A very small minority of district secretaries reported that there had been an increase in the use of ballots to record votes, primarily because of practical difficulties in organizing meetings either because of shift working or because of management refusal of time-off for meetings. Moreover, media publicity was increasing membership awareness of ballots, leading to some pressure for them. Finally, ballots were especially desirable where a show of hands was indecisive. However, the number of district secretaries reporting an increase in the use of ballots was small, and the number reporting an increase in postal ballots negligible.

The role of ballots in collective bargaining in the AUEW(E) is thus limited. The view of senior officials in the union is that ballots are neither necessary nor desirable; unnecessary because the electoral system ensures responsiveness and undesirable because they would undermine the authority of the appropriate institutions, especially the national committee, and of the full-time officers. However, balloting has been used to resolve exceptionally difficult situations, in which substantial groups of workers disagree with EC policy, as at ICI. Moreover, there is some support amongst senior stewards for increased use of ballots. In the only major example of ballots being used there was little factional organization, the difference being between groups of members and the EC rather than between left and right. However, it is likely that increased use of ballots would result in increased factional activity in collective bargaining, with a consquential increase in difficulties of intra-union management.

The four unions examined thus made very different use of ballots. The NUM has made increasing use of ballots, both in industrial disputes and on other issues, although the widespread use is a recent development. Although the TGWU and GMWU have very different philosophies, with the TGWU under Jack Jones developing a philosophy of decentralization whilst the GMWU has continued to maintain a tradition of regional centralization, there is very little difference in the extent of their use of balloting; both the TGWU and the GMWU make use of ballots in exceptional circumstances, primarily as a means of resolving major internal management problems. The AUEW(E) makes less use of ballots in collective bargaining than the other three unions, the union officials regarding balloting as a potential threat to existing patterns of decision making.

CONCLUSION

In the concluding section we examine in turn the factors which lead unions to adopt ballots, and the consequences of adopting ballots for the process of consultation and for the outcomes of the process. Both workplace and postal ballots are of interest, although our major concern is with postal ballots, since they differ most markedly from traditional union methods of decision making, and might be thought to exercise a stronger influence on collective bargaining. Balloting has an obvious impact on the process of collective bargaining, leading to greater formalization, but there is little evidence to suggest that the process in itself, as distinct from the specific circumstances which lead to its adoption, has a major impact on the outcome of the process. Finally, we examine the two major requirements for effective balloting procedures – freedom from external pressure, and adequate information.

Factors Influencing Adoption of Ballots

There is a range of options available to union negotiators in processing management offers. Seven major options exist:

(1) Accept the offer forthwith.
(2) Refer offer to national executive (or subcommittee thereof).
(3) Refer offer to delegate conference (either the annual conference or a special conference).
(4) Refer offer to regional, district or branch committee without further specification.
(5) Refer offer to senior stewards or to stewards.
(6) Refer offer to stewards and to members directly involved.
(7) Refer offer to members whether directly involved or not.

Combinations of options are also possible. As already discussed, in the majority of instances offers are referred back to the members involved. Where offers are referred to groups or individuals, there is a range of methods of voting available and used: show of hands, postal ballot, non-postal ballot; the most commonly used methods are show of hands and non-postal ballot. There is also a variety of methods possible in counting the votes cast: individual or block vote. Finally, ballots may be more or less secret. With the evidence available, it is impossible to quantify the extent to which unions follow each combination of options. As the detailed case studies presented indicate, union rules are not a precise guide to action, and unions follow different options according to circumstances. Moreover, union officials involved are often unaware of the extent of different practices, even within their own sphere of responsibility: officials are likely to become involved only in exceptional circumstances, when difficulties arise. However, although a quantitative survey of the distribution of different practices was not feasible, it is possible to indicate characteristic configurations, and the factors influencing the adoption of different procedures, drawing upon the detailed case studies and upon extensive interviews with officials of other unions.

Of unions other than those discussed in detail above (where information is available on *de facto* practices), BIFU, NALGO, NGA'82. NUS and SOGAT'82 balloted their members routinely when industrial action was involved, whilst the CPSA, EETPU, Equity, NUR, POEU and UCATT did not; in the Bakers methods of consultation were left to branches, some branches using workplace and some postal ballots. Only a small number of unions have committed themselves to mandatory ballots on agreements or strikes, as already discussed. The number is increasing slowly; BIFU amended its rules to provide for strike ballots in 1980, and in 1982 the Association of First Division Civil Servants (FDA) amended their rules to provide for mandatory ballots of the the members affected for all disputes lasting longer than 24 hours (ballots are dispatched to the address given by the member, which might be home or work, and returned through the post to the union-appointed scrutineers: signatures are required on the ballot envelope). Other unions have decided to favour ballots as a matter of policy, without amending their rules. The Bakers decided upon mandatory reference back in 1974, without introducing rule changes, and without requiring specific procedures. Finally, other unions have examined their methods of consultation without introducing general changes, as the CPSA did in 1979. Most frequently, anxiety about methods of consultation did not lead to changes in rule, especially changes providing for mandatory ballots: a variety of methods of consultation was encouraged, according to circumstances.

In general, the procedures followed are influenced by the size and distribution of the constituency voting. Where reference is made to a limited constituency (national executive, delegate conference or regional, district or branch committees), it is clear that a show of hands or non-postal ballot is likely to be used, primarily the former. It is significant that balloting is rare even when the consultative process is widened to include stewards, and postal balloting almost non-existent (see table 3.7, p. 129). In practice, variation in method occurs only when offers are referred to stewards and members, whether directly involved or not – in practice the most common procedure. The most widely used practice remains that of the traditional mass meeting voting by show of hands, which is the most commonly used method amongst manual workers. However, as already indicated, there are differences between unions in the extent to which ballots, whether workplace or postal, are used. The major environmental and structural factors influencing the likelihood of using ballots are cultural expectations, the structure of collective bargaining, the nature and coverage of the collective agreement, the union's membership distribution and organizational structure and the production process.

Throughout the 1970s pressure for the decentralization of authority and increased rank-and-file involvement in decision making came from different political groups, outside as well as inside the trade union movement. Conservative politicians saw increased membership involvement as desirable in principle, as an increase in union democracy, allowing the moderate silent majority to influence union decisions. The preferred method for increasing involvement is through increased use of ballots, preferably postal ballots. Postal ballots are seen as enabling individual members to decide their attitudes privately, free from the pressure from other members of their work group (see chapter 1). Their views have been echoed in the national and local press, and by employers; some employers have balloted workers directly themselves (e.g. British Leyland); others have offered to pay for ballots, whilst others have offered to help with the distribution of ballot papers through the wages packet (as in electricity supply in 1980). At the same time some left-wing spokesmen, outside and inside the trade unions, have seen increased membership involvement as desirable in itself, and as a way of undermining the power of often 'right-wing' union bureaucrats, and of preventing the 'sell out' of members' interests. External writers on the left have stressed the importance of collective decision making, especially through workplace meetings. Within unions different groups have preferred different methods of consultation: the left-wing leadership of the scps consults through workplace meetings, whilst the left-led combine committee in electricity supply has campaigned for half postal ballots. Both right- and left-wing views have influenced union members and officials.

However, the influence of wider cultural expectations (and propaganda campaigns) is diffuse and impossible to measure. It is unlikely to be decisive in itself, unless reinforced by other pressures: although cultural expectations are uniform, there are wide variations in practice. Similarly, the influence of employers is likely to be limited, and may be counter-productive. Employers have an obvious interest in obtaining a majority for the acceptance of offers, union officials are often resentful of suggestions that managers have a better understanding of members' attitudes than themselves, and union members are anxious about possible employer influence. More directly important are the structure of collective bargaining, the union's own membership distribution and organizational structure, the production process and the negotiators' perceptions of the best means of achieving their objectives, whether to secure a settlement, to obtain authority for industrial action or simply to avoid fostering internal conflict.

Two aspects of the structure of collective bargaining are significant: the degree of centralization and the extent of multi-unionism. The use of ballots is more likely when collective bargaining is centralized than when it is decentralized. This is partly because centralized bargaining is associated with national coverage, and the desirability of obtaining comparable opinions from different groups, and partly because centralization is associated with increased bureaucracy and direct contact between national officials and rank-and-file members. There are also practical reasons for centralized bargaining being associated with balloting. The union officials involved are likely to have the time to concentrate both upon the process of negotiations and upon disseminating relevant information to the membership. However, centralized bargaining does not inevitably lead to the use of ballots: the NUR, for example, operates within a collective bargaining structure very similar to that of the NUM (single employer, annual national negotiations, national determination of rates, including overtime and bonus rates) but makes no use of ballots.

Linked to the structure of collective bargaining is the nature and coverage of the agreement. Two elements are relevant: the effect of the agreement upon actual earnings, and the uniformity of impact of the agreement. Where the agreement determines only a national minimum, of little significance for actual earnings, it is unlikely that balloting will occur, because of the expense and time involved: if the agreement determines earnings, balloting is more likely. Hence the unions involved in the CSEU negotiations with the EEF in 1979 considered balloting their members, but the possibility was not pursued and the decision to approve the final agreement was made by a conference of executives, largely because the effect of the agreement upon earnings was thought to be limited. Balloting is also unlikely when an agreement affects separate groups differently, since it is regarded as unfair. Hence there were reservations in the GMWU about the fairness of balloting on the fibreboard carton agreement since it affected workers at Reeds, the largest company, differently from other workers because of a company grading scheme. Not all agreements directly determining earnings and affecting large groups of workers uniformly are balloted, as the contrast between the NUR and the NUM procedures indicates; however, it is unlikely that ballots would be held either where the agreement had only a limited impact on earnings or where it affected separate groups differently.

The second set of factors directly affecting the use of ballots relates to the union's membership distribution and structure. Postal ballots are more likely to be held where members are widely dispersed than where they are concentrated in large groups. Thus the only practical method of consulting managers in the Scottish hotel and catering sector in the GMWU was through postal ballot; similarly in the NUS. On the other hand, where members are concentrated in large plants there is obviously less practical need for the use of postal ballots. Moreover, where branch structure and bargaining unit structure do not coincide [as the AUEW(E)], unions may not have the home addresses of members of a specific bargaining unit available, and may be reluctant to rely upon obtaining them from management, even if management is willing to provide them. Postal ballots on collective agreements are therefore difficult in practical terms. Similar practical problems face unions organizing workers in industries with mobile workforces, as in the construction industry. The availability of alternative channels of consultation, through regional or industrial conferences, influences the extent of recourse to postal ballots; where lower level conferences are an established part of union structure, as in the GMWU, there are obvious channels for consultation available. Postal ballots are an extra cost. More importantly, postal ballots can be seen as undermining other consultative methods: hence there was some hostility to postal ballots in the TGWU because they threatened the effectiveness of other methods of consultation, including delegate conferences (public services), recorded voting in meetings (public services, London region), mass meetings (cars) and workplace ballots (oil tanker drivers).

Finally, the use of ballots is influenced by the method of choosing officials; the use of postal ballots is more likey to occur where officials are appointed rather than elected. Elected officials, especially where subject to recall or re-election, are seen as representatives of the membership and accountable through the electoral process. In the AUEW(E) ballots on national agreements were seen as unnecessary because of the electoral system (although, of course, no official stated that ballots were necessary because appointed officials had less legitimacy than elected officials). Some unions with elected officials use postal ballots on agreements; however, the unions using postal ballots are more likely to have appointed their senior officials (BIFU, NALGO).

Two aspects of the production process influence the use of ballots: the degree of conflict between occupational groups within the same bargaining unit and shift working. Balloting is likely to occur where there is sharp conflict between occupational groups in the same bargaining unit because balloting provides a means of resolving conflicts without generating tensions. Hence balloting was seen as desirable in some glass container branches in both the GMWU and the TGWU as a way of limiting the conflict between linked but often antagonistic groups. There are obviously practical advantages in using ballots in plants with extensive shift working, since shift working makes it difficult to gather the membership together (especially shifts operated on the 'continental' system). There are obvious disadvantages, even for the use of ballots, since the ballot-boxes are required to be open, and supervised, for an extended period of time to allow all shifts to participate. However, the practical difficulties involved in organizing ballots are on the whole less than the practical difficulties involved in organizing mass or departmental meetings.

There are thus environmental and structural factors which increase the likelihood of postal or workplace ballots. However, such factors are not in themselves decisive: not all centralized unions negotiating with a single employer, with an agreement affecting all members similarly, use postal ballots. For example, the POEU makes no use of postal ballots; agreements are usually approved by the annual conference, meeting in June, and the 1979 annual conference rejected a proposal that ballots should be held before strikes. Similarly, a union may use ballots in one sector because of shift working, as in the glass container sector of the GMWU, but not in another, e.g. chemicals. More important is the extent to which ballots, whether postal or otherwise, are seen as a means of resolving particular difficulties, usually tactical. As already indicated, balloting is rarely specified as being *required* by rule either on agreements or on strikes; where it is specified either in rule or in conference decision the reason is usually a specific major instance of conflict leading to tension between rank-and-file members and executive. From the interviews conducted, there emerged a general presupposition that postal ballots were not, in general, desirable: there was therefore an overall tendency against using postal ballots. However, ballots (including but not most extensively postal ballots) were seen as a desirable method of consultation in specific circumstances, either for reasons of bargaining strategy with employers, or more frequently, internal union management problems.

Organizing strike ballots can be used as an indication of seriousness of purpose in collective bargaining. Hence, the EETPU uses strike ballots as the occasion demands primarily as a means of putting pressure on management for a settlement: consultation on offers is usually with national and area industrial conferences, the executive being empowered to conclude agreements without further consultation or reference back. However, ballots have serious disadvantages as a collective bargaining tactic, since they constitute a fixed commitment and therefore reduce flexibility. Once a ballot has been taken, the room for manoeuvre is limited. Moreover, if employers know that ballots are customarily held there is a temptation to undercut the negotiating process by making the initial offer the final offer, and insisting on a ballot: if the offer is accepted the employer is satisfied; if rejected, the next offer can be put out to ballot.

More frequently, ballots are used as a means of resolving internal union problems. Ballots are seen as a particularly decisive means of resolving difficult problems, involving disagreement between important groupings; hence the use of a ballot in the AUEW(E) over participation in joint negotiations over the weekly staff agreement at ICI in 1980. Ballots are also useful in providing clear-cut answers with which there is little disagreement: ballots are seen as being decisive. The use of ballots also reduces the pressures upon officials, especially necessary during recession, in which negotiators are uncertain about the response anticipated from members involved. Ballots resolve uncertainties, and avoid personal blame. However at the same time ballots which produce unexpected results produce major difficulties, as experience in the electricity supply negotiations in 1980 indicates. Unexpected rejection leaves negotiators, who believe that there is no more money available, with a difficult task.

Moreover, the decisiveness of balloting itself limits flexibility, resulting in major difficulties in resolving differences.

The use of ballots, especially postal ballots, in collective bargaining is thus relatively limited. This is not because unions are insensitive to their members' views. Consultation is not the only priority for negotiators: effectiveness in collective bargaining, both for the specific group involved and for the wider collectivity, is also necessary. There is therefore a need to ensure that consultation procedures do not inhibit the bargaining process by limiting the room for manoeuvre, by revealing damaging divisions to employers, by causing harmful delays or by securing short-term advantages for specific groups at the expense of wider interests. There is also the need to adapt the consultation procedures to the industrial environment within which the union operates, and the collective bargaining structure. Finally, there is the particular need to avoid undercutting normal decision-making machinery by creating special procedures, whether special conferences or special ballots. The conflicting pressures upon negotiators mean that there is no universally desirable or effective method of securing membership agreement. In some circumstances it is desirable to rely upon existing institutions, and not to consult members about specific decisions: if the union political system is working effectively, specific *ad hoc* arrangements are unnecessary and may damage routine procedures. In other circumstances consultation through special conferences may be appropriate, providing means for the full exploration of offers made, and of alternative responses: two-way communication is difficult through balloting procedures. Finally, balloting may be desirable where practical circumstances require it or where particular circumstances require precise answers.

Consequences of Balloting

In assessing the consequences of balloting for collective bargaining, it is helpful to distinguish between its effect on the process and its effect on the outcomes.

The effects of increased balloting on the process of negotiations is threefold. First, it inevitably lengthens the process of bargaining. The length of time taken to carry out a ballot obviously depends upon the mechanics of the process, whether the ballot is postal, half postal or carried out at the branch or workplace; workplace ballots are the speediest, although in other respects less satisfactory. Time is obviously necessary to prepare and dispatch documentation, whether to the branch official or to the individual member, to allow the branch officer to call a meeting to inform members about the issues involved (or to hold a ballot meeting), and if necessary to allow the individual member to consider his views. At the very minimum balloting requires a week to implement: in the ASTMS a ballot was organized and carried out in eight days, with the result of workplace ballots being phoned through to the full-time officer concerned (ballot on the Legal and General offer, April–May 1982). More commonly, balloting requires three weeks or a month to allow procedures to be followed through adequately. The length of time taken of course increases if initial information is incorrect or misleading. If a single negotiation requires more than one ballot the process of referring back and consulting the membership may extend to several months. The effect of lengthening the process may be to increase the pressure for settlement, with members anxious to collect backpay where the settlement date has passed. Delay before being able to carry out industrial action may also provide time for 'cooling-off', reducing the emotional temperature surrounding an issue, and providing the employer with an opportunity to assess the situation and possibly increase the offer. On the other hand, delay may increase membership commitment to achieving initial objectives, increasing the difficulties in securing a negotiated agreement. The extent to which delay in itself reduces or increases the ease of securing a settlement is likely to depend upon events during the consultation process: but it is as likely to increase commitment to positions already taken up as to increase flexibility.

Secondly, ballots are likely to increase the formal nature of the negotiating process, especially where postal ballots are involved; similarly, complex and formal written offers by management are likely to facilitate the use of ballots. Where full postal ballots are involved it is necessary for the union to prepare a full statement of the offer under discussion, or draft agreement, and to explain the negotiators', or executive's, position. For a postal ballot the explanatory memorandum is likely to extend to at least two pages. To avoid confusion, or the need for more than one ballot, negotiators will obviously attempt to ensure that all eventualities are covered in the document. Where ballots are half postal or workplace, or where postal ballots are routinely accompanied by branch or workplace meetings (as is usually the case), there is obviously less need to detail proposals on paper: but information meetings clearly increase the influence of branch officials or stewards, limiting the role of balloting as a means of obtaining the expression of individual rather than group views. Where external bodies are used to carry out the ballot, or external pressure leads to specification of minimum levels of information being made available to the ballot, the formal character of the process is likely to increase. Such formal procedure may or may not be desirable in itself: at the very least it facilitates investigation of any subsequent complaint, and provides relatively comparable results.

Thirdly, balloting inevitably reduces the flexibility available to negotiators. Implicit understandings between management and union negotiators become difficult to sustain, firm proposals and commitments being required before the balloting process becomes practicable. Informal tests of membership opinion become more difficult to carry out. Strike ballots lead to reduced flexibility where the ballot involves specifying clearly the conditions under which strike action will be carried out. On the other hand, strike ballots on the issue of granting negotiating bodies discretionary authority to call strikes hardly increases union democracy. Reduced flexibility involves limiting the autonomy of union negotiators, and limiting their ability to tailor the negotiating process to their conception of the union's interest. Union officials become, in their view, a post-box between the employer and the membership, rather than responsible leaders. Flexibility is especially limited where balloting becomes an annual event, with routine procedures; *ad hoc* ballots do not necessarily have the same consequence.

The effect of balloting upon the outcome of the process of collective bargaining is difficult to assess because balloting is used in specific circumstances. As indicated above, the circumstances under which unions ballot their members on wage offers are highly specific: the effects of the circumstance are therefore impossible to disentangle from the effects of the process of balloting. Moreover, when considering the use of strike ballots it is difficult to distinguish the independent effects of the decision-making process used from the effects of the circumstances leading to the use of ballots: it would be misleading to attribute the growth of militancy on a national level in the NUM in the 1970s to the increased use of ballots; both the increased use of ballots and the increased militancy were the result of other pressures within and outside the union. Nevertheless, it is important to examine three issues. First, does balloting increase membership participation in decisions and therefore make outcomes more democratic? Secondly, do ballots merely reinforce decisions already made by union officials? Thirdly, does the use of ballots increase or reduce the incidence of industrial conflict?

Union members are concerned about the collective agreements relating to their bargaining units, and about industrial action which may involve them: there has been little concern about the level of membership interest in such issues, in contrast to the extensive concern about the low level of participation in union elections. Unfortunately, it is impossible to quantify the effect of introducing ballots in this area, since there is no reliable evidence on the level of membership participation in mass meetings called to discuss industrial action or to ratify collective agreements. Moreover, many union statistics on the size of the relevant constituency are imprecise. However, as in elections to union office, membership participation is likely to be higher in balloting systems, especially workplace balloting systems, because they do not require attendance at a specific place at a specific time. Moreover, the inconvenience involved is likely to be less where the ballot does not require attendance at a meeting. Hence in the NUM the level of participation in the workplace ballots held between 1969 and 1982 averaged over 80 per cent; although there is no reliable evidence on the level of participation before the extensive use of ballots, it is unlikely to have been at such a consistently high level. Moreover, balloting systems permit a more precise delineation of the relevant constituency than mass meetings, facilitating steps to ensure that only members eligible to participate in the decision do so, although ballots do not make electoral malpractice impossible. Balloting systems therefore provide reassurance, if only limited, that only union members eligible to participate in particular decisions do so. As in elections to union office, the level of participation is likely to be higher in workplace ballots than in postal ballots. In short, the use of ballots is likely to have a limited but positive effect upon the level of membership participation, but a more substantial effect upon the accuracy of the count.

There are two alternative views on the extent to which ballots are merely a means of confirming decisions taken elsewhere. On the one hand, some officials believed that, where they had a choice, union negotiators would only ballot the membership if they were confident of the outcome of the ballot; ballots were a means of conferring legitimacy on decisions made elsewhere. The consequences of unexpected outcomes were so great, both in practice and in loss of face, that negotiators would avoid going to ballot unless confident of the results; since negotiators determined the question, and had a major influence upon the relevant information available, they were normally able to ensure that balloting confirmed the negotiators' preferences, whether for acceptance or rejection. An alternative view is that negotiators only ballot when they are uncertain of the outcome; balloting in other circumstances is a waste of time and money, and could cause unexpected difficulties if mishandled. Ballots were therefore only held when negotiators were uncertain, or themselves divided. Hence ballots were likely to increase during recession because negotiators were uncertain about how far their members would be willing to support industrial action; the use of ballots would also be likely to grow in politically divided unions, where definitive outcomes were necessary to the consultation process.

Ballots are likely to be confirmatory in unions where officials are already authoritative for other reasons. Hence in the EETPU ballots tend to confirm decisions already taken. On the other hand, ballots are more frequently used to resolve continuing uncertainties with a conclusive decision, as in the AUEW(E). In particularly uncertain circumstances or for tactical reasons ballots are held without an executive recommendation. However, doing so can be risky, since it increases the uncertainties further and could be taken as an indication of leadership weakness. It is thus customary for ballots to be held with an executive recommendation. Such recommendations are thought to be accepted more frequently than rejected. On the other hand, rejections are not unknown, as the experience in electricity supply indicates. The disadvantage of ballots as a means of resolving long-standing difficulties is that they result in clear-cut decisions, but the reasons for the decisions are unclear. Where ballots result in positive majorities, whether for endorsing agreements or for strike action, this limitation on knowledge is not important. However, where ballots result in negative votes there is little basis for future policy formulation: doors are closed but none is opened. Consultation through industrial, regional, branch or workplace meetings produces less conclusive answers to specific questions, but the answers provide a basis for future decisions if there is no support for an obvious positive answer.

Does the use of ballots reduce the likelihood of industrial conflict? One union official interviewed said he would only hold a ballot where he did not want a strike; other methods of consultation would be used if he wanted to obtain approval for industrial action. It was assumed that ballots (postal or workplace) would be less likely to produce votes for strike action than consultations with stewards or with rank-and-file members through mass meetings. During a recession it is therefore likely that the extensive use of ballots is associated with reductions in the frequency of industrial conflict. Rank-and-file members are obviously fearful of the damage of industrial action to their firm's economic prospects and to their jobs. Similarly, unions losing members, and therefore facing financial pressures, are less likely to wish to pay strike benefits during a recession. However, the effect is a result of the economic environment as much as the method of consultation; even with other methods of consultation union officials would hesitate before calling for industrial action. Moreover, during periods of economic prosperity ballots are likely to reinforce the hands of union executives urging rejection, with no reduction in the level of industrial conflict. In short, decision-making procedures do not determine outcomes: in different circumstances the same procedure is likely to produce a different outcome.

Preconditions for Effective Balloting

There are two major conditions for the effective use of ballots: the individual should be able to exercise his or her vote free from the influence of others (preferably in secret) and he or she should have sufficient information to make a reasoned decision. In addition, it has been suggested that the question balloted upon should have the same meaning for all voters. Where unions fail to provide either freedom from pressure or inadequate information, union ballots are less than fully satisfactory. Both conditions are difficult to fulfil.

The organization of ballots on a full postal basis makes secrecy possible (unless the individual voter chooses to reveal his preferences). However, full postal ballots are the most demanding organizationally: the responsible union body requires comprehensive and up-to-date lists of the home addresses of the electorate, funds for postage and administrative resources for distributing and counting the completed ballot papers. Moreover, critics of postal balloting allege that the procedure maximizes the influence of the mass media, exerting pressure on the individual voter, usually either to accept the offer or to vote against strike action. Full postal ballots are also likely to require the longest time to organize and carry out. Where ballots are half postal, and even more where workplace based, the possibilities of influence by stewards or by workmates are more extensive. The ability to influence voters at workplace ballots is obviously less than in workplace meetings. Nevertheless, workplace ballots are rarely in practice secret: even where booths are provided, individuals are eager to vote quickly and get home or into work, and unwilling to queue for voting booths. Moreover, unions differ in the extent to which ballot papers require the signature of the individual voter. Since ballots on offers or on strikes are less routine than elections for union officers, fewer requirements are laid on the voter than in elections for union office. Nevertheless, where ballot papers require the voter's signature – as a rough check on fraud – it is obviously possible for individual votes to become known; it is also possible, although less likely, that individual votes can be identified when signatures are required on the ballot envelope. Finally, the effect of the media appears to be of limited importance in influencing the results of alternative decision-making processes: the media can influence voters whether the decision-making process is by postal ballot, workplace ballot or mass meeting.

The second requirement for effective balloting is the availability of adequate relevant information. The information required includes details of the offers made, of the arguments for and against alternative responses and of the negotiating body or executive's recommendation. Such information can be provided in documentary form and accompany the ballot paper. However, the circulation of extensive documentation is expensive, both in the costs of administration and postage. Moreover, there is the possibility that the documentation will not be read by some of the voters, especially if the ballot is a national one. It is therefore customary to arrange workplace meetings where practicable to explain the issues involved and to provide the opportunity for questioning, even where ballots are organized on a full postal basis. Such meetings provide the opportunity for stewards and union activists to influence the decision-making process.

The requirement that the issues should have the same significance for members participating in the ballot is impossible to satisfy. Reactions to offers are likely to be influenced by personal financial situation as well as by industrial relations matters, and will obviously vary widely. There is likely to be greater uniformity in the impact of decisions on industrial action, although even in industrial action there are likely to be different circumstances. It is therefore inevitable that union members participating in ballots will not be faced with the same circumstances, and it would be unduly constricting to attempt to confine ballots to circumstances in which they did.

In examining the role of ballots in union affairs an implicit comparison is usually made with the national political system: methods appropriate to the national system are transposed to the industrial relations system. However, the analogy is of only limited relevance: industrial relations in general, and trade unions in particular, are not comparable to the national political system, and the institutions and procedures of the one are not necessarily appropriate to those of the other. In both environments, democracy involves leaders being responsive to the interests and views of their constituents, although the interests and views are, of course, often different. There are alternative methods of ensuring this responsiveness, most markedly through electoral procedures, or through referenda. In both Parliament and trade unions, elected officials are representatives rather than delegates, with the expectation that they would use their judgement in responding to changing circumstances, whether in political affairs generally or in collective bargaining specifically. The sanction against ineffectiveness and lack of responsiveness lies in the effective working of the system of representation, not in providing for referenda on specific issues. Where the representative system does not work effectively there may be pressure for decision making by formal ballots or, in extreme circumstances, the formation of breakaway unions.

4 Ballots under the Employment Act 1980

The scheme established under the balloting provisions of the 1980 Employment Act came into effect on 1 October 1980. The Government hoped that, in due course if not immediately, major unions would seek monies under the scheme to pay for balloting. Furthermore, the scheme might increase the use of balloting either directly by persuading union officials that the substantial costs of balloting were no longer a major barrier to its use or, indirectly, by encouraging union members to urge their leaders to adopt balloting. In addition, the scheme would enable unions already using balloting extensively but worried about the expense to continue doing so, for example, most importantly, the AUEW(E). In the event, the TUC policy of refusing to cooperate with the scheme was followed by all affiliated unions, and no TUC-affiliated union has yet applied for money under the scheme (November 1983). The Government's hopes have therefore been disappointed. However, the scheme is important for three reasons. First, a small number of TUC affiliates, notably the AUEW(E) and Equity, seriously discussed seeking funds under the scheme, before deciding against doing so, for reasons discussed below. Secondly, a number of non-TUC unions sought money under the scheme. How the certification officer has operated the scheme in relation to these applications is important both in itself and as a guide to how certain key aspects of legislation (for example, 'reasonably practicable' steps to ensure secrecy) might be interpreted by industrial tribunals or by the courts when legislation enforcing ballots is introduced. Finally, the refusal of TUC unions to seek funds under the scheme, indicating an apparent lack of interest in balloting, provided a major political argument for the introduction of mandatory legislation on ballots: voluntary methods had failed, even when the costs of reform had been covered by the public purse. As the Government stressed in the 1983 Green Paper, *Democracy in Trade Unions* (p. 1):

It is because the trade unions have refused the opportunity to reform themselves voluntarily that the possibility of legislation has now to be considered. The Employment Act 1980 enables unions to claim back the costs of postal ballots on various matters from public funds, but no unions affiliated to the Trades Union Congress have availed themselves of these funds, and the opportunity to extend members' rights at small cost to the unions themselves has been thrown away.

THE 1980 SCHEME

The Employment Act 1980, section 1, provided for the Secretary of State to make regulations concerning payments by the certification officer towards certain expenditures incurred by unions using secret ballots for a prescribed range of decisions. The scheme was subsequently extended in July 1982, under the statutory instrument arrangements explicitly provided for in the Act, to include the reference back to union members of employers' proposals affecting contractual terms and conditions.[1] Regulations coming into operation in October 1980 and September 1982 detailed the decisions which qualified for a subsidy, the kind of ballot to be promoted, the conditions under which payment would be made and the payments to be made.[2]

The decisions qualifying for subsidy included: the calling or ending of a strike or other industrial action; elections to the executive committee and to the positions of president, chairman, secretary or treasurer or to any elected position held as an employee of the union; amending the rules and obtaining a merger. Thus shop steward elections were not recognized for a subsidy. The reference back of employer's proposals was narrowed by the 1982 Regulations from the Act's contractual terms and conditions to that '. . . which relates in whole or in part to remuneration (whether in money or money's worth), hours of work, level of performance, holidays or pensions'.[3]

Although the 1980 Act was not restricted to postal ballots, the scheme established under the Act has been restricted to postal ballots. In order to qualify the individual member has to mark and return a ballot paper by post to the union or some other counting agent. In 1982 'post' was limited to the postal service provided by the Post Office or a postal service which did not infringe the Post Office's privileged position.[4] This change was made to clarify the definition of 'post' after the certification officer had refused requests for subsidies from non-TUC unions using internal post or deliveries by hand when returning at least some of their ballot papers for counting.

The conditions to be satisfied when making a claim for payment require that the union's rules are not contravened, and that any rules governing the conduct of ballots are complied with. The constituency to be involved in the calling or ending of strikes is also defined '. . . so as to ensure that all members likely to be called upon to participate in the action, or participating in the action, as the case may be, were entitled to vote'.[5] A somewhat similar clause in the later 1982 Regulations governing reference back of employer's proposals also touched on the constituency and defined it as '. . . only the persons who were union members and were affected by the proposal . . .'[6] There was no reference as to who should write the question or what it should contain. The union was required to allow voting without interference or constraint, and to ensure that those entitled to vote had a fair opportunity to do so. Furthermore, reference was also made to the fair counting of votes. However, the certification officer was given some discretion to allow payment where the union had failed to comply with its own rules, if this had no significant effect upon the proper conduct of the ballot. Perhaps more importantly, the certification officer could also withhold payment if '. . . any assurance he requests from the trade union relating to the said conditions is not given'.[7]

Payment towards the cost of the ballot covered a contribution to stationery and printing, including voting papers, envelopes, and '. . . any material enclosed with the voting papers which explains the matter to which the question to be voted upon relates to the procedure for voting'.[8] Second-class postage was also included and in some circumstances first-class postage could be allowed, depending on the certification officer's judgement.

TRADE UNION RESPONSE: TUC UNIONS

The role of the certification officer in operating the scheme is reactive: whether unions apply for monies under the scheme is their own affair. The success of the scheme therefore depended upon the trade union response: if unions refused to apply for funds there was nothing the certification officer, or the Government, could do without further legislation. The Government hoped that unions which were known to be anxious about the costs of their existing balloting arrangements would either persuade the TUC to relax its policy of non-cooperation or defy the policy. Neither development occurred. Nevertheless, both the AUEW(E) and Equity discussed seriously the possibility of seeking monies, before deciding against doing so.

As discussed in chapters 2 and 3, only a small number of TUC unions are required by rule to use the kind of secret postal ballots for elections, reference back and strikes which would qualify for a refund under the 1980 scheme. Tables 4.1 and 4.2 summarize the requirement under rule to use postal ballots (full and half postal) in respect of elections, and other decisions including reference back, strikes and rule changes.

However, as was revealed by the case studies, unions make more use of postal ballots in practice for the reference back of employer's proposals than the rule provisions suggest. Many more unions than those listed above could therefore have claimed a refund from the certification officer. However, only three TUC affiliates, the AUEW(E), EETPU and Equity,

TABLE 4.1   Postal ballots and elections

Office	No. of unions using postal ballot
General secretary	8
President/chairman	10
Treasurer	6
Full-time officers	5
Executive committees	15

TABLE 4.2   Postal ballots and decisions

Decisions	No. of unions with rules requiring postal ballots
Reference back	—
National strikes	3
Local strikes	1
Rule changes	4

considered applying for a refund. The EETPU was one of the few TUC unions which welcomed the Government's support for postal ballots.[9] However, it did not seriously pursue its own application once it became clear that the AUEW (E)'s national committee, which met in May, had voted against using the fund and pre-empted the EETPU's debate arranged for June 1981. For, without the support of the AUEW(E), it was likely that the EETPU, not the most popular union in the TUC, would have been exposed to the full weight of the TUC's sanctions. Thus, the AUEW(E)'s decision was crucial to the TUC in maintaining a united front against applying for funds.

Before the AUEW(E)'s national committee meeting in May 1981 leading members of the Group within the national full-time leadership had been campaigning for some months for a vote in favour of taking Government funds for elections.[10] This policy was adopted despite the decision of the TUC in 1980 to adopt a motion expressing support for '. . . a sustained and vigorous campaign of non-cooperation with the Government . . .'[11] However, an attempt to pass a motion calling for the automatic expulsion of any union participating in the scheme was blocked before the TUC's 1980 conference, when an amendment urging such action was lost by the withdrawal of the original motion to which the amendment had been attached. Thus the AUEW(E)'s national full-time leadership was willing to risk the censure of the TUC. This was probably a calculated risk influenced by the thought that the AUEW(E), as the second largest member of the TUC, would be unlikely to be expelled for taking the money, particularly as they expected the EETPU to follow their lead.

The Group in the AUEW(E) had a convincing majority on the 1981 national committee of 57 to 34,[12] but it was clear from comments in the press that the president and general secretary were having difficulty persuading the lay members of the Group to accept that they should support an executive-inspired motion to apply for a refund under the Government's scheme.[13] Those in the Group arguing against taking the Government's money stressed the importance of maintaining a united front within the TUC against the Conservative legislation by not taking 'the carrot' offered by the balloting subsidy. Attention was also drawn to the dangers inherent in requesting a refund when the certification officer's brief (*Funds for Trade Union Ballots*, October 1980) provided that he could make '. . . other inquiries of the union as he thinks fit'. This, it was suggested, would lead to the certification officer interfering in the AUEW(E)'s internal affairs. It appeared that several members of the Group speaking against taking the money were also mandated by the divisions they represented to take this stance, and to have done otherwise could have had an adverse effect on their future careers within the union.

The president and general secretary countered by assuring the Group that the certification officer would not use the opportunity to inquire into the union's electoral system. They also stressed the cost of not applying for a refund when the union was spending approximately £290,000 a year on postal ballots. Ironically, their opponents within the Group employed the slogan 'what price democracy', originally used in the 1970s debates in support of postal ballots, to counteract the full-time officials main argument for taking the Government's money. Parallels were also drawn by the supporters of the application between the TUC's willingness to accept Government money for educational purposes and the offer of money for ballots. However, the Group's leading national officials failed to persuade their opponents, and the executive's motion supporting an application to the certification officer was lost by 55 to 36 votes.[14]

Equity's lay national leadership went one stage further than the AUEW(E)'s full-time executive in its bid for Government money. In January 1982 Equity's lay national council decided to apply to the certification officer for a refund of expenditure incurred in their ballots. An application was subsequently made but later withdrawn.[15] The union was in financial difficulty at the time, and a subsidy towards the cost of postal ballots, running at approximately £10,000 a year, would have been most welcome. However, Equity's rule book allows the membership to challenge council's decisions at the annual general meeting or a special general meeting. Further, the membership may petition for a referendum on the question at issue, the result of which is '. . . binding unless and until it is altered or reversed by a further referendum taken in accordance with this rule'.[16] The membership opposed to the council's decision to apply for a subsidy successfully challenged the council's policy under both procedures. First, they carried a majority of 394 to 89 at the annual general meeting in April 1982 and, secondly, they petitioned for a referendum. The referendum was granted, and carried out (by postal ballot). The ballot confirmed the union's opposition to the Government's scheme by 2,396 votes to 1,323.

Thus, the council's proposal to apply for a refund for its postal ballots was itself overturned in a postal ballot.

Equity's procedure for calling a referendum allows those challenging the council's decision to determine the question asked. This was an important factor in the ballot. The question actually posed widened the debate beyond the simple issue of whether or not to apply for a refund to the consequences of such action for Equity's relationship with the TUC and its member unions. The resolution in the referendum was:

> This Annual General Meeting, recognizing the extreme dangers to the interests of all Equity members in the Government's employment legislation, declares its unequivocal support for the TUC's policy of opposition to the Employment Act of 1980 as adopted by the Congress in 1980 and reaffirmed at the Congress of 1981 and, as part of this support, instructs the Council immediately to reverse its decision of 26 January to apply for Government finance for postal ballots under the terms of the Act, and furthermore to oppose similar provisions in the Employment Bill 1982.[17]

In their supporting arguments, contained in the referendum document, the opponents of seeking Government funds raised many of the arguments previously used in the AUEW(E) debate. Stress was again placed on loyalty to the TUC and independence from the state, but the main argument concerned the consequences for Equity of expulsion from the TUC. For, by 1982, the TUC had adopted a tougher policy than in 1980. As mentioned in Equity's document, the general council was now recommending that: 'Affiliated unions shall observe Congress policy and not seek or accept public funds for union ballots under the Employment Act 1980 ballot funds scheme.' Moreover, at the TUC's Conference of Executives of Affiliated Unions called in April 1982 to discuss the Government's policies, the AUEW(E) stated that it would not again attempt to take any funds from the existing Government for postal ballots. Thus Equity, a relatively minor member of the TUC, stood exposed in 1982 as the only TUC affiliate likely to fragment an otherwise united front. Expulsion was a serious threat. Moreover, in Equity's case expulsion was seen as '. . . the most serious threat to our closed shop in Equity's history'; outside the TUC Equity would be '. . . exposed to poaching from other unions', and would 'begin to disintegrate, to become a small association for the successful few. Only inside the TUC can Equity continue to fulfil its function as the sole representative body for professional performers'.[18] This argument proved conclusive in persuading Equity's members that they should not apply for a refund.

Thus in both the AUEW(E) and Equity, leadership responsible for keeping an oversight of union funds found the Government's offer of financial support tempting. The sums involved were much larger in the AUEW(E) than in Equity, but Equity's needs were more immediate. Nevertheless, the principle of union solidarity and the fear of the consequences of expulsion from the TUC enabled those not directly responsible for the unions' financial well-being to mount a successful campaign against taking the money. In the AUEW(E) this involved a minor revolt by members of the moderate Group, and in Equity a majority rank-and-file vote, by postal ballot, against the Government's scheme. Hence political and industrial concerns carried more weight than financial considerations.

OPERATION OF THE SCHEME: NON-TUC UNIONS

Among non-TUC unions the Government found a more positive response to the scheme. Between December 1980 and December 1982 the certification officer received 31 applications from non-TUC affiliates covering 36 ballots.[19] The applications were evenly divided over the two years, with 16 in the first full year and 15 in the second. Some unions made more than one application (table 4.3), and a subsidy was paid in 22 cases. The rate of rejection was much higher in the first year of the scheme than in the second. In the first full year 11 ballots failed to qualify for a subsidy. Of these, 3 were not for appropriate purposes, 2 were held before the scheme became operative, 2 failed to meet the secrecy provisions, 3 did not meet the postal provisions and 1 did not comply with the union's own rules. In the second year only two ballots, both claimed by the same union, were rejected on the grounds that they were not secret. Thus it would appear that in the second year the certification officer either made it easier for unions to qualify for a refund or the unions themselves became more proficient in their applications. A change in the regulations, which made it clear that all ballot papers had to be returned via the Post Office, also assisted claims by removing any doubt about which method of delivery would qualify for a refund.[20]

The number of individual unions applying for a refund over the two years was 19, of which 14 were successful. As a proportion of non-TUC affiliates, the 19 represented 5 per cent of the 357 non-TUC unions listed in the certification officer's 1982 Report. Non-TUC unions did not therefore flock to take advantage of the scheme. There is no evidence of the proportion of non-TUC unions using postal ballots, but given that so few opted to use the scheme, despite the wide publicity associated with its launch, it is probable that very few do.

Public sector unions comprised the majority of unions applying for money: 14 of the 19 unions requesting a refund recruited primarily, if not solely, in the public sector (table 4.3). In particular, 7 unions were in the health service and 4 in the education service. These unions generally recruited dispersed and mobile members and some had no intermediate – branch, district or regional – structure for communication and discussion with their members. However, they required and maintained membership records at head office in order to provide the training and advisory services required by their often professionally qualified members. It was thus normal to communicate with their members through the post and logical, given their position, to use a similar system for elections.

In this they had something in common with the NUS and Equity (see chapter 2).

Far more applications for money were made in connection with expenses incurred in elections than in votes on industrial action or the reference back of collective agreements: 29 out of the 36 applications concerned elections, compared with 4 concerning industrial action/reference back and 1 concerning rule-changes; the 2 remaining applications fell outside the scheme's purposes. The focus on elections is not surprising, and is largely explained by the structure of the unions concerned and their collective bargaining procedures. Small professional associations have a low level of bargaining activity, and in some cases (like the Professional Association of Teachers) explicitly eschew strike action. The four unions applying for funds in connection with the reference back of agreements and/or industrial action were the Royal College of Nursing, the British Association of Occupational Therapists, and the two banking unions, the Clearing Bank Union and Barclays Group Staff Unions.[21] In all cases the unions involved were in competition with TUC-affiliated unions, and under pressure to match rather than simply follow their competitors. The Royal College of Nursing's ballots on the Government offers in the 1982 NHS dispute were especially important, since they eventually led to the acceptance of an offer rejected by the TUC unions involved in the dispute: the College subsequently sought reimbursement of balloting expenses.

Turnout in elections varied between 11 and 73 per cent, with a median of 30 per cent. The three largest unions had the lowest percentage turnouts; the Royal College of Nursing polled 11 per cent and the Professional Association of Teachers had two polls of 16 per cent and 17 per cent. The two latter figures are not listed in table 4.3 as the certification officer for some unknown reasons conflated the two figures in his 1982 Report (see footnote [e] in table 4.3). A turnout of 4 per cent was also recorded by the RCN in a ballot on a rule change. The smaller unions tended to have the higher turnouts but there were exceptions to the general rule. For example, the Association of Education Officers polled 36 per cent in a ballot of 104 members (see footnote [g] to table 4.3). Nearly three-quarters (72 per cent) of all election ballots produced turnouts in the 25–50 per cent range. This is higher than the turnouts found in the AUEW(E), but the size of the unions was very small. The two larger unions, the Royal College of Nurses and the Professional Association of Teachers, both recorded lower turnouts than those normally found in the AUEW(E). Thus the non-TUC and apolitical unions opting to use the scheme for elections did not normally record majority turnouts.

The major practical issue faced in the operation of the scheme was the definition of secrecy. Public guidance on what is or is not recognized as secret is rather limited. In the certification officer's *Funds for Public Ballots* reference is made to '. . . the ballot [being] conducted so as to secure, as far as reasonably practicable, that those voting may do so in secret . . . by marking a voting paper; and . . . individually return the voting paper by

TABLE 4.3 Non-TUC unions applying to certification officer for refund 1980–82

Trade Union	Ballot papers			Election[a]	Question posed		
	Distributed	Returned	Poll (%)		Ref. back	Strike	Rule
Assistant Masters and Mistresses Association	560	367	66	X			
	573	418	73	X			
Association of Management and Professional Staffs	7,270	2,036	28	X			
	6,473	1,980	31	X			
Association of Optical Practitioners Ltd	4,258	1,077	25	X			
	113	32	28	X			
	4,294	1,020	24	X			
	240	88	37[b]	X			
Association of Public Service Finance Officers	2,316	741	32	X			
	2,228	650	29	X			
British Association of Occupational Therapists Ltd	4,684	1,412	30	X			
	5,926	2,681	45		X	X	
	5,759	1,366	24	X			
British Medical Association	227	143	63	X			
	611	231	38	X			
Clearing Bank Union	48,000	33,535	70		X	X	
Coventry Economic Building Society Staff Association	222	158	71	(Dissolution of Association)			
Guinness Brewing Staff Association UK	1,022	629	61[c]	X			
	1,022	569	56		X		
National Association of Head Teachers	550	335	60[d]	X			
	563	249	44	X			
	573	315	55	X			
	457	258	57	X			

Trade Union	Ballot papers			Election[a]	Question posed		
	Distributed	Returned	Poll (%)		Ref. back	Strike	Rule
Professional Association of Teachers	21,800	4,186	19	X			X
	21,200	7,107	34[e]	X			
Royal College of Nursing UK	169,914	6,064	4	X			
	194,957	21,914	11				
Society of Chiropodists	4,561	991	28	X			
	4,696	1,028	22[f]	X			
Society of Radiographers	7,884	2,211	28	X			
Association of Education Officers (2 ballots)	760	496	62[g]	X			
Association of Public Service Prof., Engineers	1,995	533	27	X			
Barclays Group Staff Union	33,805	15,256	45			X	
Chartered Society of Physiotherapy	17,569	2,960	17	X			
Institute of Journalists	2,578	737	29	X			

Source: Annual Report of the Certification Officer, 1981 and 1982.
Notes:

[a] Twenty-seven elections are listed, but in two cases this included more than one election.

[b] In a letter from the Association of Optical Practitioners the turnout was given as 73%. The potential membership vote was given as 120 and not the 240 listed in the certification officer's report.

[c] In a letter from the Guinness Brewing Staff Association the turnout was given as 96% and 81% and the potential membership was given as 703 and not the 1,022 listed in the certification officer's report.

[d] In a letter from the National Association of Head Teachers the turnout in the four elections listed was given as 67% (co 60%), 42% (co 44%), 53% (co 55%) and 58% (co 57%).

[e] In a letter from the Professional Association of Teachers the figure of 7,107 was given as two separate ballots of 3,616 (17% turnout) and 3,491 (16% turnout).

[f] In a letter from the Society of Chiropodists the number of papers returned and counted was given as 901 with 69 rejected. The percentage polling and counted was therefore 19%.

[g] In a letter from the Association of Education Officers the two ballots were given separately. In one ballot the potential membership vote was 104 and 37 actually voted (36%) and in the other the potential was 580 and 432 voted (74%).

post . . .'[22] Discretion as to what actually conforms to being reasonably practicable lies with the certification officer, but he is constrained in his interpretation by the regulations which require:

(a) that the holding of the ballot was not in contravention of the rules of the trade unions;

(b) that any requirements in the rules of the trade union as to the conduct of the ballot were complied with;

(c) in the case of a ballot containing a question for the purpose of ascertaining the views of members of a trade union as to the calling or ending of a strike or other industrial action, that, so far as reasonably practicable, the ballot was conducted so as to secure that all members likely to be called upon to participate in the action, or participating in the action, as the case may be, were entitled to vote;

(d) that those entitled to vote were allowed to vote without interference or constraint;

(e) that, so far as reasonably practicable, those entitled to vote had a fair opportunity of voting;

(f) that where the votes on any question have not been counted, the decision not to count them was taken because of a change in circumstances occurring after the first day on which voting papers were despatched or given to persons entitled to vote which materially affected the issue to which the question related;

(g) that where the votes cast have been counted, they have been fairly counted.[23]

However, the certification officer can still make payments if he believes that failure to comply with (b), the union's own rules, had no significant effect upon the conduct of the ballot.

It is the potential for conflict between a union's rules or its established procedures and the requirements for secrecy which appear to have caused the certification officer most difficulty when assessing claims for refunds. These problems arise mainly because some unions – not unreasonably – wish to ensure that only paid-up members vote in union elections. They therefore require voting members to record names and/or numbers on ballot papers and/or envelopes in order to check that the person returning the ballot paper qualifies for a vote before that vote is counted. This was the position, for example, with the Association of Head Teachers.[24] In July 1981 an application from this union failed because the member was required to sign the voting paper. By signing the papers the voter's preferences can be identified in the counting of the vote and hence it is not secret. Similarly, the Association of Education Officers was unsuccessful in an application made in December 1981.[25] The certification officer gave the primary reason for rejection as the secrecy provision, and drew the Association's attention to the difficulties of requiring members to sign the voting paper while also claiming that the ballot was secret.

In contrast to the adverse decisions affecting the Association of Head Teachers and the Association of Education Officers, the certification officer paid subsidies to a number of unions which also require members to record their names when voting. These include the Royal College of

Nursing, the Society of Chiropodists, the British Association of Occupational Therapists and the Institute of Journalists. The Royal College of Nursing requires members to sign and record their names on the ballot papers. Indeed in the reference back of National Health Service offers in 1982, the Royal College had to identify members in order to separate out those voting and working in the NHS from those voting but not working in the NHS in order to comply with the regulations requiring that only members affected by the proposal vote (see p. 172). The ballot paper was sent to all members and divided in half to provide NHS employees with one question and non-NHS personnel with another. Without some means of identifying and checking the member's right to vote those not employed in the NHS could have played a part in determining the terms and conditions of those who were so employed. The Royal College employs an independent returning officer, i.e. someone who is not a member of the College, to deal with the counting of votes.

The Society of Chiropodists had an application rejected in 1981 on the grounds that not all ballot papers were returned by post. This practice was corrected and in 1982 a refund was given by the certification officer for an election in which the voters were required to sign a certificate on the back to the envelope containing the ballot paper. Before counting the votes, the deputy returning officer was responsible for ensuring that the certificate had been signed and the member concerned was entitled to vote, having satisfied the conditions that his or her annual subscription had been paid in full. Under a detailed set of returning officer's rules the validated envelopes are opened on the day of the count and the tellers – three members of the society's staff and three outside tellers (normally college students) – count the votes. In 1982 51 voting papers were not counted because the voter's subscription had not been fully paid. Thus, without the system of checking voters' names against membership list, 51 people ineligible to vote would have done so.

The Occupational Therapists also require the back of the envelope to be signed by the voter, and they too have declared invalid votes cast by people not eligible to vote. A different method of ensuring that only paid-up members vote in elections was adopted by the Institute of Journalists, who were also successful in applying for a refund in 1982. In this union the double envelope method is used. The member is supplied with two envelopes and is required to give his name and district on the outer envelope. This is also a method approved by the Department of Labor in the United States as a means of ensuring secrecy.[26]

Unions requiring members to sign ballot papers and/or envelopes have therefore had mixed fortunes in their applications to the certification officer. Two unions requiring members' names on ballot papers failed in their applications, while one with a similar procedure succeeded, as did three unions requiring the voter to mark an envelope. But it could be argued that the differences between requiring signatures on the ballot paper and signature on the envelopes is slight. For example, it has been argued in the United States that '. . . the fact that members must put their names on the outside envelope raises the possibility that ballot counters will be able to trace how various members voted'. [27] In these circumstances, therefore, the certification officer could have ruled that the ballot was not secret, as he did in the case of the two associations requiring members to sign ballot papers.

The certification officer deals with each case 'on its merits', and there is no public explanation as to why some ballots have been accepted as being as secret as 'reasonably practicable' and others have not. However, it would appear that two factors are involved: the size of the organization and the role of external returning officers in the counting process. The certification officer has been less stringent in his requirements for secrecy in ballots held by the larger associations, most importantly the Royal College of Nursing. Secondly, the presence of an independent returning officer has also played a part. Where votes are counted by an outside returning officer, without the union having access to the papers, the ballot is likely to be regarded as secret despite the identification of the voter, although reassurances on the procedures would be required from the returning officer if it appeared that the union had access to the papers. It is also possible that the criteria became less stringent in the second year of operation of the scheme, when it had become clear that the financial costs of the scheme were likely to be small. The definition of secrecy would, of course, become of major importance if ballots were to become mandatory, and the certification officer's judgement and experience would, presumably, be relevant to future tribunal or court decisions in the area.

Some unions involved in the scheme changed their rules and/or procedures concerning ballots as a result of difficulties encountered in claiming refunds. Hence the British Association of Occupational Therapists, the Society of Chiropodists, the Association of Education Officers and the National Association of Head Teachers revised their rules and procedures. Minor alterations were required in the rules or procedures of the Society of Chiropodists, the Association of Education Officers and the National Association of Head Teachers to ensure that all voting papers were returned exclusively by post and not by some other method of delivery. More significant changes occurred in the Education Officers and Head Teachers Associations following unsuccessful claims for refunds. In both unions the practice of recording members' names and addresses on the ballot paper was ended. The possibility of non-members voting thus increased, although the secrecy of the voter was more secure.

The Occupational Therapists made a number of changes in order to comply with and take advantage of the scheme as interpreted by the certification officer. This union had its original claim for money rejected in 1981 because its application was considered not to have complied with its own rules. The argument was that, by sending ballot papers to paid-up members only, the union was contravening its rules which required that non-paid-up members remained on the register and retained the right to vote until formally removed from membership by the association's council. The association subsequently corrected this position by automatically suspending from membership any person '. . . in default for a period of three calendar months in the payment of his annual sbscription . . .' (clause 10c of the association's articles). Following the introduction of the scheme, the Occupational Therapists also chose to use a postal ballot to canvass membership opinion on salary increases and industrial action, rather than as previously using their shop stewards to sound out their members.[28] Further, they sent ballot papers direct to the home and included pre-paid reply envelopes under the influence of the scheme whereas they had previously included ballot papers in their journal and relied on members paying for their own stamps. The result was that in the first election ballot employing these new methods turnout increased by 300 per cent. Thus, for at least one union the Government's scheme assisted in, if not promoted, the adoption of new methods of balloting and substantially increased the turnout.

Even amongst non-TUC unions only a small minority applied for money under the scheme. The 19 unions which applied for money had mixed experiences. Applicants initially found it rather difficult to claim refunds, but in the second year of the scheme the position improved and at least one union changed its arrangements significantly to take advantage of the subsidy. However, there appear to be some possible anomalies in the operation of the scheme, with similar balloting methods meeting different responses from the certification officer. Trade-offs between measures which restrict voting to paid-up members, and those which guarantee secrecy in the counting of votes, have been accepted in some cases but not in others. This raises the question of whether or not the TUC affiliate, Equity, would have been successful if it had continued with its claims. For Equity, in common with the Head Teachers and Education Officers Associations, requires its members to sign the ballot paper. Thus Equity's council may have found itself in the embarrassing position of having initiated a controversial application only for the certification officer to reject it because the ballot was not secret within the terms of the scheme. It is possibie, however, that in using its accountants to count the papers Equity would have passed one of the tests initiated by the certification officer as a measure of secrecy in the counting of the vote.

CONCLUSION

The 1980 scheme to encourage the use of secret postal ballots was a failure on several counts. If it was intended to 'sugar the pill' by making unions more amenable to the less pleasant clauses in the Employment Act of 1980 it was unsuccessful. Further, by including the offer of money for ballots in what was perceived by the TUC as an otherwise anti-trade union Act the Government helped ensure that the few TUC affiliates operating postal ballots would come under intense, and as it proved successful, pressure not to use the scheme. By making the balloting provisions the one part of the Act requiring active union participation, the Government provided the TUC with a focal point for its opposition to the total package of Conservative legislation. Moreover, the stance adopted by the TUC was for the great majority of its members a painless form of opposition. They did not use postal ballots and hence suffered no financial loss by following a policy of non-cooperation. In the face of the TUC's opposition, the moderate leadership of the AUEW(E) failed to convince normally loyal supporters, and Equity failed to convince their wider membership of the advantages of applying for financial assistance, and no other TUC union seriously pursued making an application. Thus, TUC affiliates continued to elect or appoint their leaders and refer questions to their membership according to their own rules and procedures, without reference to the scheme.

Non-TUC unions responded more positively to the scheme. However, only 5 per cent of non-TUC affiliated unions applied for a refund from the certification officer, and only 4 per cent obtained one. Contrary to the fears expressed by some opponents of the scheme in the AUEW(E), the certification officer did not interfere directly in the affairs of applicant unions. However, the manner in which he interpreted what was or was not acceptable behaviour did, in some instances, lead to changes in union's rules and procedures as the unions concerned sought refunds. Conflicts between union rules and actual practice, and between attempts to ensure that members only voted and that votes remained secret, subsequently resulted in changes in union rules or procedures. However, if the unions concerned had decided not to pursue future applications there would have been no external pressure to change their rules and procedures.

Major difficulties of interpretation have arisen over the definition of secret. Although amendments to the regulations solved the problem of defining a postal vote for the purposes of the scheme, there was no attempt, at least publicly, to define what was secret. In particular, there was no recognition of the difference between secrecy in the casting and secrecy in the counting of the vote. Secrecy in the casting of the vote appears to have been assumed to exist if the person receiving the ballot paper had to return it individually by post to the union or counting agent. Secrecy in the counting of the vote was questioned in two cases where the voter was required to sign the ballot paper. No public guidelines appear to have been given as to whether or not the identity of the counting agent affects the secrecy of the count, but it appears that an independent counting agent is considered to ensure a voter of secrecy even if he or she signs the ballot form. Further, the signing of the envelope containing the ballot paper or the use of the double envelope method, with the outer envelope signed, was also accepted by the certification officer. Thus the problem which arises of ensuring that only paid-up members vote while also guaranteeing the voter secrecy has not been formally clarified.

Difficulties encountered in maintaining secrecy in the reference back of agreements, as in the Royal College of Nursing, where it was not possible to post voting papers only to members in the relevant industry and bargaining unit, have not therefore been explored. There may be some advantages in treating each case on its 'merits' when dealing with a small number of non-TUC unions, but if more interventionist measures for promoting secret ballots are introduced, as promised by the Secretary of State for Employment in July 1983, then the criteria used for assessing what is or is not secret in the counting of votes will have to be made public.[29]

The scheme has thus not succeeded in its manifest aim of stimulating the use of secret ballots, if success is judged by the number of unions applying for money. Unions which used ballots have continued to use them, for the reasons and in the circumstances outlined in chapters 2 and 3, without seeking financial assistance. However, it would be misleading to conclude that the Government has failed in its legislation. Government focus on balloting as the democratic procedure for elections and decision making has placed the trade union movement in a major difficulty. The trade union movement cannot oppose the principle of ballots; nor can it oppose the relevance of ballots to union practices, since many unions use ballots. It is therefore restricted to arguing that unions ought to be able to decide upon their own procedures, like other voluntary associations. But the failure of the trade unions to cooperate with the procedures encouraged by the 1980 Employment Act was taken by the Conservatives to indicate that the trade union movement was unwilling to reform its procedures in generally approved directions. Thus the TUC's policy of non-cooperation served to justify more direct intervention in 1983.

5 Trade Union Ballots and Union Democracy

In this concluding chapter trade union ballots are examined in the context of a wider discussion on the nature of union democracy. This discussion concentrates upon two aspects: first, union internal processes of decision making, especially the '. . . relationship between the rank and file and the union leadership',[1] and the outcome of these processes as they affect the union's ability to 'deliver the goods' to its members; secondly, the union's external relations with government, and the role of free trade unions in a pluralist society. These fundamental issues will be discussed through a general examination of the processes whereby the goals of union leaders and members are reconciled. The role of union ballots in that process is investigated, using five different models of union democracy, and the effects of ballots on the outcome of the decision-making process in trade unions is examined, especially the extent to which they produce union 'moderation'. Finally, the political consequences of legislation on trade union ballots will be discussed.

LEADERSHIP AND MEMBERSHIP GOALS

Preference for one method of decision making rather than another is rooted in the view that different levels in the union hold different views of the goals of trade unions. Three levels of membership are conventionally considered to exist within unions: the union leadership (predominantly but not exclusively full-time officials), the lay activists and the ordinary members. The leadership is considered to be preoccupied with institutional survival, the lay activists with realizing ideological goals and the ordinary members with collective organization to achieve maximum financial reward at minimum administrative cost. Conflict, or at the very least, tension is therefore considered inevitable between the three levels. In particular, the full-time leadership, and hence the unions they direct, becomes '. . . differentiated from the needs, ambitions and problems of [their] rank and file'.[2]

The objective of proponents of union elections and periodic re-elections, whether by branch or postal ballots, is to increase the influence of the members in the decision-making process and therefore restrict the full-time leadership's ability to realize its own particular conception of union goals. This analysis of leadership–members' goals is adopted, with varying degrees of sophistication and explicitness, by both Marxists and Conservatives. Marxists see leaders and therefore unions as tending to be incorporated into the capitalist system. In this view union leaders control their members on behalf of management and limit their goals to the purely economic, thus failing to pursue legitimate wider political objectives. This, for the Marxists, is a dereliction of the union's real duty. It leads the union to be '. . . concerned more with stabilizing the detail of the relationship between labour and capital than with conducting a struggle *against* the domination of capital'.[3] Leaders, preoccupied with institutional survival, come to regard the union as an end in itself rather than as a means to an end, through the familiar process of displacement of goals.

Many Conservatives also believe that the trade union movement is pursuing the wrong objectives, owing to the activities of unrepresentative leaders. In contrast to the Marxists, they criticize union leaders for being too ready to challenge the existing economic order, and of distorting the real purposes of trade unions by pursuing political objectives instead of confining their activities to the economic field. Union leaders are accused of the 'arrogant misuse of the wealth and power of trade unions' to serve their own political ambitions.[4] As Sir Geoffrey Howe asked rhetorically in a letter to *The Times* in 1978: 'Does the claim of union leaders to speak for their members stand up to critical examination? Does the political partnership between union leaders and Labour politicians mean that the former can often mishear or disregard the voice of the people and continue to pursue their own generally socialist objectives?'[5] Union leaders should concentrate upon 'responsible' bargaining and improving members' economic circumstances, negotiating conscientiously within the context of a recognition that both sides of industry have a common and over-riding interest in the prosperity of the company and nation. Unions should be 'business unions'; 'trade conscious rather than class conscious'.[6]

The above description of structured distortion of union goals, and betrayal of members' interests, is misleading: trade union decision making does not inevitably result in leadership domination, whether that domination is operating in the interest of capitalism (according to Marxists) or Socialism (according to Conservatives). All three groups – leaders, activists and ordinary members – are divided, both in terms of interests and ideology at all levels. Operating union political systems effectively requires support at all three levels. Activists without support amongst leaders are likely to find their role limited to the negative one of vetoing leadership initiatives, with little chance of implementing policies; leaders and activists without the support of members may find their membership drifting away, where this is possible, or corporate life atrophying where it is not, both undermining union effectiveness. The relationship between leaders, activists and ordinary members is thus complex, and it is misleading to portray it as simple betrayal or distortion.

In practice, differences of interest, ideology and orientation are found amongst leaders, activists and ordinary members. The major differences of interest relate to occupation and industry: in the AUEW(E) for example, fitters, whether leaders, activists or ordinary members, share common interests; in the TGWU bus workers share a comparable common interest, in industry rather than occupation. Similarly, there are obvious differences in ideology between the left and right, the extent of the differences, and their political significance, differing between unions (although the definition of 'right' is different amongst trade union activists from the definition amongst ordinary members or in politics generally). Finally, there are differences in orientation between trade unionists who, on the one hand, view their organizations in instrumental,[7] calculative[8] or bread-and-butter[9] terms, seeing unions as a type of business organization; and on the other, those who see union membership as involving a moral,[10] solidaristic[11] or radical[12] commitment. Such differences of interest, ideology and orientation obviously influence perceptions of union goals.

The influence of differences in interests and in ideology on the decision-making process in individual unions has been examined in chapters 2 and 3; this section is concerned with more general considerations. The basic participant in trade unions is the ordinary member: unions exist because of his willingness to pay union dues. Activists are drawn from the ordinary membership and union leaders are drawn from the activists. (Even where unions appoint full-time officials from outside the union they are unlikely to appoint officials who have not been active in any trade union.) Some ordinary members have an instrumental orientation to union membership, others a moral orientation. The former are likely to participate fully in union life at shop-floor level, to participate in shop steward elections and in strike meetings; they have traditionally taken little part in union life outside their immediate work environment and are unlikely to do so in the future. The latter are likely to participate in union life beyond the immediate environment, and to become activists, possibly in due course to become leaders. Such individuals are not necessarily conventionally left-wing, but they are likely to believe that trade unions are more than narrowly economic organizations.

Trade union leaders are drawn from the moral activists. To reach the level of national leader ambitious activists must become known by working their way through the branch, district and regional committees, attending conferences, educational courses and sometimes factional meetings. Members who regard the union in solely instrumental terms are unlikely to have the commitment necessary to make such progress. However, it is easy to exaggerate the importance of this restricted recruitment: it is more important to the political and organizational activities of unions than to collective bargaining activities.

Union activists are more constrained and limited in collective bargaining than in their political activities by the views of union members and by the environment, especially the economic environment: for the instrumental trade unionist collective bargaining is too important to be ignored. With the growth of plant-level bargaining in the 1970s, such influences were exercised largely at plant level. Although participation in union life outside the plant was limited, high levels of participation in plant-level decision making were reported, for example in the engineering industry.[13] Also, during the 1970s there was pressure for the reference back to the membership of those collective agreements which continued to be made above plant level (see chapter 3). A wide variety of methods of consultation and reference back were adopted, all having in common the direct involvement of the ordinary member, or of shop stewards subject to direct influence from the ordinary member. How the ordinary member decided, and will decide, on collective bargaining issues was, and will continue to be, heavily influenced by economic circumstances, at local, industrial and national level.

The basic assumption of this study is therefore that there are major differences in perceptions of union goals amongst union leaders, activists and members, which are articulated through the union political system. Indeed, occupational, industrial and ideological bonds may override interests common to leaders, activists and members. In this respect the analysis is conventionally pluralist. Union leaders are not seen as incorporated into the capitalist economy and therefore traitors to class interests, nor as ideologically committed Socialists misusing union resources for political ends. Union leaders recognize that they are operating in a mixed economy and that satisfying their members' economic interests involves recognizing the realities of economic life. At the same time, union leadership is too stressful and too unrewarding financially to be an attractive career to anyone lacking any commitment to trade unionism as a moral force. There is therefore an inevitable tension amongst union leaders, which different individuals resolve differently. Similar tensions exist, although less acutely, for union activists and ordinary members. Trade unions have both economic and political/moral goals; it is the task of union leaders to reconcile them in the light of the constraints, internal and external, to which they are subject. The models of democracy explored below will examine how far union government reconciles these differences between leaders and members and what contribution ballots make to this process.

MODELS OF UNION DEMOCRACY

Scholars have approached union democracy from a number of different perspectives,[14] but the main theoretical framework has been borrowed from political theory, and has involved applying the concepts of liberal democracy to trade unions and political parties as large complex organizations. The major framework has been set by Michels' aphorism, 'who says organizations says oligarchy'.[15] Much attention has been directed towards assessing how far union leaders' behaviour is consistent with this assumption and what checks, if any, prevent oligarchic domination. In consequence, various models have been developed to assess the degree to which certain features associated with union government promote or permit oligarchy or democracy. Since most of the approaches are concerned with the same basic problem, they overlap and are not strictly alternatives. But by selecting the most prominent features from the different studies, it is possible to construct five major models or approaches which focus on different elements in decision making: participation and competition in elections;[16] the existence and effectiveness of an opposition faction or party;[17] the division of powers and associated checks on full-time officer domination;[18] internal bargaining between leaders and conflicting groups of members;[19] and the centralization or decentralization of decision making.[20]

Each of these models will be discussed and the effect of ballots examined in respect of elections. The contribution ballots make to the process of union democracy when used in the reference back of agreements and strikes will be examined in the last model. The respective roles of formal and informal factors will also be examined.

Participation and Competition in Elections

A number of students have used the level of participation in elections and the degree of competition between candidates for office as measures of union democracy. In the simplest of models, the number and percentages of votes are counted: the higher the participation rate the more democratic the union. If a union has a low level of voting, the membership may be labelled apathetic and the leadership oligarchic.[21] This conclusion may be criticized on the grounds that abstention does not necessarily mean that the membership is dissatisfied with the leadership's performance. If members are able to participate with reasonable effort but choose not to a '. . . second test of union democracy would . . . be the degree to which such "passive" members . . . identify their leadership's policies and actions with their own interest.[22]

Competition and, in particular, closeness of elections, rather than simple measures of participation in elections, were used as the primary measures of democracy by Edelstein and Warner, who claimed that formal union structures vary in the extent to which they '. . . create equal competitors for leadership'.[23] Closeness in elections to important national office was taken as a manifestation of the effectiveness of opposition within unions. This argument qualifies the misleading view that could be gained if the focus was solely on the level of turnout; for example, a turnout of 80 per cent, divided 10 per cent for one candidate and 70 per cent for another, is not itself an indicator of a high level of democracy. Clearly, if only the candidate favoured by the established leadership and able to call on the resources of the union has the opportunity to win the contest, the level of participation is significantly less important, as the membership are not offered a real choice and the result is a foregone conclusion.

The method of voting affects both the above measures of union democracy. As shown clearly in chapter 2, changes in the physical location of the vote from geographically located branches to postal ballots delivered to the home increased participation, as measured by turnout in elections, by over 100 per cent. Also, workplace ballots (NUM 80 per cent and CPSA 40 per cent) and ballots held in workplace-based branches (TGWU 25 per cent) recorded higher turnouts than some elections conducted by postal ballot. Thus, choice of balloting method can be crucial in determining levels of participation in elections by making it more or less difficult for members to cast their votes. Unions which require members to vote in geographically based branches some distance from members' homes and places of employment at inconvenient times would, other things being equal, be less democratic than those which provided easier access to elections through workplace or postal ballots. The evidence on turnout, as described in chapter 2, therefore suggests that the NUM's pithead ballots are more democratic than those held at workplace meetings in the CPSA, which in turn are more democratic than the postal ballots held in the AUEW(E), FTAT and Equity, which in turn are more democratic than branch ballots in the ASTMS, GMWU and NUR.

However, this line of argument does not carry the same weight once the different circumstances affecting the level of turnout in individual unions are discussed, and the assumption that other things are equal is abandoned. For example, the NUM and CPSA are able to organize workplace-based votes which record relatively high turnouts because they are both industrially based unions with large concentrations of membership in clearly defined jobs and specific geographic locations. In contrast, the AUEW(E), and particularly the NUS and Equity, have dispersed, and in the latter cases, highly mobile, memberships. Moreover, these three unions have few workplace-based branches. Thus the balloting methods used in the NUM and CPSA would not have the same effect on turnout in the AUEW(E), NUS and Equity.

The voting system was one of the two major variables identified by Edelstein and Warner as affecting competition and closeness in union elections for important national office. The other and more critical variable was the presence of '. . . two or more offices of similar or identical rank at each level near the top of the hierarchy . . .'[24] This condition, it was suggested, would forestall a 'clear and "logical" line of succession . . .'[25], which tends to give an heir apparent an unassailable position in elections to the relevant vacant post. Although this is a factor assisting close contests for some senior posts, the evidence presented in chapter 2 suggests it should not now be given the weight proposed by Edelstein and Warner; in the general secretary elections in the NUS, Bakers Union and NUR, and the contests for executive positions in the AUEW(E), senior members were defeated by candidates without experience at the highest levels of government.

In the Edelstein and Warner model, the optimum voting system is one which would protect candidates against reprisals by the administration, and give ease of nomination, a fair count and elimination of preferential balloting. This, they argue, would '. . . allow oppositionists to take their case to the membership with optimum chance for a good showing'.[26]

A number of balloting methods could ensure a fair count, including postal ballots, particularly if returned to an independent counting agent. But there is little that postal ballots could do to safeguard candidates against reprisals or ensure ease of nomination. Several sanctions exist which can be used to block the future progress of unpopular candidates, many of which are clearly not associated with the formal electoral process. For example, certain candidates can be given prominence in the union journal and others ostracized; some, but not all, candidates can be invited to speak at weekend schools; preferred candidates can be supported by statements from leading officials on their suitability for office.

Edelstein and Warner also found that a 'random model' of structural variables could produce close but 'diffuse anarchic competition'[27] for office in some unions, and that this could be more prevalent in elections held under postal ballot. For example, when a postal ballot is associated with a 'limited stay in office and a rapid turnover of top leaders' competition for office could be 'random in both the nomination of particular candidates, i.e. unpredictable structurally and unbiased politically, and the irrelevant choices made by most individual voters'.[28] This is similar to the findings in chapter 2 (see p. 71) regarding the less salient elections in the AUEW(E), where few voting members appeared aware of the nature of the political choice or the record of the respective candidates.

Close contests may not therefore be any more democratic than runaway victories if the result is due to the luck of the draw. This can produce, as in the AUEW(E), the election of unknowns, possessing none of the abilities needed by full-time officials, and the defeat of experienced candidates. Thus in the circumstances in which postal ballots encourage 'randomness' they detract from democracy by reducing the element of choice, and may damage union efficiency by promoting members beyond their capabilities.

Opposition Factions and Parties

The existence and effectiveness of any opposition faction or party has, since the study of Lipset et al. in 1956 of the International Typographical Union (ITU) in the United States, tended to dominate academic discussion of union democracy.[29] The essence of the argument is that, following Michels' iron law of oligarchy, all unions are presumed to be oligarchic unless the national officials and policy makers are challenged by an internally organized opposition.[30] Lipset et al. considered that the two-party system – a governing and opposition party – operating in the ITU represented the ideal type of union democracy.

Following Lipset et al.'s seminal work, other unions studied have often been considered to be less than fully democratic unless they had similar internal arrangements. Hence, when a union has been found to contain an opposition group the Lipset et al. test has been applied and much of the argument has focused on the legitimacy of opposition, its permanence and whether or not it is institutionalized.[31] These concepts have been used to differentiate between opposition factions (less democratic) and opposition parties (more democratic). Unfortunately, this has led to a rather sterile debate of the 'when is a party not a party' kind, rather than a more fundamental discussion of whether or not the opposition group offers the membership an alternative to the leadership in policy choices and elections. It is far more useful to accept, for the purpose of assessing union democracy, that '. . . democracy exists when union executives are unable to prevent opposition factions distributing propaganda and mobilizing electoral support. It does not require that opposition be institutionalized . . . merely that it should survive as a recognized form of political activity'.[32] In adopting this approach 'parties' can be taken as being a form of well-developed factionalism by reference to the organizational behaviour of the group under discussion. Hence notions of legitimacy, for which there is generally no objective measure acceptable to both the established leadership and members of the opposition, can be dispensed with. Both factions and parties operate outside the union rules. For instance, in the AUEW(E) two of the best organized groups in the unions studied flout the rule against canvassing, and in the CPSA both groups continued to function in the period 1971–6 when the union had a rule proscribing their organization (see p. 98). Thus if the rules and the established leaders deny opposition groups legitimacy but are powerless to prevent their activities the group for the puurpose of this discussion is still recognized to exist and qualify for the title party if its organizational features warrant it.

The relationship between faction and party, by reference to the group's own behaviour, can thus be viewed as a continuum. The line between faction and party is continuous and is based on the view that there is no necessary discontinuity, based on concepts of legitimacy and institutionalization, between faction and party. Faction is in this approach on one end of the continuum and in its weakest form a '. . . comparatively unstructured conflict group whose membership fluctuates according to the issues in dispute'.[33] At the opposite end of the continuum is the party. This form of organized group has a name; selects and supports candidates in elections to all or the great majority of national elections; has existed for a sufficient number of years to have won control of government, if it had been successful in elections contested; and has a policy based on principles or ideology.[34] If an organized group has these features and behaves in this manner and the established leadership, for whatever reason, cannot prevent it from so doing, it passes the test.

The unions studied will now be assessed against the criteria used for defining parties and factions, although, it is difficult to be precise regarding the comparative standing of some of the groups within unions. The difficulties primarily lie in the lack of detail regarding some aspects of the groups' methods of organization. Although some groups are very open in their activities, others are not. This reticence does not necessarily indicate doubts about legitimacy and therefore the need to remain secret. Nor is it necessarily governed by the desire to protect the group from the established leadership's attacks. It is rather that the group's inner workings, such as nomination meetings and vetting of motions for conference, are clearly the business of group members and supporters and not open to outsiders. Therefore in allocating the groups to places on the continuum, reference is made to broad categories of organizations, rather than making fine distinctions, and the more widely known electoral successes of some of the groups are assumed to reflect effective organization and given some weight.

A number of unions analysed in chapter 2 appear at, or towards the party end of the continuum. They have had both opposition and governing groups competing for national office over a period of several years. Included in this class are the AUEW(E), CPSA, POEU, EETPU and Equity. The Group in the AUEW(E) clearly has the features associated with a party and it is probable that the Bloc in the POEU and the Moderate Group in the CPSA also come into this category. The broad left groups in these latter three unions follow a similar pattern. Indeed, they all at different times have held majority control over all or parts of their respective national governing bodies, for example, conference or executive.[35] In contrast, the broad left in the EETPU has never seriously challenged the moderates' control of the union after the ballot rigging scandal of the late 1950s. Nevertheless, the broad left regrouped and in the 1980s, despite the fierce antagonism of the established leadership, continued to contest major national elections, with some minor successes. Equity, in contrast, has had a multiplicity of groups challenging the moderate Act for Equity governing group. The Centre Forward group has probably been the most influential of the opposition groups, and in the early 1980s made a number of gains on Equity's executive. A further and important feature of all groups in this category is that they publish their own newspapers and/or election addresses and are generally successful in the more important elections in informing the wider membership of the political choice offered by their own candidates. They therefore reduce 'randomness' in elections whilst helping to promote close contests, in some instances defeating incumbents and overturning the established leadership.

In contrast to the above 5 unions, which have two competing parties or well-organized factions of broadly similar organizational strength, at least two unions, the NUM and NUR, have an imbalance in factional organization which favour the broad left. A new but weakly organized left faction in the NUR and an emergent broad left party in the NUM both successfully challenged established and moderate leaderships which in the circumstances mistakenly relied on their control of the official machinery of government, caucus meetings and a presumed natural majority for their continued supremacy. Moreover, in the NUS and Bakers Union left-wing factions were formed around specific issues, over which they challenged the leadership, and subsequently revealed more organizational ability in elections than their opponents. In these four unions, therefore, the established, and as it happened moderate leadership, has in some important national elections been successfully challenged by a left-wing opposition at varying stages of organizational development.

Unions in which the established leadership has not been subject to a significant challenge from an organized opposition include the TGWU, GMWU and ASTMS. Where political factionalism has existed, the opposition has been of the poorly organized kind, based on local and/or national caucuses coalescing around specific issues on the executive or in conference in opposition to an otherwise dominant leadership. Defeat for the national leadership or their favoured candidates in elections has been unusual. Contests for office, when they occurred, have been determined more by reference to the candidate's experience or by regional, industrial or occupational characteristics than by his or her political associations.

The role of ballots in determining the groups' positions on the various points on the continuum between party and poorly organized faction will now be examined. A framework developed by Martin for assessing factors which assist the survival of opposition factions, thus providing the opportunity for factions to develop into parties, will be selectively used for this purpose.[36] The framework contains twelve categories of constraints on leadership domination, of which four are of direct relevance to the present discussion.[37] These are concerned with variations in: (a) membership distribution, characteristics and beliefs; (b) leadership attitudes; (c) opposition expertise; and (d) union structure and processess (including method of voting).

The five unions with both highly developed government and opposition groups [AUEW(E), CPSA, POEU, EETPU and Equity], and the NUM with its effective broad left grouping, have a combination of some of the above factors in common. The three unions at the opposite end of the spectrum also share a number of factors. Most importantly, unions with well-developed factions or parties share certain membership traits. They all have greater occupational homogeneity than the TGWU, GMWU and ASTMS. Moreover, if the occupational homogeneity and stability of the historically dominant membership groups, rather than the union's wider membership is considered, the comparison is even more striking. For the two most heterogeneous of the unions with a high degree of factional organization, the AUEW(E) and the NUM, are dominated by the elite sections of their membership, that is, respectively, section 1 craftsmen and faceworkers, who are committed to the union's long term survival. Also, the two groups in the CPSA, which has a very high turnover of members, are dependent on a stable core of members who also have longer term interests in the unions. Thus unions with well-organized factions or parties, and even more so the factions and parties themselves, have common occupational interests which allow ideologically opposed groups to compete for office and power without threatening the basic cohesiveness of the union.

In contrast, the unions with a lower level of factional organization are more heterogeneous, with minor occupational and marked industrial divisions, which militate against fighting elections on ideological grounds and thus restrict the formation of political factions and parties. These basic membership differences lead members to vote primarily on the basis of a candidate's occupational, industrial or regional identity. Furthermore, they influence the processes and structures of decision making adopted and used by the TGWU and GMWU to accommodate their different kinds of membership. The resulting trade group system in the TGWU and the highly autonomous regions in the GMWU make it extremely difficult for like-minded political groups to cooperate across formal boundaries. Also, the manner in which merging unions joining the ASTMS were allowed to retain many of their previous rules, customs and practices makes it difficult to form national political interest groups which cut across industrial divisions. Finally, the widely diverse memberships recruited into these three unions may also have called for strong central leadership to bind the disparate groups into one unified whole: '. . . the large measure of autonomy granted to the TGWU's trade groups made it essential to create a strong counter poise at the centre, if the union was not to develop the weaknesses of a federation. The General Secretary represented the unity of the union'.[38] Thus the TGWU, GMWU and ASTMS have a number of barriers to the formation of well-organized factions or parties in opposition to the leadership. Not least is the belief that such developments might threaten the survival of unions already divided by occupational and industrial differences.

The impact of leadership attitudes and opposition expertise on the state of factions and parties is not consistent across the unions studied. The established moderate leaderships of the AUEW(E) and the EETPU were very antagonistic to their broad left opponents, yet the broad left survived and in the 1980s appeared to be undergoing something of a minor revival in both unions.[39] This was achieved in the face of rule changes initiated by the moderates at least partly to reduce the threat from the left. These changes included postal ballots for full-time officers' elections in the AUEW(E) and the appointment of full-time officials and the establishment of a full-time executive in the EETPU. It may be that in the AUEW(E), as in the POEU and CPSA, the antagonism shown by the moderates towards the broad left was not translated into anything more damaging than verbal criticism and rule changes because the moderates themselves are dependent on similar extra-union organizations for their own survival. Moreover, in the AUEW(E),

CPSA and POEU the broad left has managed to hold, or come very close to winning, majorities on a number of decision-making bodies, thus making it difficult for the moderates to restrict the left's organization by exploiting moderate control of the formal machinery of government. In cases where opposition candidates actually captured and established themselves as the government, as for example in the NUS and Bakers, the attitude of the previous leadership clearly proved to be no serious barrier to the survival and success of the opposition. In contrast, the national leadership of the TGWU, GMWU and ASTMS never faced such serious challenges in the 1970s and 1980s, and it may be that their claims to be the unifying force, and thus their inherent, if not declared, opposition to extra union organizations, helped prevent or restrict the rise of political factionalism.

One aspect of leadership attitudes which is common to all the unions with at least one well-organized faction is their ideological commitment. This generally originated in either Communist or anti-Communist beliefs. In more recent times the broad left embraced Communists, various Trotskyite groups and left-wing Labour supporters. On the right, the groups were normally centre/right Labour party and sometimes Roman Catholic based. It may be that the existence of a number of leaders holding strongly to one of these opposed views is a necessary precondition for effective factional organization. For example, in the NUM a commitment to broad left policies, and the Communists' willingness to work with sympathizers outside the party, helped to overcome the area autonomy which makes the organization of such groups in the NUM difficult.[40]

In unions with factions and parties the better organized have the advantage of drawing on the expertise of members or sympathizers within the ranks of the national full-time officers and executive members. However, these experts do not necessarily hold the leading offices in the faction or party as well as the union. In the AUEW(E), for example, the Group's national secretaryship and chairmanship were not always held by those moderates nominated and elected to the general secretaryship and presidency of the union. Candidates were chosen for reasons other than their position in the Group. For instance, organizational ability and a good record in recent elections influenced decisions in the Group's nomination meetings.

The willingness of leading officials to assist one faction or party, rather than another, may be a function of ambition and self-preservation as well as ideological commitment. If a member wishes to progress within the hierarchy of a union in which factions or parties are competing for supremacy and issuing election tickets there is often little room for independents. Thus parties or factions which draw on the support of full-time officials and leading lay activists may do so because they have been successful rather than because the expertise of such officials makes them successful. It is possible, therefore, for a faction or party to make rapid headway once it makes an initial breakthrough, as success brings in more expert adherents (or careerists) who in turn give the faction or party a better chance of future success. Equally, failed factions, such as those which surface from time to time in the ASTMS, or difficult individuals who insist on 'rocking the boat' by standing against incumbents in the GMWU's confirmatory elections for regional organizers (see p. 91), can find themselves on a downward spiral because such challenges can lead to ostracism and the erection of barriers against future promotion by the established leadership.

Union structure and processes have already been shown to influence the development of opposition groups when, following constitutions designed to weld heterogeneous unions into a unified whole, they raise obstacles to inter-industry, inter-regional and/or inter-occupational cooperation, and give the central officials (usually the general secretary) a dominant role. In addition, other structures and processes, unrelated to the nature of the membership, might be expected to influence the development of factions: the method of choosing leaders (appointment or election); opportunity for autonomous decision making; the voting method and the control and content of communications affecting elections (including the union journal, election addresses and ballot paper).

It appears reasonable to suggest that the frequency, regularity and status of elections should correlate with, and influence, the existence of well-organized factions and parties. Coalitions will emerge far more readily, and on a more permanent basis, when members have the opportunity to contest elections for important full-time office frequently and regularly. Conversely, in unions where the only major elections are to a tenured general secretaryship and annual lay executive posts, there will be less incentive to organize on a party basis. This is confirmed to a limited extent by the evidence. The AUEW(E), with its almost continuous electioneering to full-time officer posts, which are subject to periodic re-election, probably has the most fully developed two-party system in Britain. The NUM, with election to full-time officer posts and its executive, has one well-organized faction. However, it does not follow from this that the unions which appoint full-time officers and only elect lay executives once a year are not subject to factional organization. The CPSA, POEU and Equity which follow this pattern have well-organized factions or parties.[41] In contrast, in the TGWU, GMWU and ASTMS (the first two of which elect their general secretaries) the practice of appointing ordinary full-time officials and only electing predominantly lay executives does appear to combine with other factors to militate against factionalism.[42] Periodic elections to important full-time offices are therefore an encouragement to the development of well-organized factions and parties, but not necessary for their existence.

The opportunity for autonomous decision making within unions may assist factionalism by giving those organizing the opposition freedom to act outside the established national leadership's influence. This in turn is affected by whether or not the local full-time officer is elected or appointed. Elected full-time officials responsible to their members in the locality and to a locally elected and highly autonomous district committee, as in the

AUEW(E), can and do provide resources and support useful to an opposition faction. However, the devolution of bargaining within the TGWU since the late 1960s and the formation of district committees has not so far produced a noticeable level of factional organization in the TGWU, although the growth of shop stewards on the TGWU's executive may have limited the general secretary's discretion. Nevertheless, local autonomy does not appear to be a necessary condition for factionalism. Although the POEU and CPSA are centralized in their bargaining and union government, both have well-organized factions or parties of both right and left.

The voting method used by a union may have a bearing on the development and effectiveness of factions and parties. In addition to its potential impact on political outcomes, which depends upon several other factors, the voting method affects the role of factions in the process of elections in three main ways. First, the location of the ballot in the branch, workplace or home is a major factor influencing the number of members actually receiving a ballot paper. The location of the ballot, the union's own information system, the degree of factional organization and the media interest largely determine whether or not members realize the nature of the political choice offered in elections involving factions. If the vote takes place in branches or workplaces it is relatively easy for the factions' and parties' supporters to draw the voters' attention to their candidate's identity. This may be done by having a branch motion supporting certain candidates, by posters or word of mouth. If the voting takes place at home voters may be less aware of the nature of the choices offered. Unless the union includes an election address in which the candidates identify their own factional or party allegiance (as in Equity) or the media provides the necessary information [as in certain AUEW(E) elections] or the factions and parties have means of reaching the more fragmented membership, a considerable number of voters may cast their votes at random or according to the often very limited information on the ballot paper. It could be argued, therefore, that the introduction of postal ballots into unions in which the opposition faction is ill equipped to disseminate information to the home, but in which the established leadership is able to reach such voters by, for example, journals posted directly to the home address (as in the EETPU) the result could be a reduction in opposition effectiveness and in this union model of democracy an encouragement to oligarchy.

Secondly, the method of eliminating losing candidates affects the development of factions or parties. In voting systems in which, if there is no overall majority, the top two candidates go into a second ballot the random or non-political voting referred to earlier is much reduced, as in the AUEW(E).[43] If a first round ballot attracts a considerable number of unaligned candidates, the two organized factions' or parties' candidates, have, with only a limited degree of organization, a good chance of reaching the second ballot. In the AUEW(E)'s second or final ballot the choice is in the overwhelming majority of cases limited to the two representatives of the left and right, and the membership thus faced with a clear political choice (see chapter 2, p. 70).

In contrast, the single transferable vote as practised in the NUM does not facilitate a logical transfer of votes:

> There is no guarantee that a voter who gives his or her first preference to a left-wing candidate will order the remainder in a consistent political way . . . Under the preferential vote system it is possible for a candidate to be elected who does not represent the majority interests of members of the union. This is most likely to occur when those interests are competed for by a number of similar candidates.[44]

In this type of electoral system it is important for each faction to field only one candidate and not to confuse the electorate (see chapter 2, p. 103). There is therefore a greater need for factional or party discipline under the single transferable vote than under elimination ballots. Factions are thus more likely to influence elections where the union operates a system of elimination voting in elections which initially attract a relatively large number of candidates.

Thirdly, the timing of elections and the composition of the electorate both influence the development of factions. If factions or parties organize comprehensive 'tickets' or 'lists' of candidates there is a better chance of overturning the executive if all its members are subject to election at the same time and by the same membership. In these circumstances a faction carrying only a small majority of votes can sweep the board, or at least hope to gain a convincing majority, as in the CPSA. This stands in direct contrast to the experience of the AUEW(E). In the AUEW(E), the composition of the executive is determined by a series of by-elections held in seven different constituencies. The election dates do not normally coincide. They may be three or five years from the previous election, depending on the length of service of the incumbent, and the initial election date is an accident of death or retirement. It therefore takes an indeterminate number of years for the right or left to overturn the other's majority. In consequence, the CPSA tends to be politically volatile, unlike the relatively stable AUEW(E).

Factional and party organization is thus dependent on a number of factors. Membership distribution, particularly occupational differentiation, and the resulting union structures are much more important for both promoting and restricting the growth of factionalism than are formal rules concerning the method of election. Ideological differences are also of primary importance in causing groups to coalesce. However, where these conditions are favourable to factionalism the existence of repeated elections to major full-time office seems to encourage further the development of factions into parties. Postal ballots may hinder factional choice by making the communication of that choice to an enlarged electorate more difficult. However, if a voting system includes eliminating ballots and/or the union circulates election addresses containing evidence of factional allegiances with the ballot paper, or the factions themselves are capable of relaying this information, postal ballots need not necessarily limit factional activity. Finally, if the central concern of this particular school of thought on union democracy is that the opposition not only limit oligarchy but also have the capacity to become the government, the experiences of the AUEW(E), CPSA, POEU, NUS, NUM and the Bakers Union, all employing different electoral methods, suggest that a number of British unions meet this criterion.

Division of Powers and Associated Checks on Oligarchy

Apart from factions or parties limiting the power of the established leadership, a union may also have a formal division of powers and a number of associated checks on full-time officer dominance. In this model, power is separated between legislature, executive and judiciary – as in the United States constitution.[45] This is the system employed in the AUEW(E), discussed in detail in chapter 2 (see p. 65). The divisions written into most other unions' constitutions are those that distinguish between full-time officers, including the general secretary, executive and conference. These positions are generally filled by different methods and have responsibility for different functions in rule. Conference lays down policy, which the executive interprets and the full-time officers apply. The executive, and sometimes the full-time officers, then report back to the following conference for their approval. Each body has some discretion, but is held in check by the others.

The separation of powers does not always operate as envisaged. In practice, the full-time officers sometimes reverse the process and determine the policy of the executive and conference. 'Platform' dominance of large conferences without factional organization, such as the TGWU's with some 1,000 delegates, is facilitated by the manner in which the leading national officials can initiate the policies which are debated and influence the speakers called. By managing procedures and controlling information, the general secretary or national officers can often persuade conference to accept their proposals and reports with little criticism. However, this is not always the case. Even in the TGWU, Jack Jones, one of its most influential general secretaries, was defeated at conference on support for the Social Contract in 1977.[46] Also in the TGWU, appointed full-time officers who refused in the 1960s and 1970s to follow the union's popular policy of decentralizing power to shop stewards were brought to account, and in one case forced from office.[47] Similarly, the appointed and tenured general secretary of NALGO who failed to adapt to his union's change of character in the early 1970s was replaced in 1973 by an official more in tune with the union's executive.[48] Thus, the checks formally built into unions' constitutions to limit the power of full-time tenured officers can be exercised if the point at issue is sufficiently important to generate a strong reaction against the offending leaders.

The method of choosing leaders and type of ballot used in elections can be influential in determining the relative power of the different bodies. For example, the balance of power appears to lie with the general secretary in the great majority of unions which have elected lay executives subject to frequent and regular re-election, but selected, or appointed, tenured general secretaries with considerable experience and expertise. The general secretary is given added authority where, as in the TGWU and the GMWU, the tenured general secretary is the only full-time official chosen by a vote of the whole membership. In contrast, in the few unions with full-time executives the general secretary does not appear to have the same degree of authority or to be able to initiate policies to the same extent as his counterpart faced by lay executives.

Legislative changes requiring that appointed officials become subject to election and periodic re-election, and/or that executives normally elected by branch ballot or at conference become subject to direct election by postal ballots, could have a significant effect on the balance of power between the general secretary and the lay committees responsible for the national government of unions. If, for example, the Conservative government passed legislation requiring the periodic re-election of lay executives by postal ballots but did not change the position of appointed and tenured general secretaries, it is likely that the balance of power would move in favour of the permanent full-time officials, especially in unions without factional organization.[49] This would occur because many of the new voting membership would be unaware of the nature of any political choice or the experience of the respective executive candidates. A random pattern of voting would emerge. Since the majority of unions change their executives every one or two years, there would be a rapid turnover of executive members, resulting in an executive even more dependent on the general secretary for guidance (see chapter 2, pp. 61–2).

On the other hand, if existing general secretaries were subject to election and periodic re-election, it is unlikely that they would lose their seats, especially in unions without factional organization. As the only 'known' candidates in the election and with the support of the union machine, they could be confident of retaining office. Moreover, if they were subject to election and re-election by the whole membership their authority *vis-à-vis* a lay executive subject to a high turnover would be even further enhanced. This would be particularly noticeable if the newly elected general secretary had previously been appointed by and hence owed his position to the lay executive. Vacant general secretary seats would probably, in unions without factional organization, be contested by the leading national full-time officials, much as they are now. The odds would be strongly in favour of the most senior assistant or deputy general secretaries taking the seat.

It is in unions with well-organized factions or parties that the constitutionally prescribed division of powers is most effective in preventing domination by any one body or person. In these unions elections for national office are generally contested by candidates representing the opposition who, if successful, subsequently join their fellow faction or party members on the respective bodies and provide the potential for developing a countervailing force against the governing faction or party. This is the position in the AUEW(E). For the Group or the broad left to govern the union they ideally need majorities on the executive, national committee and final appeal court, as well as holding the position of president and general secretary. If one party fails to hold these positions, it is possible for the other to block or hinder the government of the union. Factional organization in the CPSA and the NUM makes the division between executive and conference important.

The checks on oligarchy provided by the formal division of powers are thus primarily dependent on the informal organization of faction or party for their effectiveness. Attempts to strengthen these divisions by promoting periodic re-elections and the use of postal ballots would therefore depend for their success upon the existence of factions and parties. In unions which do not have well-organized opposition factions, the proposed changes would not strengthen checks on oligarchy, and if used selectively for the election of lay executives may indeed weaken those checks.

Internal Bargaining between Leaders and Members

Internal bargaining between leaders and conflicting groups of members provides another check on oligarchy and is not dependent on the constitutional division of powers. Hemingway, in three case studies of membership challenges to the authority of full-time officials and executives in the NUS, NUR and USDAW, has shown how members may '. . . go beyond the constitutional arrangements for democracy in order to exert control over their leaders'.[50] The most extreme form of this conflict is for the dissatisfied members to threaten or actually leave the union *en masse* and establish an independent breakaway union. Between 1943 and 1972, 41 new unions were established by members breaking away from 22 established unions.[51] However, these are exceptional cases. Dissatisfied members are more likely to negotiate an accommodation with the leadership, although they may find it necessary to employ a range of sanctions including withholding union subscriptions, strikes, pickets and sit-ins during negotiations. In this model, union democracy depends on the opportunity for intra-organizational bargaining between dissatisfied groups of members and the offending officials, the ultimate bargaining lever being that the members resign and form a competing union. It is difficult to assess which unions would be most likely to provoke this kind of membership response to a perceived abuse of leadership power. Hemingway argues that such conflicts are more likely to arise in unions which have structural (horizontal and vertical) divisions of interest probably caused by recruiting over different industrial and occupational boundaries and then failing to satisfy the interests of some minority group of members. This would suggest that the TGWU and ASTMS should, in particular, experience these challenges. Recognizing that arguments have been presented above regarding the importance of occupational homogeneity for the development of factions, it would appear logical that the more heterogeneous unions would be more susceptible to this type of minority challenge, minority groups of dissatisfied members in such unions rarely reaching the status of factions. Such groups either resolve their differences with the leadership through the bargaining process or fade into insignificance because formal structural divisions prevent them evolving into factions and providing an opposition group on a more permanent basis.

Bargaining by minority groups which forces concessions from the established leadership of the less homogeneous unions may therefore help to compensate for the lack of factions and parties by limiting the practices of the existing leadership on an *ad hoc* basis without becoming a generalized opposition. This activity is not dependent on elections or constitutional mechanisms, and the groups involved may be insignificant in the formal processes. They can, however, check the oligarchic tendencies which may exist in the absence of factions and parties by bringing sanctions to bear and gaining concessions on specific issues of importance to their sectional interest and thus promote democracy.

Decentralization of Decision Making

Approaches to union democracy which analyse the centralization and decentralization of decision making within unions focus on the location of decisions at different levels of union structure rather than upon elections. Unions are recognized as being composed of several levels of government, with different issues being resolved, and different processes being used, at each level.[52] In some unions, certain questions of policy and administration may, for example, be determined nationally by the executive committee, and in others regionally by the leading full-time officials. According to this model, the lower the level of decision making, the more democratic the union. Local autonomy is taken as '. . . vital . . . if not synonymous with union democracy'.[53] It is assumed that members are able to exercise a greater degree of influence over their own interests when decisions are located at the bottom rather than the top of the union structure, thus preventing the development of a full-time officers' oligarchy. Where unions grant the district or shop-floor organization important issues to resolve, and a high degree of autonomy, there is a greater degree of democracy than where control over the same issues is confined to a higher level (regional or national) committee.

Further distinctions may also be made between the channels of government used for determining bargaining and non-bargaining issues. In some unions, for example the TGWU, these divisions are recognized in the union's formal constitution. The TGWU uses one channel for processing bargaining and another for non-bargaining decisions. Even where there is no formal distinction, as in the AUEW(E), some members and officials have a more pronounced role in bargaining than in non-bargaining decisions. It is thus possible to have high membership participation and control over issues in one channel and low participation and control in the other. For example, unions which do not elect their full-time officials, have comparatively low levels of participation and competition in elections to the lay executive, do not have factional organization and are centralized in non-bargaining decisions, may still be more democratic than these features would suggest where their members have direct control over bargaining decisions.

The four previous models examined, which concentrated on elections and checks on oligarchy, may thus not provide adequate criteria for union democracy. Their appropriateness depends on the degree to which the national full-time officers and lay executives in the unions studied make significant decisions over bargaining and non-bargaining issues. If all decisions of major importance in the bargaining and/or non-bargaining field are decentralized, it is clearly less significant for ordinary members and for democracy how the national officials and executives are chosen or elected.

Unions differ widely in the extent to which they centralize or decentralize their non-bargaining decisions. The AUEW(E) traditionally and by rule gives its lay district committees a great deal more autonomy than the comparable bodies receive in the TGWU. In contrast, the GMWU locates a large number of decisions at the regional level. However, the TGWU pursued a deliberate policy of decentralization in the late 1960s and early 1970s. District committees were formed in most regions and steps taken to integrate the growing shop steward movement into the official structure of the union.[54] The EETPU also formed area conferences, and advisory area industrial committees, both composed of shop stewards.[55] This reflected a general movement in the 1970s towards decentralization (although there were some notable exceptions, including UCATT and the POEU).

Ballots and changes in balloting methods have, not surprisingly, contributed little to the decentralization of non-bargaining decisions. The trend has been to take the decisions down to the members sitting on committees or attending *ad hoc* meetings rather than changing voting methods to bring more members into policy decisions. Unions with committees at different levels of government continue to rely primarily on representatives rather than direct participation in policy and administrative decisions. The exception is Equity, which, with its mobile and dispersed membership and lacking the normal hierarchy of committees, uses a postal referendum for determining controversial issues such as its application to the certification officer discussed in chapter 4.

Models of democracy which concentrate on the means of choosing representatives and checks on oligarchy are still appropriate tests when applied to non-bargaining decisions, for the majority of unions continue to depend on elected members for policy and administrative decisions. However, these decisions are no longer as centralized as they were twenty years ago and the opportunity for national officials to dominate the processes of decision making has thus been reduced.

The location of bargaining decisions varies from union to union and also, in some unions, between different groups within unions. Unlike elections and non-bargaining decisions, unions do not have unilateral control over the level of bargaining, which is subject to agreement with, and in some instances determined by, the employer. There may also be elements in union agreements negotiated at several different levels. For example, hours and holidays may be subject to national agreement but pay determined in the plant. However, on pay issues public sector unions are more likely to negotiate at the national, and unions recruiting primarily in the private manufacturing industry at the plant and enterprise level. Thus unions such as the CPSA, POEU, NUR and NUM are more centralized in their bargaining activities than the AUEW(E), TGWU and ASTMS, whilst the GMWU because of its extensive interests in the public sector (the GMWU has approximately 25 per cent of its members in local government) occupies an intermediate position.

The AUEW(E), TGWU, GMWU and ASTMS, all have policies, and ASTMS constitutional provisions, to promote lay involvement in bargaining at the plant level. The TGWU and ASTMS, and to a lesser extent the GMWU, were for various reasons committed to the decentralization of bargaining in the 1970s. For the TGWU and GMWU, this represented a marked move away from the centralist bargaining of previous decades dominated by full-time officers. ASTMS, with its closed branches and groups formed to deal primarily with bargaining matters, probably went further than most unions in institutionalizing its decentralized bargaining policies.

The rise of the shop steward, and the fourfold increase in full-time or professional shop stewards between 1968 and 1979 to 10,000 was directly related to the decentralization of bargaining.[56] Union reluctance to increase the number and availability of full-time officials and preference for more lay workplace negotiators also assisted the development of autonomous bargaining groups, particularly in large units in manufacturing industry. Shop stewards representing these groups negotiated and settled agreements with employers with little, if any, reference to full-time officials.[57] The result was that for many members in the decentralizing unions the shop steward became 'the union'. Participation in shop steward elections and voting on employers' offers and the taking of industrial action were thus more important and relevant actions than electing national full-time officers and executives with little influence over the bread-and-butter questions settled in the plant.

Members in unions which decentralized their bargaining activities were therefore drawn into the process of bargaining by participating in the election of their shop stewards and voting on employers' offers. The extent of membership participation in both these decisions was considerably higher than it was in the choosing of full-time officers and the election of national executives. In 1980 shop stewards were working in 75 per cent of establishments recognizing manual, and 66 per cent recognizing non-manual, unions.[58] They were elected by the members they represented and approximately 75 per cent were required to stand for re-election, although a large majority were in practice unopposed. Senior shop stewards, often the leading plant-level negotiators, were generally elected directly by union members; only 11 per cent were elected by fellow shop stewards. Very few postal ballots were used in the election of senior or ordinary shop stewards. The preferred method was by a show of hands vote, and this showed little variation across the three largest unions. Senior shop stewards in the TGWU were elected by a show of hands in 69 per cent of establishments, 78 per cent in the AUEW and 75 per cent in the GMWU. Non-postal ballots were the next most popular method: 23 per cent TGWU, 15 per cent AUEW and 10 per cent GMWU.

Acceptance or rejection of agreements and strike decisions are, as shown in chapter 3, frequently made directly by the members in both centralized and decentralized unions. However, except for the NUM, which has rules requiring reference back on certain questions, the practice is normally more prevalent when bargaining is decentralized. For example, a postal survey of the AUEW(E)'s district secretaries, while showing that reference back of offers is frequent in both general engineering and in negotiations over corporate or national agreements (apart from the EEF-CSEU national agreement), also showed that reference back is more frequent in decentralized negotiations in general engineering than in the relatively centralized national and corporate level negotiations: 84 per cent of district secretaries stated that they always referred back in the former negotiations, compared with 64 per cent in the latter. Evidence from the Department of Employment survey similarly showed that the level of consultation over wage offers was high, with only 10 per cent of shop stewards in the AUEW, 18 per cent in the TGWU and 23 per cent in the GMWU recording no consultations.[59] The scale of responses may also be thought to reflect the rank order of decentralization from the highly decentralized AUEW to the more centralized GMWU.

The method of referring questions to the membership is rarely determined by rule. Few unions use postal ballots, and workplace ballots are far more common amongst non-manual than manual unions. Nevertheless, some manual unions, including certain sections of some TGWU trade groups, use non-postal ballots in highly centralized negotiations to refer matters of real importance to members geographically dispersed over several employing units. As the tendency to decentralized bargaining and enhanced shop steward involvement increased, ballots were not considered a generally appropriate means of taking membership opinion. Tactical considerations of how best to resolve local negotiations while maintaining representative institutions led to the continued use of show of hands votes which, as discussed in chapter 3, matched the logic of the situation.

Unions which are decentralized in their bargaining structure therefore have a very high degree of membership involvement in choosing the bargainers and determining the acceptance or rejection of offers. Moreover, the lay bargainers, particularly in the larger plants in the private manufacturing sector, may frequently have a high degree of autonomy and act independently of full-time officials. Unions which recruit predominantly within this sector include the AUEW(E), TGWU, ASTMS and, to a lesser extent, the GMWU. The latter three unions tend to be centralized (regionalized in the GMWU's case) in their non-bargaining functions, to have few if any elected full-time officers and to be devoid of factions, and thus it could be suggested less democratic than some other unions. However, in collective bargaining their members frequently have the local autonomy which in this model is equated with democracy.

The five models discussed above do not assume that union leaders have any particular political axe to grind. Instead, the starting point is that unions, in common with all large complex organizations, tend to follow Michels' famous dictum. Our main concern is therefore with assessing how far postal ballots contribute to union democracy by inhibiting the emergence of an oligarchy of full-time officials, and by improving the processes whereby differing and possibly conflicting goals amongst both leaders and members are reconciled.

There are significant variations between unions in how far they 'measure up' to the different democratic models used. It is, therefore, possible to come to conflicting conclusions on the extent of democracy within unions, depending upon the model of union democracy used. The main thrust of argument since Lipset et al.'s influential work[60] has been on the role of opposition groups in restricting an oligarchy of full-time officers and/or providing an alternative government at the national level. If unions were centralized in both bargaining and non-bargaining channels, this emphasis on the national level of decision making would be appropriate. However, a number of British unions have in recent years become highly decentralized in their bargaining activities. Members in these unions depend primarily on shop stewards for their effective representation. Therefore, it may be of only limited importance for members in these unions that full-time officials are appointed or that the executive is elected by a minority of the membership. For, if the members have direct control at the workplace over the issues they consider important, they may choose not to participate in higher level, but less relevant decisions.

Thus checks on the dominance of leadership and degree of bargaining decentralization should be considered together when assessing the level of democracy in British unions. If both sets of criteria are considered, the most stringent criteria for checks on the dominance of leadership are met by many of the more occupationally homogeneous unions which have, or have had, opposition groups successfully competing for major office, and in some cases overturning the government. These unions include, amongst others, the AUEW(E), EETPU, CPSA, POEU, NUS, NUM, NUR, Bakers and Equity. The more heterogeneous and less highly factional unions, including TGWU, GMWU and ASTMS, are more decentralized in the bargaining field than many of the unions recruiting in the public sector. These three unions, with the AUEW(E) and the EETPU, have shop stewards or branch officers negotiating largely independently of full-time officials on behalf of work groups on issues of major importance to the membership.

This discussion of models of union democracy raises a number of issues regarding proposals to increase democracy by promoting secret, and particularly postal, ballots. Secret ballots as a means of determining elections and other decisions are given little attention in the models of democracy examined, probably because the models tend to concentrate on the larger issues, presumably implicitly assuming that secret ballots are used in elections. With a few exceptions, including ASTMS and GMWU where show of hands votes are recorded, this is largely the position in major British unions. But in practice the location of the secret ballot is more important than the degree of secrecy, although it is the latter which is specified in the 1980 scheme. It is not the marginal increase in secrecy gained by moving the vote from the branch to the home which causes increases in turnout (by protecting opposition voters from reprisals by the established leadership) but the ease of voting. Furthermore, relocating the voting may alter control over the communication of the choices on offer and therefore may widen the scope for external influences.

Legislation which seeks to promote union democracy will depend for its effect on democracy on the interaction between the method promoted and the union's existing processes of decision making, both formal and informal. As there is no common pattern of formal, much less informal, procedures in British unions, the result for democracy of enforcing postal ballots is problematic. Secrecy in the casting of the vote might be increased, but the conflict between secrecy and malpractice in the counting of the vote would remain a problem (see chapter 4). Even in such relatively concrete matters as turnout the results would differ according to the mobility and dispersal of membership and the levels achieved by the existing balloting method. It is probable that turnout would increase in a considerable number of unions adopting postal ballots, but in some it would decrease. More significantly, however, legislation which required postal ballots on a selective basis, for example, for the election of executives, would have a differential impact on democracy according to a combination of formal and informal factors, including the constitutionally prescribed division of powers, whether full-time officials are appointed or elected, large or small conferences, the existence of factions and parties, etc. If postal ballots generated higher turnouts in executive elections this would not necessarily increase democracy, since it would not itself limit the opportunity for government by an oligarchy of full-time officials. Indeed, increased turnout would strengthen the hands of the full-time officers and the candidates they sponsored in some unions by making it more difficult for the members of badly organized factions, of left or right, to communicate the nature of the choice they offered to the wider membership. Further, in the subsequent process of decision making the tenured full-time officer's influence could be enhanced if postal ballots, by promoting randomness in voting, increased the rate of turnover of lay executive members. Since the majority of unions surveyed have tenured general secretaries and lay executives subject to regular and frequent re-election, this is not a minor consideration. Thus the argument that secrecy and postal ballots necessarily increase democracy, even if applied selectively, is less plausible than it first appears.

Finally, formal factors are less important than informal and structural factors in promoting union democracy. As shown above, unions with many of the same formal provisions, such as similar division of powers, tenured general secretaries and branch ballots for electing conference delegates, may be more or less democratic in practice. Significantly, the development of factions and parties is not dependent on specific types of ballots or even on the election of full-time officials. Legislation cannot provide for the occupational or industrial nature of a union's membership, or the activist's ideological commitment, which shape such developments. Moreover, the decentralization of bargaining and the consequent development of autonomous work groups, which reduce the importance of national officials and limit their influence over the ordinary members is not a suitable subject for legislation. Many of the factors which exert a major influence on the level of democracy within unions cannot be legislated for.

EFFECTS OF POSTAL BALLOTS ON INDUSTRIAL RELATIONS OUTCOMES

It is more difficult to assess the effects of postal ballots on outcomes than on processes. 'Government for the members' is less amendable to external measurement than 'government by the members'. Members' interests, and perceptions of their interests, differ widely, and there is much disagreement amongst participants and observers over what they are. Moreover, bargaining outcomes are influenced by a very wide range of factors, including the state of the national economy and product and labour markets: the contribution unions themselves make to bargaining outcomes is controversial, and the effects of union decision-making processes is likely to be limited. However, Conservative policy is based upon the premise that the introduction of postal ballots would increase the influence of 'moderation' in the trade union movement, and that such moderation is desirable in the interests of trade unionists (as well as the country at large). This moderation has two dimensions: industrial and political. The industrial dimension will be considered first.

Conservative policy makers believe that ordinary union members are more moderate than activists and leaders, and that increasing the influence of ordinary members on decision making would therefore reduce the level of union militancy: the more in touch the negotiator is with the ordinary member, and the more responsive to his wishes, the more moderate the claim and amicable the settlement. If negotiators fail to conform with this pattern their recommendations are likely to be rejected in ballots on agreements or strikes, and removed from office in the next round of elections. Increased use of ballots is therefore designed to foster more 'responsible' union behaviour in formulating and pursuing wage claims, reducing the tendency of union leaders to press for wage increases beyond the reasonable expectations of the union members concerned.

Evidence justifying such beliefs is limited. First, even union members opposed to union links with the Labour party are concerned with increasing their income and improving the terms and conditions of their employment. Terms such as 'calculative', 'instrumental', and 'bread-and-butter trade unionists' convey the union members' central concern with improving their economic circumstances. Union members are intent on pursuing their sectional interests and ensuring that the union leadership 'delivers the goods' in its bargaining activities. Of course, short-run sectional interests are not always pursued regardless of long-term costs, and short-term benefits may be foregone in favour of long-term rewards. However, union leaders are themselves as likely to make such balanced calculations as ordinary members. There is no evidence to suggest, and much to deny, that ordinary union members regard union leaders who obtain below average wage settlements, or who allow their members to drift down the earnings league table, as effective.

Secondly, evidence on the effect of accountability on representative negotiators, i.e. those who do not merely act as delegates or postmen in negotiations, suggests that the greater the accountability and the '. . . more motivated their representatives are to please their constituents, the less conciliatory they will be in their dealings with the other party'.[61] Periodic re-elections may thus lead to more aggressive bargaining by negotiators, particularly when they approach re-election. If they fail to respond to the satisfaction of their constituents ('my members' legitimate aspirations'), postal ballots are no safeguard against the defeat of moderates in subsequent elections. For example, the NUS and Bakers union underwent sharp changes in political direction when the membership in the 1970s became dissatisfied with the union's industrial policy and action (or relative inaction), and opted for more militant candidates in national elections, as shown in chapter 2. Thus the Marxist arguments for periodic re-election of full-time officers, preferably by branch or workplace and not postal ballots, as a means of limiting the moderating effect of institutionalization on appointed or tenured full-time officials probaby carries more weight than the Conservative thesis. Support for the periodic re-election of officials by postal ballot may facilitate a primitive form of democracy by making negotiators more responsible to members' sectional interests, but it may also inadvertently encourage a more militant bargaining posture.

Conservative encouragement for postal ballots on the reference back of offers and on industrial action is also intended to moderate wage claims and reduce the incidence of strike action. Ballots are considered more conducive to rational reflection and to moderation than are mass meetings and show of hands votes which, as shown in chapter 3, are the most common methods of deciding such issues at present, especially amongst manual workers. Conservatives fear that members attending mass meetings are intimidated or persuaded by a sense of solidarity to pursue militant policies which are against their own 'best interests', and which they would reject if voting in the privacy of their home. On the other hand, unions find mass meetings and show of hands voting more convenient to organize than postal ballots. Moreover, some trade unionists would also claim that they are more democratic than postal ballots, in that they allow an exchange of views and the formation of a consensus or majority view in a manner which is not possible when considering how to complete a ballot paper on an individual basis. Mass meetings may also be perceived as part of the bargaining process in which the negotiator generates solidarity for the claim and mobilizes support for further action.[62] There is some evidence that union members will, as individuals, hold more moderate opinions than they are willing to express when part of a mass meeting.[63] Outside of the meeting they calculate in more personal terms the financial costs of undertaking or continuing the strike, while in a meeting they are more concerned with not appearing to break ranks and to avoid the 'moral disapproval' of their more militant colleagues.

Postal ballots therefore probably do reduce militancy by denying negotiators and/or strike leaders the opportunity to call for strike votes at mass meetings, in which appeals to solidarity can overcome concern with individual profit and loss, but postal ballots do not guarantee moderation. As shown in chapter 3, postal ballots in electricity supply, despite recommendations from union leaders to accept offers, led to rejections. The effects upon militancy are likely to be less where ballots are held at the workplace because of the opportunity for debate and discussion and the influence of opinion leaders. However, votes by show of hands at mass meetings do not automatically lead to bigger demands and strikes, even in the very large mass meetings characteristic of the motor industry (as experienced at Longbridge in 1979 during the meetings following the dismissal of Derek Robinson, or at Solihull following the decision to close the Rover assembly line in 1981).

The method and location of voting is not therefore a major determinant of outcome. If union members have a deep sense of injustice, and the economic environment is not heavily weighted against them achieving their objectives, the method of voting will be incidental to the result. Nevertheless, if the issue is finely balanced it is likely that postal ballots will result in more moderate outcomes than mass meetings as indicated in chapter 3.

Finally, if there is mandatory reference back and negotiators are forced to confer with the members by a referendum this may reduce the importance of elections. It reduces the representative role. One of the repercussions may be a change in the electorate's perceptions of the importance of elections. Individual voters may consider, perhaps somewhat irrationally, that the choice of militant leaders will have no adverse consequences in the bargaining field because, if necessary, they and other members can vote against strikes or other industrial action when the occasion requires. Thus, it is possible that the existence of requirements to ballot members on strikes, as in the NUM, releases constraints which may in other circumstances restrain the membership from voting for the more militant candidate. Mandatory postal balloting on the calling of strikes may therefore release more votes for militant candidates in elections and alter the political outcome.

POLITICAL EFFECTS OF LEGISLATION ON UNION BALLOTS

Legislation on union ballots has political as well as industrial objectives and consequences. Conservatives believe that union leaders no longer reflect the political views of union members as revealed by general election voting patterns and public opinion surveys: union leaders remain committed to the Labour party, whilst their followers do not. The use of ballots in union elections might therefore result in the election of union leaders less committed to the Labour party. Moreover, the introduction of balloting on union political funds might create financial difficulties for the Labour party, whether or not 'contracting out' was replaced by 'contracting in' for individual trade unionists. Even if the proposed legislation did not lead to long-term changes in the structure of the British labour movement the proposals would create organizational and financial problems for the labour movement. The political consequences of the increased use of ballots may satisfy Conservative objectives, in party political terms, at least in the short run; the long run consequences may be different. However, legislation regulating the internal affairs of unions for political objectives constitutes a fundamental breach of the traditional principles of liberal pluralism, breaching internationally accepted principles of freedom of association. Party political advantage is thus gained at the cost of serious damage to the political system.

Conservative legislation on industrial relations under the Heath government was not a success, industrially or politically. Weekes et al. concluded that '[The 1971 Industrial Relations Act] had little influence on the general practice of industrial relations . . . the law was judged on its utility and was found wanting'.[64] The Act did not meet the practical needs of employers, managers and employees and was therefore ineffective. Politically, the Act had more success in the short term, satisfying 1970 election pledges on union reform and defining industrial relations reform as union reform in political terms. However, the Act was not wholly successful even politically. The Act embroiled the Government in political conflict with the trade union movement on a continuing basis, and helped reconstruct relations between trade unions and the Labour party strained by *In Place of Strife* and Labour plans for industrial relations legislation: the Act reunited the Labour movement.

Conservative legislation in the 1980s avoided the worst mistakes of the early 1970s: the legislation itself was less ambitious and avoided direct long-term government involvement in industrial relations. The legislation on ballots was especially judicious. In both the 1980 Act and the 1983 Bill the Government has followed an indirect (and incrementalist) approach, establishing desirable principles but leaving the initiative for action with the unions themselves, or in default of union action with disgruntled union members (as in the 1983 Trade Union Bill proposals for ballots in union elections) or with employers (on strike ballots). The Government has thus avoided the elaborate codification, and institution building of the 1971 Industrial Relations Act. The contrast between 1971 and 1983 is clearest in the treatment of strike ballots. Under the 1971 Act the Secretary of State for Employment was empowered to ask the National Industrial Relations Court to order a ballot in specified circumstances.[65] Under the 1980 Act the use of strike ballots is entirely voluntary. In July 1983 it was proposed that:

> In the case of industrial action which is 'authorized or endorsed' by a trade union . . . immunity in tort will be conditional on the support of the union members concerned being tested in a secret ballot . . . Without immunity the trade union would be at risk of being sued for an injunction and its funds could be at risk of an action for damages'.[66]

The Government has thus avoided direct involvement in the enforcement of the approved principles.

Experience of the early 1970s is not a good guide to likely experience in the 1980s. Conservative legislation in the 1980s is likely to have greater impact on industrial relations than it had in the 1970s. The trade union movement will necessarily have to 'live with' the 1980 and 1982 Employment Acts and the prospective 1984 Trade Union Act with little prospect of repeal in the foreseeable future.[67] At the same time, the trade union movement is weaker than a decade earlier, with declining membership and financial pressures, especially amongst the major manual unions which spearheaded opposition to the 1971 Act. Economic recession obviously hinders the exercise of union power, industrially and politically. At the same time, following its victory in the 1983 election the Conservative government felt that it had received a mandate to follow through the logic of the industrial relations policy developed in its first term: frequent, individually small pieces of legislation designed to limit union power. The Conservative victory in the 1983 election led to immediate action on union ballots.

In placing trade union ballots at the forefront of political discussion, the Government has two sets of political objectives, tactical and strategic. Tactically, ballots have major advantages, and no serious disadvantages. Balloting poses few tactical difficulties for the Government. There is general agreement amongst Conservative party members that union ballots are desirable: the only controversy is over the extent to which legislation to promote them should involve mandatory requirements. Employers' organizations generally – but not invariably – favour balloting, without regarding the issue as one of high priority. At the same time, legislation on ballots poses major tactical difficulties for the trade union movement. It is impossible to oppose ballots in principle: they are undoubtedly a democratic mechanism, and many trade unions already use them extensively. It is especially difficult to oppose the principle of balloting in union elections because a majority of unions already use ballots to elect at least some office-holders, especially executive committee memberships. (There is also a powerful implicit comparison with Parliamentary elections, although a more accurate analogy would be to elections within political parties, and neither Labour nor Conservative party members are able to vote by ballot in the selection of their prospective Parliamentary candidates.) It is impossible to oppose the provision of public funds for ballot expenses, as it is merely a facility of which unions may or may not take advantage. Finally, it is difficult to oppose effectively mandatory requirements for balloting because the legislation can be presented as merely generalizing and systematizing currently accepted practice in union elections, and widening the scope of membership involvement in decisions which involve them.

Strategically, the Government's political objective is to loosen the link between the trade union movement and the Labour party. Trade unions have, of course, been institutionally linked to the Labour party since the original conference which led to the foundation of the Labour Representation Committee in 1900. The link was cemented in the party constitution, accepted in 1918, and has remained the focal point of British left-wing politics. The already close links were further strengthened by experience of the Social Contract between 1975 and 1978, and by the revision of the Labour party constitution at the Wembley conference in January 1981: the trade unions are the dominant force, organizationally and financially, in the Labour party. At the same time as trade unions have tightened their institutional links with the Labour party, significant numbers of trade union members have ceased to support the Labour party electorally, including many who believe that trade unions should not take an active role in politics: even in the majority of TUC unions which have political funds a minority of members have contracted out of paying the political levy (in unions like ASTMS or SOGAT a substantial minority). Hence, in 1979 only 51 per cent of trade unionists voted Labour, compared with 73 per cent in 1964: 33 per cent voted Conservative, and 13 per cent supported other parties.[68] In 1980 46 per cent of trade unionists agreed with the view that 'The Labour party should not be so closely linked to the trade unions'; although it would be a mistake to interpret the poll findings too precisely, evidence of union members' disillusion with union links to the Labour party is incontrovertible.[69]

There is thus a disjunction between trade union links with the Labour party and trade union members' views. Increasing membership involvement through balloting, especially on specifically political questions, would therefore inevitably weaken links between trade unions and the Labour party.

The Government's tactical political objectives have been achieved: there is widespread support for, and little effective opposition to, measures to increase the use of ballots in trade unions. Achievement of the strategic objectives may prove more difficult, and possibly even counterproductive. In assessing the impact of balloting two issues are involved: will the increased use of ballots result in the election of moderate leaders? Would moderate leaders favour loosening ties with the Labour party, either out of conviction or in response to membership opinion? Since the 1980 Act has had negligible effects, and the more substantial 1983 proposals have not yet been enacted, comment is speculative. Procedures for changing union rule books are complex and time-consuming. Moreover, even the more interventionist proposals of 1983 leave the initiative for action with the unions, or with disgruntled union members. It is therefore inevitable that any changes will be slow, and probably slight. The wider use of postal ballots in union elections might result in the election of politically moderate union leaders, although the experience of the NUS, FTAT and the Bakers union indicates that this is not inevitable. However, if more moderate leaders were elected it would not necessarily work to the political advantage of the Conservative party, and might work to its disadvantage. Moderate union leaders will continue to be drawn from that section of the activist minority of union members associated with the right wing of the Labour party rather than supporters of the Conservative party or the Liberal–SDP Alliance, as Conservatives recognize in practice: in 1976 Conservatives urged support for Labour moderates in elections in five unions.[70] Such union leaders would use their influence to extend right-wing policies in the Labour party, including tripartism, as union leaders such as David Basnett have done, rather than to weaken the links between the trade unions and the Labour party. The result would be enhanced electoral credibility for the Labour party. At the same time, the proposed requirement for confirmatory ballots on union political funds, and any weakening of the 'contracting out' arrangements, will of course reduce the financial support available to the Labour party, and give rise to financial and organizational difficulties.

By focusing upon union ballots, the Government has thus succeeded in gaining political advantages, without incurring major political costs. The 1980 Act established balloting as the desirable procedure for unions, and encouraged voluntary reform; the more extensive proposals of 1983 provide further impetus, without long-term direct government involvement. The reforms could have a beneficial effect on some trade union systems of government by increasing participation in elections or decisions on collective agreements. They might increase the number and power of industrial and political moderates in the trade union movement. But even if the legislation did not lead to any major change in industrial relations (which is likely), the Government would have fulfilled its election pledges, caused short-term political difficulties for the trade union movement and perhaps begun the process of dissolving the links between the trade unions and the Labour party.

Conservative political gains would, however, be made at major cost to the political system as a whole. Trade unions and employers' associations play a major role as independent actors in a pluralist representative democracy: they are a major means of 'interest articulation'.[71] Their effectiveness in this process depends upon their independence and ability to express the interests they represent without distortion or hindrance. Company- or state-sponsored unions which see their major roles as increasing worker productivity are neither desirable democratically nor, in the long run, effective economically, leading to cynicism and disaffection amongst the union membership. One essential element in trade union independence is the right to determine their own internal procedures, subject to the law of the land. The ILO Convention on Freedom of Association, ratified by the British government in 1949 and not subsequently denounced, outlines the basic principle:

> Workers' and employers' organizations shall have the right to draw up their constitutions and rules, to elect their representatives in full freedom, to organize their administration and activities and to formulate their programmes. The public authorities shall refrain from any interference which would restrict this right or impede the lawful exercise thereof (article 3).

In exercising their rights trade unions are subject to the law of the land, but 'the law of the land shall not be such as to impair, nor shall it be so applied as to impair, the guarantees provided for in this convention' (article 8).[72] In short, independence from government regulation of internal procedures is a basic democratic principle, the infringement of which represents a major limitation on 'free trade unionism' requiring special justification.

This analysis, of course, rests upon a particular conception of trade unions and of democracy. Trade unions are seen as voluntary associations, whose members pay subscriptions to achieve objectives outlined in union rules (or to avoid social ostracism or to satisfy the requirements of closed shop provisions).[73] As Allan Flanders has argued:

> The first and over-riding responsibility of all trade unions is to the welfare of their own members. That is their primary commitment; not to a firm, not to an industry, not to the nation. A union collects its members' contributions and demands their loyalty specifically for the purpose of protecting their interests as they see them, not their alleged 'true' or 'best' interests as defined by others.[74]

The ability of unions to express the interests of union members becomes distorted where internal procedures are arranged to satisfy government (or employer) requirements: external concern to increase internal democracy becomes inextricably entangled with the desire to achieve specific outcomes:

increased productivity or moderate wage settlements. The entanglement may be explicit or implicit; in either case organizations established and funded by their members to achieve one set of objectives are being, in effect, misappropriated.

As the terms of the ILO convention on Freedom of Association indicate, the normal assumption in a democracy is that trade unions are free to establish their own rules and procedures, external regulation requiring special justification. The first justification for restricting such freedom is the general law of the land; legislation concerning racial or sexual discrimination has obvious implications for union internal procedures. Alternatively, such justification might be based on the need to eliminate corruption, as in the Landrum-Griffin Act in the United States in 1959. More generally, it could be justified where trade unions are accorded special legal privileges, as in the Australian Conciliation and Arbitration system.[75] In the British context, unions possess legal immunities, most importantly the protection of the 'golden formula' in industrial disputes, whereby unions are protected against action for tort in certain circumstances. Moreover, the unions acquired an influence over government policy during the period of the Social Contract (1975–8) which exceeded that of any other group, including employers. Where unions claim the right to political influence on the basis of their representing 'the majority of ordinary working people', governments have a responsibility to ensure that such organizations have effective systems of representation. However, since 1979 Conservative policy has been to narrow the scope of the 'golden formula', in both the 1980 and 1982 Employment Acts, and to reject union claims for a distinctive political role. Unions are to be treated as other economic interests groups, to be listened to or ignored according to the Government's particular policy priorities. To the extent that Conservative policy succeeds in reducing the unions to the status of other economic interest groups, the justification for external intervention in their internal decision-making procedures grows weaker.

The balloting provisions of the 1980 Act are uncontroversial: trade unions remain free to adopt ballots or not as they think fit. However, the 1983 Trade Union Bill raises more substantial issues. The principles laid down for trade union elections require unions to administer their affairs in a particular manner on penalty, ultimately, of prosecution for contempt of court. Where unions do not carry out elections in a specified manner disappointed candidates, or other union members, are entitled to apply to the ordinary courts for a declaration stating that a specific election has not been carried out according to the union's statutory obligations. If the declaration is made, the court grants the union a specified time period to carry out the election according to the specified principles; if the election is not so carried out, the members concerned will be able to seek enforcement of the order, under sanction of contempt of court proceedings. The proposal clearly involves state authorities specifying the internal procedures of trade unions, in breach of ILO Convention 87.

In 1977 the CBI commented:

Legislation affecting power groups is inevitably subject to party political considerations. But if it is to be effective and lasting it must be supported by a broad consensus. We have learnt to our cost that we cannot have industrial relations law treated as a political shuttlecock. The current widespread complaints from employers about the bias and burden of the present legislation relate as much to the problems caused by continually changing requirements as to the nature and volume of the law itself. The CBI's main concern is to find practical industrial solutions, divorced as far as possible from party politics.[76]

Such a plea would have enthusiastic support from the TUC in 1983.

APPENDIX: Rule Book Survey and Classification of Unions

Total of 103 unions surveyed by rule book in 1980 and classified according to manual, non-manual, craft or craft origins.

MANUAL UNIONS (NON-CRAFT)

Amalgamated Association of Beamers, Twisters and Drawers (Hand and Machine)
Amalgamated Felt Hat Trimmers, Woolformers and Allied Workers Association
Amalgamated Society of Textile Workers and Kindred Trades
Amalgamated Textile Workers Union
Amalgamated Union of Asphalt Workers
Associated Metalworkers Union
Cloth Pressers Society
Confederation of Health Service Employees (COHSE)
Fire Brigades Union (FBU)
General and Municipal Workers Union (GMWU)
General Union of Associations of Loom Overlookers
Iron and Steel Trades Confederation (ISTC)
National Association of Theatrical, Television and Kine Employees (NATTKE)
National Society of Metal Mechanics (NSMM)
National Society of Operative Printers, Graphical and Media Personnel (NATSOPA)
National Union of Agricultural and Allied Workers (NUAAW)
National Union of Blastfurnacemen, Ore Miners, Coke Workers and Kindred Trades (Blastfurnacemen)
National Union of Dyers, Bleachers and Textile Workers
National Union of the Footwear, Leather and Allied Trades (NUFLAT)
National Union of Hosiery and Knitwear Workers
National Union of Mineworkers (NUM)
National Union of Public Employees (NUPE)
National Union of Railwaymen (NUR)
National Union of Seamen (NUS)
National Union of Tailors and Garment Workers (NUTGW)
Northern Carpet Trades Union
Pattern Weavers Society
Power Loom Carpet Weavers and Textile Workers Union
Prison Officers Association

Rossendale Union of Boot, Shoe and Slipper Operatives
Scottish Prison Officers Association
Screw, Nut, Bolt and Rivet Trade Union
Society of Graphical and Allied Trades (SOGAT)
Tobacco Mechanics Association
Tobacco Workers Union
Transport and General Workers Union (TGWU)
Union of Communication Workers (UCW)
Union of Shop, Distributive and Allied Workers (USDAW)
United Road Transport Union (URTU)

MANUAL UNIONS (CRAFT OR CRAFT ORIGIN)

Amalgamated Society of Boilermakers, Shipwrights, Blacksmiths and Structural Workers (ASB)
Amalgamated Society of Journeymen, Felt Hatters and Allied Workers
Amalgamated Society of Wire Drawers and Kindred Workers
Amalgamated Union of Engineering Workers, Engineering Section [AUEW(E)]
Amalgamated Union of Engineering Workers, Foundry Section [AUEW(F)]
Associated Society of Locomotive Engineers and Firemen (ASLEF)
Association of Patternmakers and Allied Craftsmen (Patternmakers)
Bakers, Food and Allied Workers Union (Bakers)
British Roll Turners Trade Society
Card Setting Machine Tenters Society
Ceramic and Allied Trades Union
Electrical, Electronic, Telecommunication and Plumbing Union (EETPU)
Furniture, Timber and Allied Trades Union (FTAT)
Military and Orchestral Musical Instrument Makers Trade Society
National Graphical Association (NGA)
National Society of Brushmakers and General Workers
National Union of Domestic Appliance and General Metal Workers
National Union of Gold, Silver and Allied Trades
National Union of Scalemakers
National Union of Sheet Metal Workers, Coppersmiths, Heating and Domestic Engineers
Post Office Engineering Union (POEU)
Sheffield Sawmakers Protection Society
Sheffield Wool Shear Workers Union
Society of Lithographic Artists, Designers, Engravers and Process Workers (SLADE)
Society of Shuttlemakers
Union of Construction, Allied Trades and Technicians (UCATT)

NON-MANUAL UNIONS

Amalgamated Union of Engineering Workers, Technical, Administrative and Supervisory Section [AUEW(TASS)]
Association of Broadcasting Staff (ABS)
Association of Cinematograph, Television and Allied Technicians (ACTT)
Association of First Division Civil Servants (FDA)
Association of Government Supervisors and Radio Officers

Association of Professional, Executive, Clerical and Computer Staff (APEX)
Association of Scientific, Technical and Managerial Staffs (ASTMS)
Association of University Teachers (AUT)
Banking, Insurance and Finance Union (BIFU)
British Actors Equity Association (Equity)
British Air Line Pilots Assocation (BALPA)
British Association of Colliery Management (BACM)
Civil and Public Services Association (CPSA)
Civil Service Union (CSU)
Educational Institute of Scotland
Engineers and Managers Association
Greater London Council Staff Association
Health Visitors Association
Hospital Consultants and Specialists Association
Inland Revenue Staff Federation (IRSF)
Institution of Professional Civil Servants (IPCS)
Merchant Navy and Airline Officers Association
Musicians Union
National Association of Colliery Overmen, Deputies and Shotfirers (NACODS)
National Association of Cooperative Officials
National Association of Licensed House Managers
National Association of Schoolmasters and Union of Women Teachers
National Association of Teachers in Further and Higher Education (NATFHE)
National and Local Government Officers Association (NALGO)
National Union of Insurance Workers
National Union of Journalists (NUJ)
National Union of Teachers (NUT)
Post Office Management Staffs Association
Radio and Electronic Officers Union
Society of Civil and Public Servants (SCPS)
Society of Post Office Executives
Transport Salaried Staffs Association (TSSA)
The Writers Guild of Great Britain

OTHER ABBREVIATIONS

ACAS, Advisory Conciliation and Arbitration Service
ACTTS, White collar section of TGWU
BIM, British Institute of Management
CBI, Confederation of British Industry
CSEU, Confederation of Shipbuilding and Engineering Unions
EEF, Engineering Employers Federation
EESA, White collar section of EETPU
IPM, Institute of Personnel Management
MATSA, White collar section of GMWU
NCB, National Coal Board
NIRC, National Industrial Relations Court
NJIC, National Joint Industrial Council
STAMP, White collar section of UCATT
TUC, Trade Union Congress
UCG, Unquoted Companies Group

Notes

CHAPTER 1   CONSERVATIVE INDUSTRIAL RELATIONS POLICY AND TRADE UNION BALLOTS

1 R. Lewis and B. Simpson, *Striking a Balance? Employment Law after the 1980 Act* (Martin Robertson, 1981), p. 2.
2 Ibid., p. 22.
3 Ibid., p. 224.
4 In 1976 Peter Walker accepted the Labour government's policy of making tax allowances conditional on the incomes ceiling figure the unions were prepared to accept: 'I disagree with those who consider it wrong to make this type of approach to the unions' (*Hansard*, 7 April 1976). Sir Geoffrey Howe and Mrs Thatcher thought otherwise. According to Mrs Thatcher, '[the Chancellor] surrendered the power to decide fiscal policy and the power to determine the course of the economy to an outside body' (*Hansard*, 9 June 1976).
5 *The Right Approach: a Statement of Conservative Aims* (Conservative Central Office, 1976), p. 44.
6 *The Conservative Manifesto 1979* (Conservative Central Office, 1979), p. 21.
7 *The Right Approach*, p. 11.
8 Ibid., p. 22.
9 Ibid., pp. 37–8, 44.
10 *The Conservative Manifesto 1974* (February), in *British General Election Manifestoes, 1900–74*, ed. F. W. S. Craig (Macmillan, 1975), p. 381.
11 *The Conservative Manifesto 1979*, pp. 7–8.
12 Ibid., pp. 11–12.
13 J. Prior, 'Industrial relations – approaching the year 2000', *Granada Guildhall Lectures 1980: the Role of the Trade Unions* (Granada, 1980), pp. 11–12.
14 Ibid., p. 17.
15 *The Right Approach to the Economy* (Conservative Central Office, n.d.), p. 19.
16 Ibid., p. 20.
17 *The Conservative Manifesto 1979*, p. 9.
18 Prior, 'Industrial relations', p. 18.
19 *Report of the Royal Commission on Trade Unions and Employers' Associations* (Donovan) (HMSO, 1968), Cmnd 3623, pp. 114–15.
20 Industrial Relations Act 1971 (cap. 72), sections 12, 49 and 141.
21 *The Conservative Manifesto 1974* (February), (ed. Craig) p. 376.
22 *The Conservative Manifesto 1974* (October), (ed. Craig) p. 434.
23 *The Right Approach*, p. 44.
24 P. Walker, *The Ascent of Britain* (Sidgwick & Jackson, 1977), pp. 69–70.
25 *Guardian*, 16 September 1978.
26 *The Times*, 28 September 1978.

27 *Hansard*, 7 November 1978. See, for example, *Guardian*, 9 November 1978.
28 *Financial Times*, 27 December 1978.
29 *Hansard*, 16 March 1979.
30 *Hansard*, 20 March 1979.
31 *The Conservative Manifesto 1979*, pp. 6, 7, 9.
32 *Working Paper on Support from Public Funds for Trade Union Ballots*, p. 1; *Industrial Relations Legal Information Bulletin*, no. 142, 8 August 1979, p. 4.
33 *Financial Times*, 10 July 1979.
34 *Observer*, 15 July 1979.
35 CBI Memorandum of Views on Proposed Industrial Relations Legislation on Picketing, the Closed Shop and Finance, September 1979.
36 *Britain Means Business 1978* (CBI, 1978), p. 47; *Britain Means Business 1977* (CBI, 1977), p. 35.
37 Letter from Electrical Contractors Association of Scotland to CBI, 17 August 1979.
38 EEF Representation on Support from Public Funds for Union Ballots, 17 August 1979.
39 Ibid.
40 *Personnel Management*, November 1979, 11, 11, p. 15.
41 TUC Circular to Affiliated Unions, 27 July 1979.
42 *Observer*, 15 July 1979.
43 *TUC Congress Report* (TUC, 1979), p. 440.
44 Ibid., p. 633.
45 For polls on the legislation see the *Guardian*, 3 September 1979: for Gallup poll see the *Daily Telegraph*, 18 September 1979.
46 *Hansard*, 17 December 1979.
47 *The Times*, 23 January 1980.
48 Committee A Official Report, 24 January 1980, col. 18.
49 Ibid., col. 22.
50 Ibid., col. 24.
51 Ibid., col. 33.
52 Ibid., col. 40.
53 Ibid., col. 64.
54 Ibid., col. 94. The fears were largely justified, see p. 43. *Notices of Questions and Motions*, 6 February 1980, no. 375, p. 4723.
55 *Notices of Questions and Motions*, 4 February 1980, p. 4610.
56 *Notices of Questions and Motions*, 21 February 1980, no.448, p. 5385; *Hansard*, 21 February 1980.
57 CBI, *Trade Unions in a Changing World: the Challenge for Management* (CBI, 1980), p. 5.
58 Ibid., p. 11.
59 Ibid., pp. 11–12.
60 Ibid., p. 22.
61 Ibid., p. 26.
62 Ibid., p. 28.
63 *Hansard*, 22 April 1980.
64 Ibid., col. 279.
65 *The Times*, 31 March and 22 April 1980.
66 *The Daily Telegraph*, 21 April 1980.
67 *The Times*, 20 April 1980.
68 *Hansard*, 22 April 1980, col. 311.
69 Ibid., col. 313.
70 *The Times*, 24 April 1980.
71 *Hansard*, 22 April 1980, col. 271.

72 Ibid., cols. 241, 258.
73 *Official Report, House of Lords Debates*, 3 June 1980.
74 *Conservative Party Annual Conference Report*, 1976, p. 56.
75 *Democracy in Trade Unions* (HMSO, 1983) Cmnd 8778, p. 20.
76 James Prior, Standing Committee A, 5 February 1980, col. 209.
77 *TUC Report 1980*, p. 599.
78 *Trade Union Immunities* (HMSO, 1981), Cmnd 8128, p. 66.
79 Ibid., p. 62.
80 Ibid., pp. 6–7.
81 *Democracy in Trade Unions*, p. 16.
82 Ibid., p. 20.
83 Ibid., p. 4.
84 Ibid., p. 17.
85 *Proposals for Legislation on Democracy in Trade Unions*, 12 July 1983.
86 *Trade Union Bill 1983* (HMSO, 1983).
87 Under the 'golden formula' trade unions are immune from prosecution from certain actions which would otherwise be actionable when acting 'in contemplation or furtherance of a trade dispute'. See P. Davies and M. Freedland, *Labour Law: Text and Materials* (Weidenfeld & Nicholson, 1979) pp. 602 seq.

CHAPTER 2 THE ROLE OF BALLOTS IN UNION ELECTIONS

1 *The Right Approach*, p. 45.
2 1983 Green Paper, *Democracy in Trade Unions* (HMSO, 1983), Cmnd 8778, p. 3.
3 Statutory Instrument 1980/1252.
4 Ibid., clause 4(c). Note this clause does not include any reference to the water representatives originally specified under Section I, 3(c) of the Employment Act 1980.
5 *Proposals for Legislation on Democracy in Trade Unions*, 12 July 1983.
6 The GMWU and the ASB are discussed as separate entities throughout as the survey was concluded before their amalgamation in 1982.
7 See Appendix for a list of the unions surveyed, classified according to manual, non-manual, craft and craft origins.
8 A. Bullock, *Life and Times of Ernest Bevin* (Heinemann, 1960), vol. 1, pp. 198–207.
9 J. B. Jefferys. *The Story of the Engineers* (Lawrence & Wishart Ltd, 1945), pp. 136–9.
10 H. A. Clegg, *General Union in a Changing Society* (Basil Blackwell, 1964), pp. 102–24.
11 G. S. Bain and R. Price, 'Who is a white-collar employee?', *British Journal of Industrial Relations*, 10, 3 (1972), pp. 325–39.
12 There is no consistent relationship between the method of choosing the president/chairman and the lay or full-time nature of the post. However, 6 of the 10 full-time president/chairmen are elected by the membership.
13 These are the BACM, NUM, AUEW(E), Patternmakers, Merchant Navy and Airline Officers Association, Blastfurnacemen, NGA, NUFLAT, Hosiery & Knitwear and the Bakers.
14 It should also be noted that two teacher unions, the National Union of Teachers (NUT) and the National Association of Teachers in Further and Higher Education (NATFHE), have a vice-president who is elected by a half postal ballot and who later automatically progresses to the post of president.

226 *Notes*

15 The CPSA subsequently changed its rules in 1981 to elect its senior full-time officials by a workplace branch ballot.
16 A. Bullock, *Life and Times of Ernest Bevin*, p. 203.
17 R. Undy, V. Ellis, W. E. J. McCarthy and A. M. Halmos, *Change in Trade Unions* (Hutchinson, 1981), chapters 4–8.
18 V. L. Allen, *Power in Trade Unions* (Longmans, 1954), p. 198–215.
19 AUEW(E) *Journal*, March 1982, p. 2.
20 The union does not have figures for its craft membership, but by 1970 the number of members in the craft exclusive section had shrunk to 25 per cent of the total. However, craft members may opt to join the other non-exclusive sections which carry lower subscription rates and hence the total number in the union is not known.
21 H. A. Clegg, A. J. Killick and R. Adams *Trade Union Officers* (Basil Blackwell, 1961), pp. 9–10.
22 R. Undy, 'The electoral influence of the opposition party in the AUEW engineering section 1960–75', *British Journal of Industrial Relations*, 27, 1 (1979), pp. 19–33, and a criticism of the term 'party' used in relation to the AUEW(E) by M. Dickenson, 'The effects of parties and factions on trade union elections', *British Journal of Industrial Relations*, 29, 2 (1981), pp. 190–200.
23 H. A. Clegg, A. Fox and A. F. Thompson, *A History of British Trade Unions Since 1889, Vol. 1, 1889–1910* (OUP, 1964), p. 143.
24 See p. 193 for a discussion of the definition of party and faction as used in this chapter.
25 H. A. Clegg, *The System of Industrial Relations in Great Britain*, 3rd ed (Basil Blackwell, 1976), p. 101.
26 For a brief period, 1981, the national committee had 91 members.
27 AUEW(E) *Rule Book 1980*, rule 2(10).
28 *IRIS* is one of the publications which supports Group candidates.
29 It should be noted that full-time officer posts increased from 160 in 1963 to 182 in 1973.
30 Undy, 'The electoral influence of the opposition party', p. 29, for details of branch voting.
31 Interview conducted in 1982.
32 *Financial Times*, 10 October 1981.
33 These positions are president, general secretary, assistant general secretary, executive council and national organizer.
34 J. D. Edelstein and M. Warner, *Comparative Union Democracy* (Allen & Unwin, 1975), pp. 178–9.
35 Ibid.; Undy et al., *Change in Trade Unions*, pp. 105–6.
36 This also includes the now defunct section two membership which was also craft exclusive.
37 These figures are based on calculations of the membership voting at the branch in the three named years in elections of TUC delegates. This election takes place at the same time each year and therefore provides a useful guide to branch attendance.
38 These figures are taken from the AUEW(E) *Journal*, June 1980, p. 7. The elections used for the calculations in both periods, i.e. 1964–72 and 1972–80 were identical and included 4 executive councillors, 1 assistant general secretary, 3 national organizers, 3 regional organizers, 4 divisional organizers, 9 assistant divisional organizers and 17 district secretaries.
39 AUEW(E) *Journal*, May 1976, pp. 2–4.
40 AUEW(E) *Journal*, December 1973, p. 553.
41 AUEW(E) *Journal*, June 1982, pp. 2–4. This lists votes in 25 contests. The range

of turnout varies from 13.7 to 25.1 per cent and includes the figures for the first final appeal court election held under postal ballots.
42 This was the executive division seven seat which includes the London area. The seat was won and retained by a leading member of the Group, Jack Whyman, on Reg Birch's retirement. Before Birch, the seat was held by other members of the left, i.e. Berridge, Scott and Tanner. Tanner subsequently became disillusioned with the left and helped form the Group and *IRIS*.
43 Later in 1983 the Group suffered a surprising set-back when it lost the vacant Scottish executive seat to Jim Airlie, a leading member of the broad left.
44 The defeated incumbent, a leading Communist, was subsequently re-elected unopposed.
45 In 1980 the rules were changed to include, on the second ballot form only, the election address. A book containing election addresses is sent to the branch.
46 Undy et al. *Change in Trade Unions*, pp. 293–6.
47 See *The Times*, 2 August 1981, for comment on the Group's constitution.
48 AUEW(E) *Rule Book 1980*, rule 12(21).
49 C. H. Rolph, *All Those in Favour: the ETU trial* (Andréw Deutsch, 1962).
50 The executive was made full time in 1965.
51 *Socialist Challenge*, 18 February 1983, p. 9.
52 *Financial Times*, 17 December 1982.
53 In 1976 the Bakers Union changed its name to the Bakers, Food and Allied Workers Union.
54 For comment on the history of FTAT see H. Reid, *The Furniture Workers From Craft to Industrial Union* (Unpublished PhD thesis, Warwick University, 1982). A number of the comments on the history of FTAT are based on this thesis.
55 *Our History – A History of the Bakers Union 1849–1977* (Bakers Union, 1977), p. 112.
56 Ibid., p. 107.
57 J. Hemingway, *Conflict and democracy* (OUP, 1978), p. 38.
58 Ibid., p. 73.
59 Ibid., p. 69.
60 Ibid., pp. 48–73, for comment on the development of the left in the NUS.
61 Harold Wilson, Labour Prime Minister, made this statement in the House of Commons in 1966 when the seamen's strike was threatening to breach Labour's incomes policy.
62 Equity Elections 1982: statements by candidates and voting paper, pp. 5–7.
63 AUEW(E) *Journal* – June 1982, pp. 2–4.
64 See p. 113 and Undy, 'The electoral influence of the opposition party', for a discussion of the features causing the two opposing groups in the AUEW(E) to be best defined as parties.
65 See p. 194.
66 TGWU *Rule Book*, rule 16(1).
67 The regions elect representatives on the basis of 1 per 50,000 members or less, 2 per 50,001–150,000 and 3 per 150,000 members or more. Each of the trade groups also elects a representative.
68 TGWU *Rule Book*, rule 13(3).
69 H. A. Turner, *Trade Union Growth, Structure and Policy* (Allen & Unwin, 1962), pp. 289–91.
70 R. Undy, 'The devolution of bargaining levels and responsibilities in the TGWU 1965–75', *Industrial Relations Journal*, 9, 3 (1978), pp. 44–56.
71 J. England, 'Shop stewards in Transport House', *Industrial Relations Journal*, 12, 5 (1981), pp. 16–29.

72 Undy et al., *Change in Trade Unions*, pp. 95–6.
73 England, 'Shop stewards in Transport House', p. 24.
74 There was some evidence, gained in interviews, that caucuses on the executive had become better established in the 1980s.
75 ASTMS *Rule Book*, rule 24(6).
76 See, for example, the *Financial Times*, 24 May 1982, for a report on the 1982 annual conference when the executive was heavily criticized over its handling of financial affairs.
77 The broad left renewed its efforts to influence ASTMS in July 1983 when it held an inaugural conference of the various left-wing groups in ASTMS.
78 ASTMS *Journal*, July/August 1978.
79 GMWU *Rule Book*, rule 5(8).
80 H. A. Clegg, *General Union in a Changing Society* (Basil Blackwell, 1964), pp. 122–3.
81 Ibid., pp. 140–41.
82 GMWU *Rule Book*, rule 5(1).
83 Although the executive is in theory a lay body, its members all work virtually full time on union business.
84 *The Structure and Democratic Procedure of the NUR*, NUR Educational Leaflet, 1982, p. 2.
85 Ibid., p. 4.
86 P. S. Bagwell, *The Railwaymen: the History of the National Union of Railwaymen* (Allen & Unwin, 1982), vol. 2: *The Beeching Era and After*, p. 93.
87 Bagwell, *The Railwaymen*, p. 84.
88 *Financial Times*, 14 October 1982.
89 *Financial Times*, 23 March 1983.
90 Bagwell, *The Railwaymen*, p. 109.
91 F. Bealey, 'The political system of the Post Office Engineering Union', *British Journal of Industrial Relations*, 15 (1977), pp. 376–9.
92 Ibid., p. 385.
93 In 1983 the broad left won a majority on the executive in a period when the Conservative government's policy of privatization was causing the union much concern and generating calls for militant industrial action.
94 Edelstein and Warner, *Comparative Union Democracy*, pp. 305–6.
95 E. Wigham, *From Humble Petition to Militant Action* (CPSA, 1980), pp. 174–5.
96 Ibid., p. 9.
97 Ibid., p. 195.
98 Ibid., p. 199.
99 *Red Tape* (CPSA Journal), July/August 1980, p. 316.
100 *Red Tape* (CPSA Journal), July/August 1981, p. 316.
101 *News of the World*, 15 November 1981; *Newcastle Journal*, 16 November 1981.
102 *Socialist Worker*, 21 November 1981.
103 *Financial Times*, 6 December 1982.
104 In 1983 the conference agreed to periodic elections.
105 Aspects of these developments are described in V. L. Allen, *The Militancy of British Miners* (The Moor Press, 1981) and T. Hall, *King Coal* (Penguin Books, 1981).
106 Allen, *The Militancy of British Miners*, p. 127.
107 *The Times*, 3 February 1981; *Morning Star*, 3 February 1981; *Financial Times*, 12 February 1981.
108 J. Gormley, *Battered Cherub* (Hamish Hamilton, 1982), p. 176.
109 Allen, *The Militancy of British Miners*, p. 126.
110 *The Times*, 2 September 1981.

111 Edelstein and Warner, *Comparative Union Democracy*, p. 221.
112 *Financial Times*, 30 October 1981; *Sunday Times*, 23 October 1981.
113 *The Standard*, 23 November 1981.
114 Allen, *The Militancy of British Miners*, pp. 118–35.
115 Gormley, *Battered Cherub*, p. 207; *The Times*, 12 December 1980.
116 *The Times*, 9 November 1980; *Financial Times*, 30 September 1980.
117 See p. 133 for comment on the mechanics of pithead ballots.
118 Since the survey was completed, as noted in the study of the CPSA, the CPSA moved to elect its senior full-time officials by a vote of the membership.
119 Allen, *Power in Trade Unions*, p. 213.
120 *Proposals for Legislation on Democracy in Trade Unions*, 12 July 1983.
121 J. Goldstein, *The Government of British Unions* (Allen & Unwin, 1952), p. 100.
122 See pp. 192–201 for a discussion of factional organization and its contribution to union democracy.
123 For a discussion of the factors influencing factionalism see H. A. Clegg, *Trade Unionism Under Collective Bargaining*, (Blackwell, 1976), pp. 44–51.
124 Undy, 'The electoral influence of the Opposition party', pp. 27–8.
125 Edelstein and Warner, *Comparative Union Democracy*, pp. 319–36.
126 England, 'Shop stewards in Transport House', p. 26.

CHAPTER 3   THE ROLE OF BALLOTS IN COLLECTIVE BARGAINING

1 Industrial Relations Act 1971, sections 141(1), (2) and 138(2).
2 *Report of the Royal Commission on Trade Unions and Employers' Associations* (Donovan) pp. 114–15.
3 Lewis and Simpson, *Striking a Balance?*, p. 133.
4 By the time of writing SLADE had merged with the NGA to form NGA'82 and NATSOPA with SOGAT to form SOGAT'82.
5 BIFU *Rules 1982*, p. 16.
6 Ibid., p. 17.
7 Ibid., p. 48.
8 Ibid., p. 17.
9 W. W. Daniel and N. Millward, *Workplace Industrial Relations in Britain* (Heinemann, 1983), p. 194.
10 Calculated from data kindly made available by Professor A. W. J. Thompson, University of Glasgow.
11 Calculated from data kindly made available by Mr Neil Millward, Department of Employment, gathered through the Workplace Industrial Relations Survey. The data related to the 1979–80 pay round.
12 Gormley, *Battered Cherub*, p. 166.
13 NUM *Rules 1978*, pp. 21, 22.
14 See Allen, *The Militancy of British Miners*, for an extended discussion of the rise of the left in the NUM.
15 NEC recommendations on the March 1976 ballot calling off the overtime ban, and the July 1977 ballot on the concessionary coal scheme are not available. For extensive accounts of the 1977–8 negotiations over productivity see Allen, *The Militancy of British Miners*, pp. 272–83, and L. J. Handy, *Wage Policy in the British Coal Mining Industry* (Cambridge University Press, 1981), chapter 13.
16 TGWU *Rules 1980*, p. 22.
17 Note to minute 46, TGWU Rules Revision Conference 1980.

18 TGWU Rules Revision Conference 1974.
19 *Report of a Court of Inquiry into a Dispute between the Parties Represented on the National Joint Industrial Council for the Electricity Supply Industry* (Wilberforce) (HMSO, 1971), Cmnd 4594, pp. 43–4.
20 The most celebrated use of ballots to resolve local difficulties occurred in the Ansells Brewery dispute in Birmingham in 1981. Regional officials were in conflict with local officials and shop stewards over the correct response to the company's proposals to introduce new working practices, and wages and hours reductions, under threat of plant closure. Two ballots were organized. The first, organized by the company, was aborted following opposition from the union members involved. The second ballot was organized by the union, but sent out by company post. The second ballot resulted in a majority for accepting the company's terms. However, local officials organized a special meeting of the members concerned shortly afterwards, which resulted in a substantial majority against accepting the company's terms. As many members voted in the meeting as had voted in the ballot. The company closed the brewery. Among the many lessons of the confused Ansells dispute is the lesson that ballots carried out over the heads of local officials and shop stewards are unlikely to produce tidy and conclusive answers. A subsequent internal union inquiry was critical of both officers and members concerned.
21 GMWU *Rules 1979*, p. 36.
22 AUEW(E) *Rules 1980*, p. 29, rule 13(10).
23 Ibid., pp. 24–5.
24 Based on a postal questionnaire to AUEW(E) district secretaries: 68 district secretaries replied, giving a response rate of 55 per cent.

CHAPTER 4   BALLOTS UNDER THE EMPLOYMENT ACT 1980

1 Statutory Instrument 1982/953.
2 Statutory Instruments 1980/1252 and 1982/1108.
3 Statutory Instrument 1982/1108, 4(f).
4 Ibid.
5 Regulations 1980/1252, 11(c).
6 Regulations 1982/1108, 5(h).
7 Regulations 1980/1252, 10(b).
8 Ibid., clause 13(b).
9 *Financial Times*, 22 May 1983.
10 *Financial Times*, 18 March 1981.
11 TUC *Report 1980*, p. 390.
12 The national committee had been increased to 91 in 1980 but was reduced to its previous size of 52 in 1983 following High Court action by the TASS section of the AUEW.
13 *Financial Times*, 25 April 1981 and 5 May 1981.
14 Ibid., 8 May 1981.
15 *Annual Report of the Certification Officer 1982*, p. 34.
16 Equity *Rules*, section 34 (5b).
17 Equity Referendum May 1982.
18 Ibid.
19 The figures provided are taken from the certification officer's annual reports of 1981 and 1982, and further details were obtained through correspondence with a number of the unions participating in the scheme.

20 Statutory Instrument 1982/1108, 3.
21 The 1982 RCN ballot is not listed in table 4.3 since it was not lodged until after December 1982.
22 *Funds for Public Ballots*, was first issued in October 1980 and was not subject to revision before June 1983.
23 Regulations 1980/1252, 11 (a–g).
24 IDS Brief 214, September 1981, p. 16.
25 IDS Brief 226, April 1982, p. 16.
26 D. Pearlman, 'Union elections and the LMRDA: thirteen years of use and abuse', *The Yale Law Journal*, 81, 3 (1972), p. 469.
27 Ibid., p. 469.
28 IDS Brief 217, November 1981, p. 17.
29 *Proposals for Legislation on Democracy in Trade Unions*, 12 July 1983.

CHAPTER 5 TRADE UNION BALLOTS AND UNION DEMOCRACY

1 R. Herding, *Job Control and Union Structure* (Rotterdam University Press, 1972), p. 45.
2 A. M. Ross, *Trade Union Wage Policy* (University of California Press, 1948), p. 23; quoted in R. Hyman, *Industrial Relations: a Marxist Introduction* (Macmillan Press, 1975), p. 66.
3 Hyman, *Industrial Relations*, p. 91.
4 N. Tebbit, 'Industrial relations in the next two decades: government objectives', *Employee Relations*, 5, 2 (1983), pp. 3–6.
5 *The Times*, 29 September 1978.
6 R. E. Hoxie, *Trade Unionism in the United States*, quoted in M. Perlman, *Labor Union Theories in America* (Greenwood Press, 1976 ed), p. 131.
7 J. H. Goldthorpe, D. Lochwood, F. Bechofer and J. Platt, *The Affluent Worker: Industrial Attitudes and Behaviour* (CUP, 1970), pp. 93–115.
8 M. Moran, *The Union of Post Office Workers: a Study in Political Sociology* (Macmillan, 1974), pp. 2–3 and 45–51.
9 Hoxie, quoted in Perlman, *Labor Union Theories*, pp. 129–30.
10 Moran, *The Union of Post Office Workers*, p. 3.
11 Goldthorpe et al., *The Affluent Worker*, p. 114.
12 Hoxie, quoted in Perlman, *Labor Union Theories*, pp. 129–30.
13 W. Brown (ed.), *The Changing Contours of British Industrial Relations* (Basil Blackwell, 1981), chapter 4.
14 See for example, Herding, *Job Control*, pp. 47–53; M. Poole, *Theories of Trade Unionism* (Routledge & Kegan Paul, 1981), pp. 149–62; Hemingway, *Conflict and Democracy*, pp. 1–12; R. Martin, 'Union democracy: an explanatory framework', *Sociology*, 2 (1968), pp. 205–20; S. M. Lipset, M. Trow and J. S. Coleman, *Union Democracy* (Glencoe, Ill., Free Press, 1956); Edelstein and Warner, *Comparative Union Democracy*; R. Martin, 'The effects of recent changes in industrial conflict on the internal politics of trade unions', in *The Resurgence of Class Conflict in Western Europe*, Vol. 2, ed. C. J. Crouch and A. Pizzorno (Macmillan, 1978), pp. 101–26.
15 R. Michels, *Political Parties* (Glencoe, Ill., Free Press, 1962), p. 365.
16 Edelstein and Warner, *Comparative Union Democracy*.
17 Lipset et al., *Union Democracy*.
18 Clegg, *The System of Industrial Relations*, pp. 79–118.
19 Hemingway, *Conflict and Democracy*.

20 Undy et al., *Change in Trade Unions.*
21 Goldstein, *The Government of British Unions*, p. 269.
22 H. A. Turner, *Trade Union Growth, Structure and Policy* (Allen & Unwin, 1962), p. 303.
23 Edelstein and Warner, *Comparative Union Democracy*, p. 63.
24 Ibid., pp. 81–2.
25 Ibid.
26 Ibid.
27 Ibid., p. 68.
28 Ibid.
29 Lipset et al., *Union Democracy.*
30 Michels, *Political Parties.*
31 See Dickenson, 'The effects of parties', for a recent discussion of some of these arguments.
32 Martin, 'Union Democracy', p. 207.
33 Ibid.
34 Dickenson, 'The effects of parties', p. 191, refers to 'permanence' rather than a period needed to win control of the union concerned. However, permanence is subsequently defined as something which the members of the group concerned conceive of as permanent. As there is no evidence of what members perceive as permanent, this is of doubtful utility.
35 The broad left in the POEU gained control of that union's executive in 1983. See chapter 2 for reference to the AUEW(E)'s and CPSA's broad left successes.
36 Martin, 'Union Democracy', 208–14.
37 Ibid. The twelve are: political culture; government attitudes and behaviour; pattern of membership distribution, past, present and future; industrial setting, including the degree of ownership concentrations and the collective bargaining system; economic environment; technology and rate of technological change; source of union's bargaining power; membership characteristics; membership beliefs; opposition expertize and resources; leadership beliefs; and union structure. Some of these, e.g. industrial setting and collective bargaining, vary widely between unions with similar kinds of opposition groupings. For instance, the AUEW(E) is decentralized in its bargaining and deals with a large number of employers which is in direct contrast to the CPSA and POEU. Yet all have well-organized factions or parties.
38 Bullock, *Life and Times of Ernest Bevin*, p. 205.
39 The broad left won a vacant executive councillor's position (Scotland) in the AUEW(E) in 1983 which had previously been held by the Group. See chapter 2 (p. 75) for the broad left's view of their standing in the EETPU after the general secretary elections in 1982.
40 Allen, *The Militancy of British Miners*, pp. 126–35.
41 As mentioned in chapter 2 (p. 99), CPSA only changed to election of some of its full-time officers in 1981.
42 The GMWU's confirmatory elections for regional organizers are ignored in this argument as the appointed incumbent is rarely challenged.
43 Edelstein and Warner, *Comparative Union Democracy*, p. 73.
44 Allen, *The Militancy of British Miners*, p. 119.
45 Clegg, *The System of Industrial Relations*, p. 99.
46 Undy, 'The devolution of bargaining levels', p. 56.
47 Undy et al., *Change in Trade Unions*, p. 270.
48 Ibid., p. 236.
49 See discussion document of July 1983.
50 Hemingway, *Conflict and Democracy*, p. 3.

51 Ibid., pp. 174–5.
52 Clegg, *The System of Industrial Relations*, p. 101; Undy et al. *Change in Trade Unions*, p. 20.
53 Herding, *Job Control*, p. 51.
54 See I. Boraston, H. Clegg and M. Rimmer, *Workplace and Union* (Heinemann, 1975), chapter 3, for discussion of the impact of this policy on three districts of the TGWU.
55 Ibid., p. 81.
56 G. S. Bain (ed.) *Industrial Relations in Britain* (Basil Blackwell, 1983), p. 70.
57 Boraston et al., *Workplace and Union*, pp. 168–71, argue that size of establishment was an important factor giving work groups independence from full-time officials.
58 This information and much of the following detail is taken from Daniel and Millward, *Workplace Industrial Relations*, and from additional data made available by the authors.
59 Ibid.
60 Lipset et al., *Union Democracy*.
61 D. G. Pruitt, *Negotiating Behaviour* (Academic Press, 1981), p. 44.
62 T. Clarke and L. Clements, *Trade Unions Under Capitalism* (Fontana, 1977), p. 303.
63 Ibid.
64 B. Weekes, M. Mellish, L. Dickens and J. Lloyd, *Industrial Relations and the Limits of the Law* (Basil Blackwell, 1975), p. 232.
65 Ibid., pp. 190–91.
66 *Proposals for Legislation on Democracy in Trade Unions*, 12 July 1983, p. 3.
67 Although the Engineering Employers Federation commented in June 1981: 'Under the British political system it is virtually certain that immunities taken away by a government of one complexion will be at least restored by another government more sympathetic to the cause of union power. There is no merit therefore in initiating this kind of debilitating struggle in industry merely to make use of temporary political advantage. However desirable in principle the wholesale radical reform of union immunities may seem to be, there is no advantage in attempting it unless the British political system can deliver the prospect of its durability.' Quoted in R. Taylor, *Workers and the New Depression* (Macmillan, 1982), p. 184. The EEF neglected the fact that durability in political life is measured in months or years, not decades.
68 Taylor, *Workers and the New Depression*, p. 194.
69 Ibid., p. 191.
70 The *Financial Times*, 26 March 1976.
71 For a discussion of pluralism see the various works by R. Dahl, especially *A Preface to Democratic Theory* (University of Chicago Press, 1956); for 'interest articulation' see G. A. Almond, 'A functional approach to comparative politics', in *The Politics of Developing Areas*, ed. G. A. Almond and J. S. Coleman (Princeton UP, 1960), pp. 33–8. Interest articulation is the process of translating individual grievances into collectively manageable demands. The use of the terms does not, of course, involve acceptance of the general assumptions of functionalist theory.
72 International Labour Organization, *International Labour Conventions and Recommendations*, 1919–81 (ILO, 1982), pp. 4–5.
73 It could have been argued before recent Government legislation restricting the operations of the closed shop (see Department of Employment Code of Practice, *Closed Shop Agreements 1983*) that intervention in unions' internal government was justified by union membership agreements which led to

involuntary union membership. However, this argument has had much less force since the passing of the 1982 Employment Act.

74 Allan Flanders, 'What are trade unions for?' in *Management and Unions*, ed. A. Flanders (Faber & Faber, 1970), p. 40.

75 B. Dabscheck and J. Niland, *Industrial Relations in Australia* (Allen & Unwin, 1981), pp. 128–31.

76 *Britain Means Business 1977*, CBI First National Conference, Brighton, 13–15 November 1977, p. 33.

Index